Mary,
The light you shine forth
light up the whole world.

PRAISE FOR

LIGHTED CLEARINGS FOR THE SOUL

Lighted Clearings for the Soul is just what the title suggests. In a wonderfully clear and pragmatic style, Dr. William Yoder lights the way for us to live a more spiritual life in our troubled times. This book comes just at a time when we so deeply need a no-nonsense approach to the values of forgiveness, tolerance, and compassion. It offers us comfort, inspiration, and hope. Read this book for yourself, for your family, and for the world community.

Gail Straub, Executive Director, Empowerment Training Programs; author of *Empowerment*, *The Rhythm of Compassion*, and *Circle of Compassion*

Lighted Clearings for the Soul is a wise and discerning book. Through a comprehensive description of human perception and experience combined with a loving attitude, Yoder shows us how we all have the capacity for joy and unconditional love — and helps us to find our way there.

Barry Neil Kaufman, author, *Happiness Is a Choice*, and director of The Option Institute, Sheffield, Massachusetts

Lighted Clearings for the Soul is filled with practical spiritual nuggets that will inspire the reader to new heights.

Gerald G. Jampolsky, M.D., author of *Love is Letting Go of Fear*.

This book opens an inviting doorway to a whole new dimension of possibility, while at the same time offering greatly needed practical tools to help people actually **experience** this dimension for themselves.

Sandra Ingerman, M.A., author of *Soul Retrieval* and *Medicine for the Earth*.

The provocative distinction between the Spiritual-Holistic and Separative-Technological perspectives clearly distinguishes between an empirical and spiritual view of the self and world, and opens the mind and heart to the personal experience of a larger reality. The Spiritual-Holistic view, coupled with exercises for directly experiencing the world of immediate experience as essentially spiritual, overcomes traditional

dualism and makes spirituality available for everyone. I heartily endorse this work, and encourage all seekers to immerse themselves in it.
Harville Hendrix, Ph.D., author: Getting the Love You Want: A Guide for Couples, and co-originator with Helen Lakelly Hunt of Imago Relationship Therapy.

In his excellent book, William Yoder challenges us in a variety of ways to re-vision our relationship with life and free us from ways of thinking that bind and prevent us from seeing deeply into the presence of spirit within our lives.
David Spangler, author of Blessing: The Art and the Practice.

William Yoder, a philosophy professor turned Healer, guides you through models that will help you to choose that which will truly serve you in life, and find your greater purpose. Through Yoder's approach you can find your personal reference point for life and live in a garden of choice. **Lighted Clearings for the Soul** *is a philosophic and practical guide that is full of brilliant ideas that can assist you to reclaim the joy of living.*
Donald M Epstein, author of Healing Myths Healing Magic and The 12 Stages of Healing, and developer of Network Spinal Analysis

I am not usually very much interested in books in the category of "Self-help Spirituality." Most of them seem to be either trite or unbelievable. William Yoder's Lighted Clearings for the Soul, *however, is neither trite nor unbelievable. Rather it is both philosophically astute and spiritually penetrating. It is also quite readable and accessible to the general public. The author does not give arguments for the way things "are" but rather proposes possibilities for viewing the world and the self which are different from the usual technological view that sees everything as "It." One selects among many such possibilities to make a lighted clearing in which to live in this world of mystery. The ultimate criterion for the worth of such a lighted clearing is not some hypothetical factuality, but whether it fosters depth and richness in your experience. To anyone interested in a deeper and fuller everyday life, I recommend this book. It opens doors to new ways of seeing the world, doors that can lead to a life of meaningful peace and compassion.*
Dr. Jay G. Williams, Professor of Religious Studies, Hamilton College

There is an intelligence at work in this book, and Bill Yoder also recognizes and respects the intelligence of his reader, which I appreciate.

I found it clear, well thought through, honest, stimulating, challenging, and well-worth reading.

Rev. Douglas Wilson, Executive Director, UU Rowe Camp & Conference Center.

By helping us to remember and actually experience our deeper spiritual truth, this book lays a foundation for forgiveness, tolerance, and unconditional love, which is so important in our world today.

Bob Wittman, M.A. Marriage & Family Therapist

Through an awakened perspective and heartfelt compassion William Yoder guides the readers to a deeper and richer experience of the spiritual dimension of their lives. His writing truly illuminates the spiritual journey we all share.

Thank you for being such a clear channel for truth to me and hopefully for countless others.

Mark Tucker, founder of Healing Heart Productions

Charting a course between the Charybdis of New Age enthusiasm and the Scylla of the orthodox scholar's antipathy for moral advocacy, Bill Yoder's book is an untiringly positive reflection on the existential value of the cultivation of unconditional love. Even what is most perplexing has served me, as Dr. Yoder hopes it will, as a friend's Socratic provocation to take stock of my own life choices.

Mitchell Miller, Ph.D., Philosophy Dept., Vassar College

This book opens readers of all religions or no religion to the very essence of Spirituality: unconditional love. It is an extremely timely publication for a world in dire need of the core human values of forgiveness and tolerance flowing from unconditional love.

Father Fred Daley, St. Francis de Sales Church, and recipient of national Jefferson Award for community service 2003

A book both mentally challenging, and spiritually awakening, with concrete, comprehensive examples on how to shift one's negative perspective toward life, to a world open with possibility. I loved its celebratory approach to life!

Rev. Kaaren Anderson, Unitarian Universalist Church of Utica

LIGHTED CLEARINGS
FOR THE SOUL

Reclaiming the Joy of Living

William Yoder, Ph.D., D.C.

 Alight Publications, New York

Lighted Clearings for the Soul
Reclaiming the Joy of Living
by William R. Yoder, Ph.D., D.C.

Published by
Alight Publications
Post Office Box 524
Sauquoit, New York 13456
alightpublications@msn.com

Order @ http://www.alightpublications.com

Publisher's Cataloging-in-Publication
(Provided by Quality Books, Inc.)

Yoder, William R. (William Robert)
   Lighted clearings for the soul : reclaiming the joy
of living / William Yoder. – 1st ed.
   p. cm.
Includes bibliographical references and index.
LCCN 2003106993
ISBN 0-9721556-3-5

   1. Self-actualization (Psychology) 2. Spiritual
life.   I. Title.

BF637.S4Y64 2004   158.1
                             QBI33-1401

Printed in Canada on acid-free paper

Cover photo, Mark Tucker, Healing Heart Productions, http://mtt3hheart@aol.com

To Mary,
My life partner and soulmate.
Her love, wisdom and humor
have helped me to discover and realize
the truest and best part of myself,
and to enjoy the process along the way.

Also by William Yoder

Toward An Ontology And Epistemology Of Mysticism. Ph.D.
Dissertation, SUNY Buffalo, 1978.

Glimpses into a Lighted Clearing, Alight Publications, spring 2004

The Lighted Clearings for the Soul Workbook, Alight Publications, fall
2004.

Opening the Present, Alight Publications, fall 2005.

ACKNOWLEDGEMENTS

A loving, supportive group allows more truth to shine through than could come through any one person alone.

I want to thank my friend Charlie Felsenthal for his tough-love honesty on the first draft of this book. Because of his comments, the second draft was a quantum leap forward. And then Charlie brought a scholar's mind and proofreader's critical eye to the second and third drafts, and taught me a lot about the fine points of grammar and vocabulary. I want to thank Kathy and Bruce Richmond for holding me to a rigorous standard of intellectual honesty. Dr. Michael Pearson, a longtime friend, provided important philosophical and psychological insights. Bob Wittman, a wonderful and loving counselor, read the second draft and gave me enthusiastic reassurance when I was beginning to doubt the project. Sara Bakert read the second and third draft meticulously, with a critical editor's eye and a good feel for fine-tuning the rhythm and flow of the text.

I want to thank Mark Tucker for generously giving me the beautiful photo for the cover of the book. He is a genuinely kind and loving person, and his inspirational photography and music programs have been presented to international acclaim over the years (Healing Heart Productions, http://mtt3hheart@aol.com).

I also wish to thank my children, Liana, Tamaryn, and Adam. While they never read any of the drafts of this book, they patiently let dad have his hours and hours of writing time. And through the years, they have been some of my greatest teachers about unconditional love.

I am deeply, deeply grateful to my wife, Mary, for her hours and years of patient help. Without her on-going support and inspiration, this book could not have been written. Her wisdom and honesty were always mixed with a sparkling sense of humor, which made criticism easier to hear for my sometimes insecure ego. Her comments and suggestions about the content and style of the book were invaluable. She has an amazing editorial talent that I am in awe of — often by simply changing one word, or slightly rearranging a phrase, she introduces a whole new level of insight and beauty. In its final form, this book is as much her doing as it is my own.

Finally, I want to thank all of my friends and family members whose love and encouragement have given me the confidence and trust to see this project through over the course of eight years. I am truly blessed and grateful to share my journey with such bright and beautiful souls.

CONTENTS

PREFACE

Peace, love, joy, a sense of connectedness, a feeling of participating in a greater whole — humans have sought these things since the dawn of self-awareness. This search for a deeper, richer, and truer quality of life is an on-going journey of personal growth and spiritual discovery. Although the particulars of each individual's quest may be unique, every person's journey takes place within a cultural-historical context, which largely defines both the form of the questions asked and, as well, the kinds of answers that can be discovered. In our modern culture of critical thinkers, for instance, many people are generally not willing to accept any answers that seem dogmatic — not willing to accept unsubstantiated theories or opinions about "how things really are." But this standard of intellectual integrity has led us to a psychological and spiritual dilemma.

People are weary of the cynicism and materialism of our modern culture. They seek to find a deeper meaning for their lives, a sense of participating in a greater whole — seek to actually *experience* the profound spiritual dimension of life promised by so many religions and philosophies. But virtually all of these religions and philosophies seem to carry a price tag of dogmatism. Traditional religious approaches as well as more modern New Age theories all tell us how things really are, and we must simply accept these descriptions on faith, or not. Many of today's best-selling authors in the fields of personal growth and spirituality take a basically assertive and declarative approach. In some cases, the authors profess special powers, such as the ability to see energy fields. In other cases, the authors say that higher powers and entities actually dictated their books. Some writers simply assert with great conviction that what they are saying is "The Truth." Readers who are hungering for answers are drawn to such certainty. But ultimately, even if such claims are valid, to merely accept a belief based on someone else's certainty cannot be truly satisfying.

Even the widespread popular theory that thought creates reality is a metaphysical assumption that must be simply accepted on faith or not. No proof is offered (or perhaps even possible) for this claim of mental creation — we are told that this is just how things are. The thought-creates-reality model is used as the theoretical foundation for many inspiring and transformative practices, such as creative visualization and assuming personal responsibility. But the unproveable nature of this metaphysical theory is often troubling for a critical thinker, for it seems that the cost of admission to these wonderful practices is a metaphysical leap of faith. Those who are willing to make this leap sometimes feel vaguely uncomfortable, worried that they may have merely traded in the dogma of traditional religious thought for the dogma of New Age secularized spirituality. Their discomfort tends to undermine their commitment to the practical applications, and this in turn undermines the effectiveness of those practices for them. Many are not willing to make such a leap at all — not willing to just accept some arbitrary description of reality on someone else's authority. Therefore, they tend to dismiss much of the modern literature on spirituality and personal growth as mere New Age airy-fairy speculation — and as a result, they cut themselves off from a wealth of ideas and practices that could transform the quality of their life experience. Even though they may be dissatisfied with the separative and materialistic beliefs of modern culture, they are unwilling to compromise their intellectual integrity.

My point here is not that traditional religions or the more modern New Age alternatives are false or wrong — indeed I believe that they can enrich and deepen our life experience immeasurably. But the fact that they are presented dogmatically undermines their potential to positively influence people's lives. Many critical thinkers in our contemporary scientific culture tend to reject the topic of spirituality whole-cloth as dogmatic opinion — and thus they end up cut off from a valuable dimension (some would say the most valuable dimension) of human experience. Others decide to believe a religious or metaphysical doctrine solely on someone else's authority — but ultimately this is an arbitrary decision, swayed by the charisma and passion of the writer or speaker. In short, it seems that we must choose between blanket rejection and dogmatic acceptance.

Thus a pressing question for our contemporary culture is, *"Can a thinking person experience true happiness?"* — can a thinking person experience a deep and rich quality of life, a spiritual dimension of experience, without giving up his or her intellectual integrity?

This is the question that has guided my own on-going search, and has eventually led to the ideas presented in this book. Although the particulars of my own journey may be unique to me, the general issues, I believe, are common to many in our modern culture.

My earliest experience of a deeper and richer dimension of life was within the framework of traditional Christianity — my mother was a dedicated Methodist, and I attended church regularly for many years as a child. Church for me was a private experience — a personal communion with something deeper than my everyday ego, something that was a source of peace and love.

My academic interests in high school and college were strongly slanted toward science and math. There was a reassuring comfort in knowing the principles and laws of a science — they allowed you to predict and control events with certainty, and could be easily demonstrated and proved in the laboratory. As I moved through college, I became more and more aware of the dichotomy between the empirical certainty of science and the dogmatic faith of religion. I drifted away from the church, because it seemed too soft-headed and un-rigorous for an intellectually sophisticated mind. I reveled in the exactitude and certainty of my scientific world — although as I learned more about relativity theory and quantum mechanics, those seemingly solid beliefs began to feel rather shaky too.

But my relatively precise scientific world of atoms and molecules mechanically interacting according to fixed physical laws lacked something — that dimension of experience I remembered from my childhood religion. However, I was not willing to accept a seemingly dogmatic belief system just to feel better. In my scientific frame of mind, I turned to psychology, hoping to find a rational basis for a deeper level of experience. But throughout my entire undergraduate psychology major, virtually every course offered was in the field of behaviorist psychology — a strictly empirical study of stimuli and responses (and even to call them "responses" was an overstatement, because basically there seemed to be little or no room in that scientific model for true creativity or freedom of choice). That model of psychology presumed that the human mind worked according to fixed mechanical principles just like the physical universe — and psychology was the science of empirically determining which reaction was mechanically elicited by which stimulus. One psychology professor told us that the mind was like a black box. We couldn't possibly have any idea of what was going on in that box — we could only observe patterns of stimuli and reaction. (I remember thinking at the time that there was indeed a way to know what was happening in that so-called black box — because I lived in there! But for that scientific paradigm, my subjective experience was not considered to be hard data.) In my several years of psychology courses,

I remember only one class that was not behaviorist — but it was presented as a mere speculative theory about the mind, without any definitive proof of its truth. (It is important to note that the field of psychology itself is much larger and deeper than I have presented it here — this was simply my own earliest academic experience of it.)

By the end of my college years, I turned to Zen Buddhism (or at least the popular version that was so big in the late 1960's) in my attempt to find something more to life than the mechanical laws of physics and chemistry — which, for all their exactitude, felt lifeless and joy-less. Zen appeared to be the perfect answer to the intellectual dead-end I seemed to have reached. I saw human life as an on-going koan — one of those one-hand-clapping riddles whose purpose is to confound and eventually stop the intellect, so that pure being can take over. The ultimate answer to my intellectual dilemma was to simply let go of the intellect altogether, for even though the rational mind might be very handy for balancing one's checkbook, it was completely irrelevant to the search for Truth — because Truth was not a theory but a direct experience (or perhaps the very experience of experience itself). My mantra in those days became, "Don't think — just be!"

But this sense of completion was short-lived for me for several reasons. Basically I wasn't ready to simply give up thinking. For one thing, I enjoyed thinking — it felt like part of my nature and my path. Moreover, I believed that the human capacity for thinking was not just a mistake, or a mere illusion to be overcome and discarded, but rather a gift. The issue for me was to discover how to properly use this gift, to use it in a way that improved the quality and depth of my life experience. The fact that thinking could be misused was not reason enough to throw it out altogether.

At this point in my journey, I discovered the world of Western philosophy. It is important to note that there is much more variety and depth to Western philosophy than the empirical-mechanistic tradition which is often parodied. For years I studied the history of Western philosophy to better understand how the worldview of my culture had evolved. Eventually I wrote my doctoral dissertation on comparative mysticism (although from one point of view, that phrase could be considered an oxymoron). My thesis was that the writings of the mystics were intended to evoke an experience rather than to "describe" Reality.

One important outcome of my years of philosophical study was a healthy respect for the relativity of the different philosophical theories I had studied. Each one was a possible way to see the world, and each one had its own limited truth. Eventually I came to see that even the scientific worldview, which had been for me the bedrock of certainty, was also just one possible way of seeing the world (as was pointed out by many thinkers, from Berkeley's and Hume's critiques of Locke, down through Kuhn's theory about scientific paradigms).

But the recognition of the relativity of all philosophical and religious theories was a mixed blessing. It did relieve the pressure and anxiety of trying to find the one true theory about how things really are, since I now believed that there was no one absolute truth. But the other side of the coin was that I couldn't wholeheartedly believe in anything (except of course, in the belief that "everything is relative"). I found myself envying those naive souls who had never thought long and hard about relativism, and so were able to enjoy their philosophical and religious beliefs without question — they simply assumed that their views were right, and were unaware of and untroubled by the possibility of equally valid alternative views.

For a while, I was very excited about the thought-creates-reality model that is the theoretical foundation of many New Age philosophies. Within that paradigm, I didn't have to be concerned with whether or not my belief was true in the sense that it accurately described some external reality. Since my beliefs literally created my reality, there was no higher authority of truth. This gave me both a wondrous sense of freedom and an awesome responsibility. On the one hand, it promised that I could choose and create any reality I desired. On the other hand, it said that I was completely responsible for everything in my current reality that was less than perfect, less than desirable — it was, after all, my own doing. But despite the practical advantages of this model for my life, ultimately it was unsatisfactory for me. After all, those who promoted this theory did not just say that it made good practical sense to believe it — they claimed that it was true, that it simply described how things really are. But there was no way for me to prove that this theory was true — thought-creates-reality was a metaphysical assertion about the absolute nature of reality, and as such was ultimately a matter of faith. Moreover, my own experience did not always seem to bear it out. Often it seemed that other factors beyond my own separate individual mind somehow contributed to my reality (although the thought-creates-reality model could always appeal to the creative force of my subconscious beliefs that I was unaware of). Not only did my own experience seem to show me that I wasn't the sole creative force in my universe, but I didn't really want that to be the case either. I wanted to participate in a universe where there was the possibility of feedback, the possibility of grace and guidance. (For a while, I toyed with the idea that if I simply chose to believe that there was a level or dimension of reality that was not created by my thought, my thinking it would make it so — but ultimately that tack seemed self-contradictory.)

I still vividly remember one particular incident that brought my whole intellectual dilemma into sharp focus. I was attending a weekend workshop with Wallace Black Elk, a wise and deeply spiritual Native American teacher. I remember when I first arrived at the workshop, I felt like an outsider. Many of the other participants who were not Native American by race, were wearing headbands and moccasins and little leather medicine bags. They all seemed to talk the same talk — using phrases like, Mother Earth, Grandfather Sun, and talking about all the various kinds of "people," such as the two-legged people (humans), the four-legged people, the winged people, the finned people, the creepy-crawler people, the plant people and the stone people. They talked about the directions of the compass as spirits — the spirit of the East, and the spirit of the West. I remember thinking that this gathering was a wonderfully safe place that allowed all of these wanna-be Native Americans to pretend together — just like, for instance, the Renaissance Fair that allows people to dress up and playact. But it seemed like the workshop participants were not aware that they were pretending — since they were in a group where everyone else was pretending the same thing, they thought it was true (just like the stereotype of the asylum where none of the inmates has to "face reality"). I remember seeing one person hugging and talking to a tree. The skeptical and materialistic part of me thought, "Doesn't she know that's just a tree? Trees can't think or feel or communicate — they're just elaborate photosynthesis machines."

But the critical voice in my mind was a cover for a deeper longing. Those people were experiencing a *living* world, a world of spirit and love, whereas I seemed to be stuck in the so-called "real world" of atoms and molecules. I envied them their naiveté, and the passion and richness of their experience. In contrast, my own experience seemed lifeless, mechanistic and lonely. But then the question occurred to me, "What if *my* belief in the lifeless atoms-and-molecules theory was only a pretense?" Perhaps it seemed real to me only because nearly everyone else in my culture also believed it. Perhaps the only reason why the workshop participants' beliefs seemed to me to be playacting was that those beliefs were out of synch with my cultural norm. Ultimately I had no proof that the atoms-and-molecules model was the one and only absolute truth. But one thing was very clear to me — as long as I believed that a tree was *only* lifeless atoms and molecules, I would never be able to discover whether trees could talk to me and give me guidance, comfort, and friendship. My very belief in the thing-like nature of a tree would close me off from experiencing any other possibilities. And yet it was difficult for me to choose to believe the trees-can-talk model just because I wanted a sense of connection and participation. After all, a person with intellectual integrity believes things because they are true, and not merely because they feel good. I envied those people at the workshop who, untroubled by these kinds of questions, were having the time of their lives talking to trees, and even to rocks.

It is out of these kinds of wonderings and questions that the ideas of this book grew. For me it was not merely a theoretical intellectual game, but a passionate and sometimes even desperate desire for a deeper, richer quality of life — a quality of life characterized by peace, love, joy, and a sense of connectedness. For me, the ideas of this book such as the Possibility Model, the lighted clearing, and understanding truth as unhiddenness, have given me a way to re-discover such a quality of life — to re-discover what I call the "spiritual dimension" of experience. These ideas are not so much alternatives or competitors to the other ideas and theories in religion and philosophy, but rather can serve as a valuable complement to them. They give us a new way or a new "how" to think, while allowing us to freely choose what we want to think and believe. Moreover, many people with whom I have shared these thoughts over the years have told me that these ideas have been life-transforming for them. In the final analysis, this book does not present a theory about how things really are, but rather offers a way of thinking about our life experience, and suggests concrete beliefs and practices that can create "lighted clearings for the soul" — clearings which can open us to the possibility of experiencing a dimension of peace, love, and joy that is perhaps our deepest and truest birthright.

INTRODUCTION

Over the years, I have read many wonderful books on the subjects of spirituality, philosophy, and personal growth. These books usually paint a beautiful and inspiring picture of reality. They speak of the underlying unity of all things, of the goodness and light that shine in and through every creature and every event. They discuss deeper realities like "soul" and "Spirit," and assure us that there is a profound meaning behind the seeming chaos we often experience in our daily lives. They encourage us to live in harmony with Nature — to live with unconditional love, patience, forgiveness, and reverence for all things. They speak of peace and harmony — for the individual person, for nations, and for the whole planet.

But often, after the inspiration of the book had faded, I found myself asking, "Wouldn't it be wonderful if reality were like that?" The very grammar of my question betrayed my disbelief and despair. What I would have liked to say was, "Isn't it wonderful that reality *is* like that!" But often I didn't actually experience reality in such a beautiful and spiritual way. Moreover, I lived in a culture that constantly seemed to tell me how ugly and dangerous and threatening the world really was. I turned back to my inspiring books, desperately looking for some kind of proof that these beautiful visions were true. As a reflective and thoughtful person, I didn't want to adopt a belief simply because it sounded noble and inspiring. But for the most part, I found that these books did not provide any kind of proof at all — I had to either accept their wonderful theories on faith, or not.

Wouldn't it be wonderful if the world were really as good as all these books proclaim it to be? Not overly cute or cloyingly sweet, but just fundamentally positive and good. Wouldn't it be nice if we really *knew* in our hearts that everything was for the best — that every event and situation in our lives was somehow guided by a loving wisdom, so that it would turn out for the good of everyone involved? Wouldn't it be wonderful if we knew that every seeming crisis and tragedy in our lives was somehow a blessing in disguise?

What would have to change so that we could actually *experience* our lives like this? Would we have to change the people and circumstances in our lives? Even if we changed our immediate circumstances, would that be enough? Would we also have to change national and global circumstances? All of the news media seem to tell us that the world is a dangerous and hostile place, and that it is getting worse every day. If we listen to television and read the newspaper, it is easy to believe either that there is no God at all, or that He (She, It) doesn't really care all that much about what happens here on earth. One currently popular theological explanation claims that God takes no active role at all in the affairs of the mundane world, except to give us the strength and courage to somehow survive the negativity and hostility that permeate our lives every day.

Perhaps the answer lies in simply changing our perception of reality. Is it possible to experience a more wonderful world merely by changing our beliefs and attitudes? In the children's movie, *Pollyanna*, Pollyanna believed that everything that happened was intrinsically good. She believed that every event presented opportunities for joy and growth. As a result, she experienced a wonderful, positive world, no matter how negative her circumstances seemed to be. No matter how much scarcity seemed to pervade her life, she believed that the world was essentially abundant. No matter how petty and mean others seemed to be, she trusted in their inner goodness. Not only did her beliefs affect her own perception of reality, but in time they affected the perceptions of everyone around her. The people in her town became more loving and forgiving, and the town became a happier place to live.

But is such a shift of attitude realistic? Are these kinds of beliefs about the goodness and abundance of the world really true? Do they accurately represent reality? Is this Pollyanna view of the world merely a fool's paradise? Is this approach to reality even safe? If the world really were hostile and negative, wouldn't all of this positivity and optimism be potentially dangerous, especially if we let down our defenses? If we close our eyes to the real dangers and hostility of the world, won't we be hurt? Won't others take advantage of us?

We could just as well ask the converse questions. Is the fearful negative view of the world realistic? Is it true? Does it accurately represent reality? Is the Ebenezer Scrooge view of the world merely a fool's hell? If the world really is friendly and positive, wouldn't all of this negativity and pessimism rob us of our full potential for growth and joy? If we close our eyes to the underlying essential benevolence of the world, wouldn't we cut ourselves off from enjoying the good and the beauty that surround us?

Or maybe neither of these views is correct. Maybe the truth lies somewhere in between. Maybe the world is neither intrinsically good nor intrinsically bad. Maybe the world is essentially like some large, indifferent machine — the gears simply go round and round, and sometimes things work out well for us and other times things work out badly. Maybe the most realistic approach is to simply accept the fact that you have to take the bad with the good, the thorns with the roses. But even if this half-and-half view of the world were correct, how would we decide if a particular event in our lives is good or bad — or at least, good or bad for us? How would we know whether this particular relationship, or this particular financial situation, or this particular political state of affairs is really for the good of ourselves and others, or actually presents a hostile, threatening situation? Is there some criterion we can use to evaluate each particular situation, or do we have to rely solely on our (sometimes fallible) first impressions? Merely to make the generalization that reality is a mixture of good and bad does not help us to interpret the concrete particular events of our lives, nor does it give us any guidelines for how to feel or how to respond in any particular situation.

Or maybe reality is simply neutral — maybe it has no intrinsic value at all. Maybe the goodness or badness of any particular situation is simply what we make of it, how we interpret it. But does that mean that our decision about what to believe is completely arbitrary? Maybe even our decision to believe in the neutrality of the world is itself an arbitrary choice. Are some decisions about meaning more true or valuable or useful than others? Wouldn't the choice to affirm the neutrality of the world at the same time be a choice to deny any possible intrinsic goodness or badness? Insofar as it was a denial, wouldn't it also run the risk of blindness and prejudice?

One possible alternative that is very popular in today's New Age literature is the theory that thought creates reality. From this perspective, it makes no sense to ask questions like, "What's *really* going on out there? Is the world *really* spiritual, or is it *really* only material and mechanistic? Is the world *really* purposeful and benevolent, or it *really* only random (or even hostile)?" According to the thought-creates-reality model, there is no reality out there apart from what is created by our thoughts. In some mysterious way, our thoughts create all of the things and circumstances and relationships and values of our world. Reality is only what we, quite literally, make it to be. At first glance, this theory seems to solve all of our dilemmas about the nature of reality in one bold stroke. From this perspective, we don't need to torture ourselves with questions such as, "what is *really* going on out there?" because nothing exists besides our thoughts, in their various mental and materialized forms — there is no "what's really going on" apart from what is being created by our thoughts.

Several years ago, I attended a personal growth workshop, which explored how we could use tools like creative visualization and positive affirmations to improve the quality of our lives. The metaphysical presupposition and foundation for this whole workshop was the thought-creates-reality theory. At one point, I was feeling somewhat desperate and unsure of myself, and I found myself doubting everything — including even the claim that thought creates reality. But I knew that without this foundation, much of the rest of the positive and inspiring content of the workshop would not have a theoretical leg to stand on. I privately asked the workshop leader how I should best deal with my doubts about this matter. I assumed that he could provide some kind of proof, or at least a few convincing arguments, that this model was true. I assumed that the only reason he had not already covered that topic was that he thought it was much too elementary for our group. But when I asked, I was told that I simply had to accept the basic truth that thought creates reality. There was no way to prove it, any more than we can prove that the grass is green or that birds can fly — it's simply how things are. The bare assertion that it was true, however, did not really answer my doubts and questions.

The thought-creates-reality model does have the advantage that it gives us an active role in the process of our lives — we are no longer victims of some external, fixed reality. Thus it can provide a framework of hope. I am never just stuck with my life — I can always think new thoughts and believe new beliefs, and rebuild my reality from the ground up. But the cost of admission to this bright promise seems to be the dogmatic acceptance of an essentially unverifiable metaphysical presupposition — another metaphysical leap of faith. It seems to me that the only way I could possibly verify this theory for myself would be to somehow get outside my experience, in order to see the process of my thoughts in the midst of actually creating reality — to somehow catch the still unreal pre-reality (that nebulous, unstructured, and unexperiencable stuff) in the very process of becoming "real-ified" by my thoughts. Thus, for all of its power and efficacy to psychologically motivate us to think positively and to try harder, the thought-creates-reality model is really not a satisfactory answer to our dilemma — at least, not for me. It merely trades in one metaphysical absolute (e.g., reality consists of material atoms out there) for another (e.g., reality consists of materialized thoughts), without providing any proof. (For all I know, the thought-creates-reality model may be entirely true. Many well-respected teachers and deeply revered spiritual authorities claim that this is exactly what's going on. But for me, the real question is, can I accept a belief just because it is inspiring and just because someone else tells me it's true?)

I believe that the questions we ask ourselves about the nature and meaning and value of reality are fundamentally important. The answers we discover and create in response to these questions form the basis of all of our life decisions. They affect every area and aspect of our lives, including how we feel, what we say and do, our relationships with each other, and our relationship with Nature — they play an important role in determining the content and quality of our life experience. But many people, when confronted with the bewildering variety of competing metaphysical dogmas, none of which can be conclusively proved or verified, decide to simply give up asking such questions at all — decide to simply live their lives, without really thinking too much about it. At other times in our history, there have been generally accepted religious and metaphysical beliefs about the nature and value of reality — beliefs that everyone simply took for granted without question. Even now, there are some cultures and sub-cultures in the world that share unquestioned religious or metaphysical presuppositions. In our modern culture of rational, independent thinkers, however, we have no commonly accepted metaphysical foundation. But simply not thinking about questions of the nature and value of reality does not make them go away. Our day-to-day choices about what to think and say and do, about how to respond and what to feel — all of these simply-living-our-lives choices presuppose some overall context of belief and meaning. To merely ignore questions about the nature and value of reality is, in effect, to choose to live a life based on whatever hodgepodge of beliefs you have simply inherited from your childhood, your parents, and your culture. It is not that you have no beliefs, but merely that you are unaware of your beliefs. By not consciously and deliberately choosing your beliefs, you choose by default — you choose to live a life on automatic pilot. This is the dilemma that a rational, reflective person faces in our modern culture. He is caught between a rock and a hard spot — either choosing a sleepwalking life of unexamined beliefs, or choosing some arbitrary metaphysical dogma; either not thinking about his life at all, or fruitlessly and frustratingly thinking about questions that seem to have no answers.

These are more than just theoretical questions that you might ask yourself if you happen to have a taste for philosophizing. How you answer and resolve such questions and dilemmas for yourself will profoundly affect the content and meaning and quality of every moment of your life experience.

PART ONE
POSSIBILITIES

CHAPTER 1

THE POSSIBILITY MODEL

The spiritual dimension of life has been explored throughout human history, from the theologies and cosmologies of traditional religions, to the metaphysical theories of contemporary spiritual literature. But without some direct experience, all of these ideas and theories can seem like just so much dogma competing for your allegiance. Ultimately, *the real measure of the truth and value of a spiritual or religious idea for you is the degree to which it helps you actually* <u>experience</u> *the spiritual dimension of your own life.* The word "dogmatic" means "opinion without foundation in direct experience." In this sense, dogmatic always means dogmatic for a given individual. Whether or not someone else's religious or spiritual idea is dogmatic for you does not depend on the consciousness and intent of the person who created or presented that idea, but rather on the consciousness with which you understand it — it depends on whether *your understanding* of the idea is experiential or dogmatic. The real question isn't, "Where can I find the 'right' book (teacher, seminar) that will tell me how things really are?", but rather, "How can *I* approach and understand spiritual books and teachings experientially rather than dogmatically?"

Mystics have often pointed out that the spiritual dimension of your life is not some distant "there" you have to travel to from your mundane, everyday "here" — it is the very truth and essence of the on-going process of the "here-ing" of the here and the "now-ing" of the now. Becoming aware of the spiritual dimension of your life is waking up and remembering — not just intellectually, but *experientially* — who you, in truth, *already are.* The true value of any spiritual theory or practice is to facilitate this process of direct awareness. But the real guru and teacher is always truth itself — your own inner truth, your own direct experience.

❖ The Possibility Model

Several years ago, my wife and I designed and built a new home. When it came to selecting the fluorescent lighting fixtures for our kitchen, we discovered that there was a bewildering variety of fluorescent tubes to choose from. To illustrate their different properties and lighting effects, our friend at the local electrical store set up a "light box" for us. This was a large wooden box, approximately four feet wide by two feet high and two feet deep. The front of the box was open, and looking into it we could see two identical large color photographs of a woman's face, which were separated by a vertical partition in the middle of the box. Each half of the box had six different fluorescent tubes mounted across its top or "ceiling." By turning on different tubes in each half of the box, we could compare how the different lights affected the appearance of the photographs.

I was surprised that subtle changes in the tone and warmth of the light could have such a dramatic effect. Sometimes the two photos looked so different, it was difficult to believe that they were really the same. Different kinds of light would highlight or hide different colors, and dramatically affect how they appeared. What appeared red under one light, for instance, might appear orange under another. Two colors that contrasted starkly under one light, might be indistinguishable from each other under another light. Color, tone, warmth, and even distinction itself varied dramatically under different lighting conditions. Finally, after going through many combinations of lights, I stepped back and asked, "Wait! What does the picture *really* look like?" By this time, my head was spinning with all of the different possibilities, and I desperately wanted a reference point — I wanted to know what the photo really looked like, so that I could choose the light which was the most realistic, the light which showed the photo most true to life. But as soon as I asked the question, "What does the picture *really* look like?", I felt embarrassed. I had, after all, been a philosophy professor for years, and I had patiently helped many students through such naive questions.

At the time, the question, "What does the picture *really* look like?", felt like a completely natural thing to ask (even though I felt like a fool for asking it publicly). Why did this question feel so natural? I think it is because the presuppositions underlying this question are the same presuppositions that are shared by most of our culture. We tend to assume that reality exists out there in some definite, "actual" form — it simply is what it is. From that point of view, our goal as human perceivers and thinkers is to experience that actual reality as realistically as possible, and then to describe it as accurately as possible. When we describe reality accurately, we say we have spoken the "truth" — where truth is understood to mean, "the correct or accurate conceptual re-presentation of reality." The very word, realistic, presupposes that there is some one, definite reality out there, and that we can correctly perceive it or not. Being unrealistic, on the other hand, is considered to be a fault or a shortcoming of someone who is unable or unwilling to see things as they really are. I call this view the Actuality Model of reality — it is the belief that there is some one actual reality out there, and that our goal is to perceive it and describe it as accurately as possible.

But my experience with the light box made it clear to me that the Actuality Model of reality was an inadequate paradigm for understanding my life experience. I realized that there was no way to tell what the photo really looks like, because the appearance of the photo is not a piece of objective data. The appearance of the photo always involves a combination of at least two factors. First, there is the photo-in-and-of-itself — the objective "given" fact prior to any actual experience of it. Exactly what this consists of, however, cannot be completely specified, since any concrete experience of the photo always involves the other factor as well. (Of course it may be possible to give an abstract scientific description of the photo, detailing what wavelengths of light are reflected from which areas of the picture under a certain carefully controlled set of lighting conditions. But all of these numbers would be only one possible *abstraction* — they would not describe my actual *experience* of seeing the picture.) The second factor is the light shining on the photo. In the light box, I saw how different kinds of light dramatically altered my experience of the photo — altered its color, warmth, tone, and even what colors and forms were visible at all. (One reader raised the question, "Wouldn't sunlight let you see what the photo really looked like?" It could be argued that sunlight is only one possible kind of light, albeit the kind we usually call "normal." Perhaps more to the point is that sunlight itself has many variations, depending on such factors as time of day, weather, season, and the particular reflective surfaces of your environment — as any painter or photographer will readily attest.)

For me, the light box provides a wonderful analogy for understanding our experience of ourselves and the world. My actual concrete experience is always a combination of factors. On the one hand, there are the so-called "data" I encounter in the world, although it seems impossible to define exactly what these are, in and of themselves. On the other hand, there is the light I shine out ahead of myself, which allows me to discover and understand the meaning of the things and events in my world. In this analogy, the light would be my beliefs and expectations, my view of the world. Any given interpretation will highlight some aspects of my world, and cast others into shadow; it will emphasize some differences and distinctions, and conceal others. My beliefs will affect where I look, what I focus on, and how I interpret it. They help determine what I am able to see and what I am blind to. What I choose to believe about reality will be the light I use to guide my way through the world — it will illuminate my possible options, and influence my choices among them. In this context, what is important for me to ask is whether the light I am currently using truly serves my own best interests (and here it should be noted that the phrase, "my own best interests," is not necessarily egocentric — depending on how I define my relation to the world, my own best interests may include the interests of other people, and even the interests of the whole Earth itself).

I call this way of understanding our life experience, the Possibility Model of Being. In this model, Being or what-is exists not as one actual reality, but rather as a vast, indefinite range of possibilities — a range of possible life experiences.[1] Our beliefs act as an interpretive filter, which allows some of the possibilities to be actualized as concrete, meaningful experiences of ourselves and the world. To be consistent, the Possibility Model itself must be seen as but one possible way to interpretively understand what is. It is not some accurate description of how things really are, but rather *one possible way of thinking about* and experiencing the world — a possible way that allows us to understand the world in terms of possible experiences that we help to define, rather than as fixed actualities that are merely "given."[2]

Earlier I said that the question, "What does the picture really look like?" felt like a completely natural thing to ask. From the perspective of the Possibility Model, any time I am in the midst of actual life experience, I am experiencing the actualization of one of the possibilities of what is. What that means is that I am *always* experiencing the world as an actual definite something. Therefore, it seems natural to believe that reality, in and of itself, exists as something actual, inasmuch as every experience of the world is an experience of the world as an actual reality.

❖ Different from the Thought-Creates-Reality Model

One theory about how things are is the thought-creates-reality model, which has become very popular in New Age literature. The Possibility Model we are discussing here, however, is different from the thought-creates-reality model in several important respects. First, thought-creates-reality claims to describe how things *really* are (i.e., reality, in and of itself, consists of materialized thoughts) and what's *really* going on (i.e., my thoughts really are "creating" reality itself). The problem with such an absolute claim about what's-*really*-going-on is that there is no way for me to prove or verify it for myself. For me to verify it, I would have to somehow get outside of reality, in order to see it actually being created — watching, for instance, as my thought energy somehow caused molecules to materialize out of nothingness, or perhaps magnetically attracted and coalesced some amorphous quantum soup of pre-reality into solid, tangible forms. The Possibility Model, on the other hand, does not address the metaphysical question of the nature of reality itself, but rather focuses on my life *experience*. According to the Possibility Model, my beliefs help to determine the structure, meaning and content of my life *experience* for me. (But this is not to say that the Possibility Model is merely a form of subjectivism — because my life experience includes the objective as well as the subjective, out-there as well as in-here.) [3]

One of the main practical values of the thought-creates-reality model is that it reminds us of the active role we play in determining our lives — reminds us that we are not just passive victims at the mercy of some fixed external circumstances. From the perspective of the Possibility Model, we could say that the value of the thought-creates-reality model is that it enables us to discover our own active-creative possibilities. But for me, to say that my thoughts "create" reality implies that my thoughts (or even human thoughts in general) are the only active component in the whole process, the only creative power in the universe. Some New Age thinkers, in fact, seem to go so far as to claim that the ego is God (again, if thoughts really do unilaterally create reality, would merely thinking that my ego is God make it so?). The real question here is whether or not I choose to believe that there is some creative force at work in my life, above and beyond the willfulness of my ego. For me, one advantage of the Possibility Model is that it is a way of thinking about my life that reminds me to remain open to the possibility of deeper sources above and beyond my conscious thinking ego — it explicitly includes a component of receptivity to complement and balance the activism and willfulness of my ego.

I am not saying, of course, that everyone who believes in the thought-creates-reality model is an egocentric megalomaniac. In fact, the thought-creates-reality model tends to be the philosophical starting point for many thinkers and teachers who are deeply spiritual, and whose lives are dedicated to such ideals as service and unconditional love. But for me, the idea of "creating reality" carries the implicit danger (although some might call it an advantage) of egocentricity. The Possibility Model, however, focuses on our *co-creative* partnership with the field of possibilities, and explicitly reminds us to remain open to something beyond ourselves — an openness which includes the whole spectrum from what my mother used to call, "an attitude of gratitude," in which I appreciate the blessings and beauty of the world (without busily creating them, and without trying to take credit for them), to my reverent receptivity to deeper spiritual sources of grace, wisdom and guidance.

The differences between the Possibility Model and the thought-creates-reality model are especially clear to me when I am in the midst of personal stress, doubt or despair. It is precisely at these times that I need some helpful way to think about myself and the world, which can allow me to see my life in a more positive or constructive light. At such times, the thought-creates-reality model does not serve me nearly as well as the Possibility Model. When reality seems especially dark or tragic, the belief that I have created all of the ugliness and evil in the world can tend to be very dispiriting, and to add guilt and shame to my stress. Moreover, in times of doubt and despair, I tend to be quite cynical and skeptical. As I set out to rebuild my worldview and attitude from the ground up, I am especially unwilling to have my very first foundation stone be an absolute and unverifiable dogmatic claim about how things really are — it is simply too much of a metaphysical stretch at such times to believe that my thoughts are literally creating reality. But I can always accept the more modest claim that my beliefs and ideas filter and interpret my experience, and thereby help to determine its content, meaning, and value for me. From this starting point I can begin to make changes in how I look at myself and the world, and hopefully begin to change the quality of my life experience. Also, when I am helping another person through his own dark times, the Possibility Model seems to be a more plausible starting point, than some absolute metaphysical claim of mental creation.

It is important to remember that I am explicitly not discussing which model of reality accurately describes "how things really are" — which one is right, and which one is wrong. I am not claiming that the thought-creates-reality model is false (to either affirm or deny an unverifiable metaphysical position would be equally dogmatic), or that those who profess this belief are somehow wrong. Many highly respected spiritual authorities say that our thoughts really do create reality, and I am not so presumptuous as to assume that I know more than they.

I believe that the Possibility Model and the thought-creates-reality model are just two possible ways of thinking about my life, whose true value and meaning lie only in the quality of life experience they make possible. For me, the Possibility Model provides a more plausible foundation for the on-going enterprise of choosing and re-choosing the beliefs and attitudes that can improve the quality of my life, and contribute to the quality of others' lives as well — and it does so without metaphysical dogmatism, and without the danger of falling into egocentric activism.

CHAPTER 2

TRUTH AS UNHIDDENNESS

Within the context of the Possibility Model, we have to redefine our idea of truth. In the Actuality Model of reality, truth means accuracy — what I say or think is true if it is an accurate description or copy of reality itself. But according to the Possibility Model, any given thing or being or situation, in and of itself, exists as a constellation or range of possible experiences. Our beliefs and ideas filter, interpret, and actualize some of these possible experiences. There may be several different, and even contradictory, beliefs about the "same" thing or event that could be equally valid — that could accurately correspond to possible experiences of that thing or event. Moreover, since each belief tends to interpretively filter and define its own corresponding life experiences, our experience will naturally tend to validate our beliefs. This means that our beliefs will usually seem to us to be accurate representations of our experience, since they were the interpretive filters that determined and conditioned that experience in the first place. Given these considerations, defining truth as simple accuracy is not very helpful in the context of the Possibility Model — because there may be many equally accurate views of any given situation or event.

We find a more useful definition of truth by turning to the ancient Greek word for truth, "aletheia." Aletheia literally means unhiddenness.[5] From this perspective, the truth of an idea or belief for me is determined by the openness or unhiddenness it creates in my life experience — the truth of an idea is evaluated in terms of the range and kinds of possibilities that it reveals to me. In this context, untrue no longer means simply false or inaccurate — here, an untrue idea is one that tends to hide or conceal possibilities. From this perspective, we might say, for instance, that racial prejudice is a relatively untrue perspective, insofar as it denies and hides the possibility of seeing the full humanity of another person.

❖ The Lighted Clearing

The poetic metaphor of "the lighted clearing" can help us to better understand the Possibility Model. Imagine that you are sitting in the midst of a dark forest. You have a lantern with you that casts a circle of light. Within that circle you can clearly see yourself and the things that surround you. At the edges of your circle of light, things begin to get fuzzy and indistinct. Beyond the light, the wilderness lies in darkness and mystery. I can think of my very being as a kind of lighted clearing, within which some possibilities are unhidden or revealed. Beyond my lighted clearing is the darkness, where other possibilities remain hidden from my sight. In this metaphor, where you focus your attention would correspond to where you choose to place your lantern. Your worldview, as the context of meaning and significance which you bring to your experience, would correspond to how bright your lantern is, how large a circle of light and unhiddenness it casts, and the color and tone of its light which affects how you experience and understand everything you see in your clearing. From this perspective, instead of saying that your thoughts create reality, it would be more appropriate to say that your thoughts create a lighted clearing of discovery.

I am using the poetic metaphor of the lighted clearing rather than the term "awareness" for two reasons. First, "awareness" tends to imply a purely mental reality. But the lighted clearing, as I am defining it, involves the openness of my whole being — including an open heart as well as an open mind. Second, and even more important, we tend to interpret "awareness" as a definite descriptive term — as such, "awareness" is defined only relative to "objects of awareness." But this distinction between "awareness" and "objects of awareness" is a distinction I make *within* the lighted clearing of my being — within this clearing, I encounter *both* awareness *and* objects of awareness. In general, any descriptive term will tend to distinguish between things or qualities found within the unhiddenness. We can speak of the unhiddenness itself only in metaphorical or poetic terms, since it is the openness within which every distinction and description is possible at all. Therefore, the metaphor of "a lighted clearing" is not only more appropriate, but also much richer and deeper, precisely because it does not pretend to accurately describe the openness of my being — it is *explicitly poetic*.

My very be-ing is the on-going creating of a lighted clearing — and the truth of my existence is the unhiddenness of the clearing I am creating. Within the truth or unhiddenness of my being are revealed and discovered all of the beings and qualities of my experience, including "myself" (at all of its levels: ego, superego, subconscious, higher Self, soul, etc.), "others," "things," "events," "situations," "the world," "mind" and "matter," "subjects" and "objects," "awareness" and "objects of awareness." The truth or unhiddenness or lighted clearing of my being is the very possibility of every possible experience of myself and my world.

We can make this analogy even more dynamic by imagining that you are walking through these dark woods, and shining your light out ahead of yourself. The light you are shining in front of you is the context of meaning and significance you project ahead of yourself as you proceed along the path of your life. This context of meaning and significance is what allows you to comprehend and understand all of the individual things and events you encounter. Just as the meaning of an individual word can be defined and understood only within the context of all the other meanings and definitions of the whole language, so too can the meaning of an individual thing or event in your experience be defined and understood only within a greater context of meaning and significance. This greater context is your worldview or your overall understanding of the world — it is the context that allows you to understand the meaning and significance of each individual thing or person or event you encounter. For instance, when you interpret some particular event as good for yourself, this judgment is possible and makes sense only within a larger context of meaning — a context which includes what "good" means to you, the belief that good things can and do happen at all, and the belief or the faith that this event will ultimately fit into your life in such a way that all of its consequences are truly in your best interests. This overall context of meaning is not something you can directly perceive "in" your world — it is rather something you bring to your world. It is the context of understanding that enables you to experience a meaningful world at all — the context that allows you to discover, interpret, judge and make sense of the things and events in your world. You pro-ject (literally, "throw before") your worldview ahead of yourself, like a beam of light — and the brightness and color of your light, as well as where you choose to shine it, will determine what you are able to see and understand, and what it will mean to you.

As you change your worldview and your basic beliefs, you become aware of different things and qualities in your world, and your world can take on a different meaning or significance for you. A story from the Buddhist literature illustrates this point. A certain monastery in Japan found itself in decline — with each passing year, it had fewer and fewer monks, and was visited by fewer and fewer pilgrims. Finally, the head monk went to visit a renowned Zen master, to ask for advice and help. After the Zen master heard the monk's story, he became very quiet and thoughtful, and looked deeply into the Mystery in his heart. Finally he said, "I have just had a revelation, and it is amazing! One of the monks in your monastery is a reincarnation of the Buddha himself, disguised as an ordinary person! How fortunate we are to have the Buddha reincarnate in our own lifetime! And how extremely fortunate for you, that he has chosen your monastery." The head monk excitedly rushed back to his monastery. He called together all of the monks, and told them the wonderful news. Among themselves, the monks began to ask, "Who could it be? Is it the meditation master — he certainly seems very kind. Or, might it be the cook — he is often rude and disagreeable, but that may merely be the Buddha's disguise. Or, might it even be myself — the disguise might be so good, that the Buddha is actually fooling himself." Since each monk regarded everyone in the monastery, including himself, as a potential Buddha, he treated them and himself with love and reverence, and was on the lookout for every detail that could possibly be interpreted as an expression of the sacred. By the same token, he discounted anything that seemed to be ordinary or petty as just another part of an elaborate disguise. Within a few years, this monastery became the largest one in Japan, and people from all over the country visited it simply to experience the kindness and compassion of its inhabitants.

In the analogy of walking through the woods, I said that you pro-ject your worldview ahead of yourself like a beam of light as you move along your life path. "Ahead," in this sense, implies the future. What you are experiencing now, and how you are experiencing it, is determined in large part by the worldview you *have already projected* ahead of yourself in the past. What you choose to believe and project ahead of yourself now will help determine how you can experience your life and your world in the future. But usually you are unaware of the interpretive framework that you project ahead of yourself, since you tend to focus your attention on what is already interpreted and filtered through that framework — you tend to think of your already-interpreted experience as simply "given." In our light analogy, we could say that we don't see the light itself — we see only what is made visible by the light. Light itself is invisible — its function and purpose is to enable objects to become visible, to bring them out of darkness and hiddenness into unhiddenness. Likewise, our beliefs and our worldview tend to be intrinsically invisible or self-hidden — their function and purpose is to illuminate and reveal the various possibilities of Being. Insofar as they are doing their job, they remain in the background of awareness. Moreover, since our beliefs pre-filter and pre-interpret our experiences, our experiences tend to support and validate our beliefs. Therefore, it can seem that our beliefs are merely "descriptive" of the "given facts" of experience — merely copies of how things really are.

❖ Views, Filters, and Clearings

I said that in the Possibility Model, "what is" exists as an indefinite range of possibilities or possible life experiences, and my worldview serves as an interpretive filter, which helps determine which possibilities are realized, and which are not. But it must be noted from the outset that terms like "view" and "filter" are not meant as accurate descriptions of how things really are — the intent and value of these ideas is to create a lighted clearing of possible experience. In this context, it is important that we not interpret these metaphors too literally. The filter metaphor, for instance, seems to imply that I am somehow "in here," looking outwards "through" a filter toward some nebulous cloud of possibilities that exist "out there." This filter allows some of these "objective" possibilities to come through to me "in here," so that I am able to experience them as my perception of reality. Similarly, the "view" metaphor seems to imply that I am somehow "in here" viewing the pictures of an objective world "out there." But in the broader context of the Possibility Model, the possibilities of what-is are not merely out there, like some amorphous cloud of possibility-things. The possibilities of what-is include everything I can possibly experience. *"I," too, exist as a field of possibilities.*[5] Moreover, my relationship to the world, and to the people and things outside myself, also exists as a field of possibilities. How I think of my relationship to others, or how I understand the relationship between "in here" and "out there" plays a crucial role in determining what possibilities I am able to realize — plays a crucial role in defining who "I" am and how I experience myself. My belief choices do not stand "between" me and the world, nor is my worldview merely a way of gazing "outwards" at objective things and events "out there." My beliefs about the world, about human nature, about myself, about the relation of myself to other people and things — all of these beliefs form the context of understanding, which colors and shapes the lighted clearing of my experience, the truth or unhiddenness of my existence. My beliefs thus help determine what possibilities of the world and what possibilities of myself I can experience. The clearing is not "in" me (or in my head, or in my mind). Rather, "I," as a distinct ego or personality or consciousness, am one of the beings discovered in the clearing. (Just as in a dream, my dreamed self that I experience and identify with is only one of the actors in the whole drama, only one of the faces and voices of my dreaming consciousness.) The true value of metaphors like "filter" and "view" is that they remind me of the *co-creative* role my own belief choices play in defining the clearing of my life, which embraces all of my internal as well as external experience.

We must also take care not to interpret the *poetic metaphor* of "the lighted clearing" itself too literally — the purpose of the idea of "the lighted clearing" is to create a lighted clearing of discovery. In explaining this metaphor, it is helpful to differentiate among its various component elements: the clearing or openness itself; the light choice (or belief choice) which defines the location, size and coloring of the clearing; and those life possibilities which we discover "in" the clearing. But it is important to remember that in my concrete experience, I do not encounter these elements separately — I always experience "the lighted clearing and its meaningful contents" as an integral whole. Again, the primary purpose of these various distinctions is to remind me of the important role that my own belief choices can play in determining the form, content, and quality of my life experience.

CHAPTER 3

CHOOSING YOUR BELIEFS

❖ No Choice Whether to Choose

It is important to recognize that we have no choice whether to choose our basic beliefs or not. Insofar as we already experience a world that is meaningful for us, and insofar as we are self-aware beings who are able to make our day-to-day decisions, we are *already* choosing, interpreting and filtering — we are always already in mid-choice. But even if we cannot choose whether to choose, we can choose whether to choose our beliefs consciously and deliberately, or merely by default. Ways of choosing by default include letting someone else choose for us (which is really a choice to let them choose for us); merely reacting to the world according to our personal history and our childhood experiences; or letting ourselves be passively influenced by general public opinion ("you know what *they* say"), or by television and other public media.

We may, of course, be unaware that we have any choice at all. Since our beliefs work in the background, pre-filtering and pre-interpreting our experience, we tend to be unaware of them — that is to say, we tend to think that our experiences are simply "given" in their current form and meaning, and that our ideas are merely copies after the fact. As I said above, we don't see the light itself — we see only what is made visible by the light. Moreover, this seeming lack of choice can give us a certain comfort. As much as we may complain about what we are experiencing, there can be a comforting security in believing that the world is simply given. Facing the radical freedom of choosing the meaning and content of your life experience can evoke a strong sense of anxiety and insecurity. When you have to choose your beliefs on your own, you always seem to run the risk of making a "wrong" choice (whatever that may mean).

But this feeling of insecurity may ultimately arise from an illusory idea of "security." An analogy from the Zen Buddhist tradition claims that trying to find security in the ever-changing world of form is like trying to catch a moving river in a bucket. Of course, as soon as it is in the bucket, it is no longer the moving river. Our typical response to this is either "I need to fix my bucket!", or else "I need a newer and better bucket!" But the real problem is not in the quality of the bucket, but in the illusory goal of trying to catch a moving river in a bucket in the first place. This story implies that if we are not aware of the illusory nature of security, we will be locked into the desperation and anxiety of our insecurity — for no matter how hard we look, we will never be able to find a real solution to an unreal problem. "In-security" is a good example of a concept that seems to be negative and seems to imply lack or deficiency — but the analogy of the moving river raises the question whether the thing that is supposedly lacking is only illusory in the first place. In the framework of the Possibility Model, we could say the same about the concept, "un-realistic." "Un-realistic" seems to be a negative term, because we presume that it is possible to be "realistic." But if we no longer believe that there is only one actual reality out there, then being realistic loses most, if not all, of its meaning. Perhaps the general lesson here is that before we bemoan or feel anxious about the apparent lack of something, we want to first question whether or not that something is only illusory — only a mental construct we have made up, which has no corresponding or validating life experience.

❖ Criteria of Choice

"Objective Evidence"

If we want to consciously and deliberately choose our basic beliefs, what criteria can we use? Our current modern culture tends to offer us two kinds of criteria for making such choices. The first is objective evidence. But there is a fundamental problem when we try to use objective evidence as a criterion for choosing our basic life beliefs and worldviews. As a selective interpretive filter, my worldview allows me to experience (it unhides) those possibilities that are consistent with it, and tends to exclude (conceal, blind me to) those possibilities that are inconsistent with it. Thus, the selective filter of my worldview tends to allow in only its own supportive objective evidence. But in the richness of the total possibilities of Being, many different beliefs may well yield equally supportive objective evidence. What this means is that you can't defend a given belief choice simply on the basis of the evidence that is currently staring you in the face, since your beliefs have helped determine this "evidence" in the first place. In this situation, appealing to objective evidence would be, at least in large part, circular reasoning. Nor can you use a current lack of evidence as a valid reason to not change your beliefs — since the appropriate evidence might not become available to you until after you have already changed your interpretive filter.

Not only does every belief system tend to generate (filter and interpret) its own supportive evidence, but it also tends to explain away any apparent inconsistencies. Several years ago, a friend of mine was diagnosed with a particularly deadly form of cancer, and was given three months to live. He embarked upon a holistic regimen of a healthy diet, stress reduction, positive thinking, prayer, and so forth. At the end of a year, he returned to his doctor, and the exam and X-rays revealed no trace of the tumor. The doctor explained these findings away by saying that the initial diagnosis must have been wrong — because in that doctor's frame of reference, cancer could not simply disappear, nor could the body heal itself without medical intervention. I had another friend who, despite all of her holistic efforts, nonetheless died of her cancer. One of her New Age acquaintances, who believed that every disease could be cured through repeating positive affirmations, claimed that her death must have been due to unresolved, subconscious feelings of self-hatred. What is important to note here is that both the traditional medical doctor and the New Age positive thinker had their own explanation for the apparent inconsistencies in their experience, and thus each was able to maintain their own dogmatic belief without contradiction. Every "fact" that could possibly be interpreted as supportive was marshaled as evidence for their own beliefs; every "fact" that could not be interpreted as supportive was somehow explained away.

Two Worldviews

Another example of the self-validating nature of our basic life beliefs can be illustrated by comparing two people with very different worldviews. The first is a person I met several years ago. At the time, she was in her sixties, and she was closed off, distrustful, and defensive. She had grown up in a home with very little love or affection, and she had developed a very cynical view about people. She was convinced that everybody was simply out for himself, and that nobody really cared about anyone else. She believed that any apparent demonstration of love always had an ulterior motive — the other person was simply pretending, in order to get something for himself. Sooner or later, the pretense would be dropped, and the other person would show his true selfish colors. As a result of these beliefs, this woman was very distrustful, and she looked upon everyone with a suspicious eye — she always had her guard up, ready to strike out to defend herself.

Even though this approach to life made her miserable and lonely, she felt she had no choice. She believed this was the way the world was, and that she was simply being realistic. Moreover, all of her "evidence" seemed to verify and confirm her theory. On the one hand, since she focused only on the negative and the selfish aspects of other people, that was all she experienced. Everything she saw that could possibly be interpreted as selfish and loveless was further support for her cynical, distrusting vision. Everything she saw that seemed to be loving and good, was interpreted as mere pretense and hypocrisy. On the other hand, her attitude toward other people actually influenced them to be less loving and open. When she looked at you with her suspicious and hostile glance, you could almost see her holding her fists up as a warning not to get too close. No matter how nice you were acting at the moment, she was always waiting for your mean and petty inner self to emerge. Sooner or later, whatever seeds of fear and distrust might be in you began to blossom forth into your own full-blown defensiveness. The more withdrawn, suspicious, and defensive you became, the more evidence you provided her for her own frightened vision. Thus, this woman's view of the world both limited what she was able to experience, and actually influenced others to speak and act in ways that would confirm her view.

I want to emphasize here, however, that I am not saying that this woman's defensiveness "caused" other people to be defensive. Whenever we meet a frightened, hostile person, we have a choice as to how we will respond. A typical response is to simply react with our own defensiveness — in a Darwinian survival-of-the-fittest worldview, we best take care of ourselves by reacting to every perceived attack with our own defense and counterattack. But we also have the choice of responding with forgiveness, understanding, compassion and love. In fact, from a certain spiritual perspective, meeting a suspicious, defensive person is seen as a kind of gift, for it can teach us of the limits of our current capacity to love and forgive. Whenever I feel a reaction of hostility and defensiveness arising in myself, I can use that feeling as a clue to discover my own beliefs of separateness and fear. As I discover these beliefs in myself, I am able to change them if I choose.

As a contrast to this defensive woman, we could consider the life of Jesus. Without getting into questions of theological doctrine, we could say that Jesus regarded everyone he met as basically good and worthy of love. Even though he associated with some of the most reviled people in his society, such as prostitutes and tax collectors, he regarded and treated each one with love and respect. What other men considered to be "sins," Jesus forgave as mere mistakes arising out of ignorance and fear. Nothing that anyone could do could possibly disprove this vision for him, or cause him to adopt a negative, hostile approach to the world. His unconditional love and forgiveness not only affected his own perception of the world, but it also had a positive influence on others. Because of his unwavering faith in their inner goodness, others were inspired and encouraged to discover it for themselves, and their lives were transformed.

Note that each of these two people would consider their own worldview to be accurate or realistic, since virtually all of their experiences validated and confirmed their beliefs — and those few exceptions that didn't seem to confirm their beliefs could be explained away. Moreover, each person would criticize the other person for being unrealistic. The defensive woman might criticize Jesus' worldview as being naive, head-in-the-clouds," Pollyanna optimism. She would claim that the naively trusting love and forgiveness of such an approach would make one vulnerable to all of the hostile people and forces in the environment — he would be taken advantage of and beaten down in the dog-eat-dog competition of the "real world." His illusory happiness would be shattered when it encountered the harsh realities of a selfish world based on the survival of the fittest. His lack of defensive self-protection would result in an unsuccessful life, lacking in the power and possessions that could provide what little happiness and fulfillment were possible in this harsh world. She might even point to Jesus' crucifixion as further proof that his perspective was unrealistic — he simply wasn't shrewd enough or ruthless enough to protect himself from the hostilities of those around him.

If this woman were questioned about all of the unhappiness involved in her own distrustful and defensive way of life, she would reply that negativity and unhappiness are simply the most true and realistic reactions to a hostile and dangerous world — in such an environment, a happy, trusting, defenseless attitude would be insane and dangerous. To further verify her belief in the hostility and dangers of the world, she could appeal to all of the various news media, which are full of stories of tragedy, selfishness, and inhumanity.

Jesus, on the other hand, would consider this woman's approach to be a partial and distorted view of the world. He would claim that her belief in separateness blinds her to the unity and commonality of all things; her fear blinds her to the reality of love; her pessimism blinds her to the truth of goodness. Moreover, her selfish and defensive actions also influence others to be more selfish and defensive. As those around her become more selfish and defensive, she will feel that her own defensiveness is even more justified. Thus, her view not only leads to her own individual unhappiness, but can also contribute to a defensive and unhappy world. From his point of view, this fear and unhappiness is ultimately unnecessary, inasmuch as it is based on a fundamental ignorance about the nature of humanity and the world. He might well argue that others' hostility toward him was merely a reflection of their own fear in the face of his more expansive vision. Moreover, he might argue that it made more sense to live a joyful, loving life worth dying for, than to live a frightened, defensive life merely to avoid offending someone else's selfish and paranoid sensibilities. Living in constant fear of alienating others' affections might or might not have prolonged his life a few years — but for him, it would have been an untruthful life, not really worth living. (Moreover, from his point of view, he might even argue that the destruction of his physical body was not any real loss.)

Earlier I said that my belief system shines ahead of me like a searchlight, and helps to determine where I look, what I see, and how I see it. In this context, it is not possible to simply "be objective" — I cannot see at all without a light, and the light I choose affects how and what I see. Whatever beliefs I choose will illuminate and color my experiences, and will help to create the evidence which supports and confirms my beliefs. The individual things and events I perceive cannot prove or disprove my overall context of meaning — for it is only within this context of meaning that a "meaningful fact" can be perceived and understood as "evidence" at all. How, then, am I to decide between two such worldviews, such as that of the defensive woman and that of Jesus, inasmuch as each view seems to provide its own evidence? Note that this is not merely a decision about how to interpret some particular thing or event in my world — it is a decision that affects the whole structure, meaning, and tone of my life experience. Such a choice can affect every aspect of my life — it will affect my perceptions, my thoughts, my actions, my emotions, my social relationships, and my spiritual life. If I cannot appeal to objective evidence, how am I to decide what to believe about the value and meaning of the "facts" in my life? How can I decide what to believe about the meaning of the world in general? Even if I don't want to think about such generalities, I am still faced with day-to-day questions about the meaning of particular things and events — and every particular interpretation implies a prior choice of a larger context of meaning.

The point I am making here is not that objective evidence is worthless or that it should be simply ignored. In choosing our own worldview, we do of course want to choose one that is as consistent as possible with all of our perceptions and experiences. But at the same time, we want to recognize that there is a necessary interdependence between our overall context of interpretation and the interpreted evidence we use to support and confirm this context. We must realize that any "fact" that has emotional content for us, or is valuable or meaningful or significant for us, has already been interpreted — it is not merely a bare datum of experience. Ultimately, the art of choosing a worldview has to involve some kind of balance between open-minded observation and consciously chosen interpretation.

An important implication of the Possibility Model is that we may have more alternatives to choose from than we previously thought. A typical person in our culture does not believe that there is any real choice — he believes that his understanding of the world is simply "true," since all of his objective evidence confirms it. Furthermore, he believes that reality is simply "out there" — it is what it is, and we are just stuck with it. But from the perspective of the Possibility Model, we always have some degree of choice as to what possibilities we will focus our attention on, and how we will interpret them. Within this framework, our meaningful life experience is always seen as a synthesis of the possibility field of what-is, and our own belief choices — in other words, all of our seemingly "objective" evidence is *interpreted* evidence, and by changing our beliefs, we can change the content and meaning of our experience.

Logical Certainty

Objective evidence is one of the two main criteria used in our culture to determine validity. The other one is logical certainty or logical proof. In traditional logic, there are basically two kinds of logical proof: inductive and deductive. Inductive logic starts with particular examples, and proceeds to establish a general principle. This is how empirical science operates — after observing many individual events, the scientist formulates a general law. But we have already shown how this kind of logic cannot be used to help us decide between two differing worldviews. Any individual event that I would use as evidence to "prove" one view or the other has already been interpreted within the projected context of that view. For instance, I cannot amass enough evidence to inductively prove that human nature is either basically good or basically bad or even a mixture of the two — because the process of gathering and interpreting my evidence would already be colored by my beliefs.

Deductive logic, on the other hand, starts from a general principle, and proceeds to prove what must be the case in each individual instance. The classic example of this kind of proof is the syllogism, "All men are mortal. Socrates is a man. Therefore, Socrates is mortal." We can never use deductive logic, however, to establish our initial general principle. Yet in deciding between basic worldviews, that is exactly what we are trying to do — to establish our initial general principles.

Therefore, we cannot use either inductive or deductive logic to prove which of two worldviews is right. Each view, from *within* its own system of beliefs, can provide various arguments in favor of itself and against the other view. But the arguments cannot help us make the prior choice of which view to adopt in the first place.

This is not to say that we should simply throw out logic and rational thought. The real question for us is, what is the proper use of these tools and gifts? It seems that we cannot use logical thinking to prove the validity or the non-validity of, for instance, an idea such as "Spirit" or "goodness." But we can use rational thinking to help us discover this very fact — to help us discover the limits and the proper use of logical thinking itself. By discovering that logical certainty is not a valid criterion for deciding between basic worldviews, we are freed to use other, more appropriate criteria. It is, of course, valuable to give any new belief choice some thoughtful consideration before simply jumping in. But if we believe that we must logically prove to ourselves that it is right before we try it out, we have set ourselves an impossible task. For many people, the very impossibility of proving the validity of an alternative view keeps them locked in their old familiar beliefs — even when those old beliefs no longer truly serve them, and even though they are no more provable than the alternatives.

❖ Anxiety of Modern Times

It is part of our own historical destiny to live in a culture which tends to use logic and empirical evidence as the ultimate criteria for deciding truth. We find the beginnings of this belief with the ancient Greeks, and it is later developed more explicitly by the philosophers of the 16th and 17th centuries. Today, we often simply take it for granted that empirical evidence and logic are the best tools for making any decision about truth. But the downside of this exclusive emphasis on logic and empirical evidence is that we sometimes rely on them to do things that they cannot do. Many people today are looking for some alternative to the frightened, defensive worldview that seems to be so pervasive in our culture. They look to logic to provide arguments that the world is somehow spiritual or good or purposeful— and indeed, many of the books of philosophy and religion try, and ultimately fail, to provide a compelling "proof" of these ideas. This very failure causes still more frustration for those who are seeking an alternative view. They often interpret this failure to prove the existence of spirit as a kind of reverse proof that spirit does not exist. In desperation, they turn to their own life experience, hoping to find some kind of *conclusive* empirical evidence of the unity and goodness of all things — evidence so strong that it can justify the seemingly huge leap of faith involved in changing their basic life beliefs. But the very fearfulness of their search affects their perception of meaning, and tends to preclude the possibility of a more positive kind of experience.

We are left with the pervasive anxiety of modern times, which desperately asks such questions as, "How can I *know* whether I am alone, or God is with me? How can I *know* whether the world is random or purposeful? How can I *know* whether the world is fundamentally cruel and hostile, or good and benevolent? How can I *know* whether forgiveness, compassion and love is the most authentic way to live, or is merely foolish and weak? How can I *know* whether my thoughts really affect reality, or merely remain in the privacy and isolation of my own separate mind? How can I *know* whether the natural world is simply a collection of things to be used as man sees fit, or is a great family of life to be reverenced and loved? How can I *know* whether my intuitive sense about something is a real inner knowing, or is simply a wishful imagining?" Sometimes our concern with the meaning and value of reality is reflected in questions about particular topics. For instance, one friend of mine, who had just taken a workshop on shamanism, asked the question, "How can I *know* whether the shamanic journeys I am taking are 'real', or are just a product of my imagination?" Another friend, who was attending a dream workshop, asked, "How do I *know* if my dreams are meaningful spiritual journeys and messages from a friendly Unconscious, or are merely arbitrary mental fantasies and random firings of neurological circuits?" Another who had recently lost a close relative asked, "How do I *know* if there is an underlying purpose and good to this loss, or if it is simply a cruel and meaningless pain?"

I think that much of the desperation we often feel in asking such questions arises because our culture tends to interpret the word "know" exclusively in terms of objective evidence and logical certainty — and, as we have seen, these are simply inappropriate tools for making these kinds of choices. Trying to insert a screw with a hammer is frustrating — and simply hammering harder only makes the situation worse. The solution lies not in using the wrong tool more forcefully, but in finding a tool more appropriate to the task. Perhaps it would be more helpful to ask such questions as, "What do I want to believe? Is this belief consistent with my values and my life purpose? Does this belief make my life more satisfying, happier, and more peaceful? Does this belief somehow help me to better contribute to others and to the world? Why do I want to believe this? Does this belief serve a positive or constructive role in my life? What kinds of possible life experiences could be revealed by this belief? What kinds might be hidden or concealed by it?"

Since I cannot use the criteria of objective evidence and logical proof, my choice of a worldview may seem to be somewhat arbitrary, in the sense of "not having any objective basis." But it is certainly not arbitrary in the sense that "it makes no difference." My basic belief choices will affect what I see, how I see it, what I think about it, and how I feel. It will affect me mentally, physically, emotionally, ethically, socially, and spiritually. It will affect not only how I experience the world, but also how I experience myself. Even if every window is equal as a "window," it is possible that some windows can offer more expansive and more desirable views than others.

When we do not have objective criteria for our basic belief choices of value and meaning, then it seems as if they are a leap of faith. But it is important to recognize that we have no choice whether or not to make such a leap — as self-aware human beings deciding our day-to-day lives, *we are always already in mid-leap.* Our choice is not whether to leap — we can only choose the whither of our on-going leap. It is important to remember that we are always already in mid-leap, especially whenever we are considering changing one of our basic life beliefs. When facing such a decision, we are acutely aware that the new choice seems like a leap of faith. But the old belief choice, the one that we already believe and live, does not seem like such a leap at all — in fact, it often does not even seem like a "belief." Because it filters and interprets our current life experience, we are already encountering a wealth of supportive objective evidence. It seems as if our old belief is merely a reflection of what is there in front of us, staring us in the face. It seems to us that we are not making any "choice" at all — we are just being realistic. From that perspective, adopting a new and different belief that doesn't match our current objective evidence seems to involve a tremendous and unwarranted leap of faith. Even if the new belief could substantially improve the quality of our lives, it still seems foolhardy to fly in the face of the facts, and to blatantly ignore our current life experience. What is important to remember in such a situation is that our current belief is just as much of a leap of faith — even if we have temporarily forgotten that it is a leap because we have come to take it so much for granted.

PART TWO

CHOICES

CHAPTER 4

MAKING YOUR OWN CHOICES

❖ Thinking for Yourself

So far, we have explored the Possibility Model of Being — a general theory for understanding the role our beliefs play in helping to define and color our life experience. We noted that even this "Possibility Model" itself is but one possible belief choice — a choice to see the whole of "what is" as a range of possible experiences, rather than as some actual fixed reality. Within the context of the Possibility Model, objective evidence and logical proof are not adequate criteria to use in choosing our basic life beliefs.

In the absence of these objective standards, it seems that we must rely on more personal and individual criteria in making our basic belief choices. In the following chapters, I will discuss some of the theories and belief choices I have found helpful, and some of the questions and reflections that have led me to these choices. But when I talk in terms of "my" questions and "my" answers and "my" belief choices, I am not trying to claim exclusive ownership of, or take all of the credit for, these ideas. I have myself borrowed freely from many other thinkers in arriving at what works best for me. And even if I wanted to claim credit for my particular synthesis of all of these ideas, their meaning and significance will be transformed as soon as you think them through for yourself and integrate them into your own unique understanding — at that point, they will truly become your ideas, not mine. My questions and my answers are intended only as a starting point for your own self-reflection — the point of reading this book is not to become an expert on my truth, but to discover or create your own. What are your own truest and deepest questions? What are your own best answers? I can't give you the "right answers," or tell you "how things really are," or provide you with an accurate metaphysical description of the ultimate nature of reality. I don't even believe that there is some one theory or answer that is universally right for everyone; I don't believe that there is only one accurate description of "reality" — in terms of the light box analogy, there is no one way the picture really looks.

My purpose in writing this book is both more modest, and, at the same time, more profound than any possible "telling" could be. My intent is that my ideas and my questions will help craft for you a lighted clearing, within which you can discover the light choices which will best serve your own unique life journey. I say "help" craft a clearing, since your own participation is an essential part of this process. Your unique lighted clearing will be created by a synthesis of the words I write and the unique understanding you bring to these words.

In this spirit, I ask you to listen carefully to the truth of what I say. If I had said this at the beginning of the book, it would have sounded incredibly presumptuous. That is because we usually understand "truth" to mean an accurate description. Therefore, it would have sounded as if I thought I had some special knowledge about the absolute nature of reality — and I was advising you to take good notes, just in case there was a final exam before your "enlightenment." It would have sounded as if I were planning to create some kind of word painting, which was to be an accurate copy or re-presentation of ultimate reality. But now it is understood that I am using the term "truth" in the sense of unhiddenness. Therefore, when I ask you to listen to the truth of what I say, I am asking you to move into the *clearing* created by my ideas, rather than simply analyzing the words themselves. So whether you agree or disagree with my ideas, remember that the real goal of your reading and reflecting on this book is your own self-discovery. Instead of thinking of my words as an opaque painting or copy of reality, I invite you to approach them as a stained glass window — a window which invites you to gaze through it into the truth of your own being.

One very important aspect of any belief or idea is to be found in the *questions* it generates for us. A question is a way of creating a horizon of discovery — what I ask and how I ask it define the range and kinds of possible answers I can discover, but do not necessarily determine which particular answer I will find. A question is a quest into the clearing created by the underlying beliefs of the question. The following example can clarify this. Suppose you have just experienced a situation in which someone seemed to treat you unfairly. There are many kinds of questions you could ask, in order to better understand what happened. You might ask, "Why is that person so rotten?" This question assumes that the person is indeed rotten, and opens up the horizon of possible explanations for his rottenness — e.g., psychological factors, environmental factors, a difficult childhood, lack of moral integrity, etc. Or you might ask, "Why did such a rotten thing happen to me?" This question again assumes that what happened was bad, and searches for some explanation for your suffering — for instance, "Bad karma," "Rotten things always happen to me," or "It's a dog-eat-dog world." You could ask, "Why did I react to this rotten thing by getting so upset?" Again you assume that what happened was bad, but now you have shifted your focus to understanding how your own beliefs and attitudes may have caused your unhappy reaction. Or you could ask, "Why did I think this person or event was rotten in the first place?" This question no longer assumes that what happened to you was bad in and of itself, and now you are opened to the possibility of discovering alternative interpretations. Or you might ask, "How can this seemingly awful situation be seen as a blessing in disguise, as an opportunity for personal growth? How is this apparently terrible person really a disguised manifestation of Spirit — a teacher and a messenger?" These questions would open up yet another range of possible discovery.

We can see that even though each particular question does not necessarily determine the exact form and content of the answer, it does circumscribe a horizon of possible answers. Therefore, whenever we ask a question, it is important to pause for a moment to *examine the question itself*, before rushing straightaway to look for an answer. What are the underlying beliefs presupposed in the question? How do they limit and define your possible answers? Listening to the *truth* of a question means dwelling in its clearing with an open heart and an open mind, and discovering what reveals itself to you there. You don't want to become so preoccupied with the answers you are finding, that you forget that you yourself play a crucial role in creating the horizon of possible answers — you don't want to become so caught up in what you find in the clearing that you lose sight of the clearing itself. As you remember to focus on the truth or unhiddenness of your questions, you will take care to craft them so that they allow you to discover the kinds of answers you are truly seeking.

Theories, like questions, also create and define clearings of discovery. The word "theory" comes from the ancient Greek word "theoros," which meant "a view of the divine." In that context, a theory served as a specific window, through which the divine could partially reveal itself to a properly receptive mind. The thinker looked *through* the theory rather than "at" it — the words and ideas of the theory served as openings to a deeper vision. The truth of any theory (the unhiddenness created by it) depended not only on the ideas that made it up, but also on the intent of the person thinking that theory — most importantly, on an attitude of reverent openness. This reverence was not for the theory or for the person who created the theory, but for that deeper Mystery which could reveal itself through the theory. In terms of our Possibility Model, we would say that every theory exists as a range of possibilities, and that the attitude and intent of the thinker helps to determine which possibilities will be actualized. How we approach a theory will determine whether it will be simply an interesting intellectual construction to be figured out and argued for and against, or will be an opening to a deeper vision.

In English, the words "think" and "thank" are etymologically related.[6] In its most radical (root) sense, "thinking" does not mean merely figuring out the logical implications and internal consistency of a collection of ideas. It is not that calculating or figuring out is a "wrong" form of thinking — in fact in some situations, it may be very appropriate. Calculative thinking, however, never leaves the arena of the familiar — it merely explicates (unfolds) the implications of (what is already enfolded in) what is already known. But there is also another kind or level of thought that goes beyond just figuring things out — a thankful openness to the Mystery. This is the dimension of creative or original thinking. What makes a thought truly origin-al is not that it is necessarily new or different from everything that has gone before, but rather that it comes from the origin itself. In this kind of thinking, we allow the origin of thought to speak through us in its own way. My theories and questions are the light I actively shine ahead of myself, to create a specific lighted clearing. But this actively directed creative focus must be counterbalanced by a receptivity — a mindful and heartful openness to what reveals itself in the clearing. Ultimately, this is an openness to the Mystery itself, to the possibility of discovering what we cannot even conceive or imagine from our present frame of understanding — a reverent receptivity, which can allow the unspeakable Mystery to somehow speak through us. When I discover for myself what reveals itself in the truth (clearing) of my being, and I find the ideas that best express my discovery, then it truly becomes "my theory" "in my own words." To call something "my theory" does not mean that I own it like a possession. It means that I discovered it myself within my own openness, rather than merely accepted it on someone else's authority. To express my theory "in my own words" means that I have chosen those words which best re-create for me the specific clearing of discovery for that insight. In this sense, it is irrelevant whether anyone else has ever expressed a similar thought in similar words or not. The issue here is not "newness" or "difference" — what makes "my theories" and "my own words" origin-al is that I myself have gone to the origin of my thought to discover them for myself.

When I ask you to listen to the truth of what I say, I am encouraging you to think for yourself (which is the only way you can truly think anyway). I am asking you to focus on what I am talking about, rather than merely on what I am saying — to be receptive to the subject matter itself, rather than merely to the particular form of its expression. I am inviting you to see through me and my words — to see through them into that unique lighted clearing created by the synthesis of what I say and how you understand it. Remember that your own experience of this clearing and what you discover within the clearing may well be very different from mine. The goal here is not that you agree with me, but that you explore your own truth.

I believe that my responsibility as a writer here is to remain attentive to the truth of the subject matter itself. Only in this way can I discover and create the original meaning of my ideas for myself. To be sure, I have been influenced by many others in my life, both in the formal context of study and in the informal context of life in general — and I am grateful for the gifts and lessons they have shared with me. Some of the ideas I have learned from others have been and continue to be valuable searchlights in the process of illuminating and exploring the openness of my life. But original thinking is never just a matter of rearranging borrowed ideas in new combinations. I believe that I fulfill my responsibility as a thinker and a writer only by remaining focused on the truth of my own experience, and speaking in words that grow out of that truth for me. Likewise, you fulfill your creative responsibility as a reader only insofar as you use my words to illuminate and explore the truth of your own experience.

Often in my own process of self-exploration, I am unsure whether I am "discovering" or "creating" my answers, whether I am "finding" answers or "making them up." It may not always be possible to know whether we are doing one or the other, or a mixture of both. But we might want to ask whether it really makes a significant difference. This is a good example of questioning a question, before running off to look for an answer. Why would I want to ask whether I am "discovering" or "creating" my answers? For me, the intent behind such a question is that I want to know whether the answers I find are "really there," or are *merely* something I have "made up." "Merely" implies that anything that comes from my own creative imagination is somehow inferior to what is simply "given" to me from "the outside." But the truth for me is that *I don't know* whether one alternative is inferior to the other. Perhaps what comes to me from my own deepest wellsprings of creativity and imagination — the stuff that I "make up" — is just as (or even more) valid and true as what I "discover" already existing "out there." Or maybe there is no real difference between them — maybe "in here" and "out there" are only relative distinctions within some greater whole. The point here is that often

I don't know whether I "discovered" or "created" a given idea or theory, and furthermore, *I don't know* if it makes any difference anyway.

For some people, "I don't know" implies powerlessness and lack. It can even be a source of insecurity, which paralyzes someone who is afraid to begin or commit to anything without first "knowing all the answers." For instance, I have met people who are unable or unwilling to formulate a statement of their own basic life purpose, because they are afraid that they might just be "making it up" — and that would mean that it was "not really true." Since there's no way to conclusively prove to themselves whether they're just making it up or not, they simply never begin at all. For me, however, there is a tremendous power to "I don't know" — it is a source of openness and discovery, and it can give me an exhilarating sense of freedom. In terms of our Possibility Model, we could say that "I don't know" exists as a constellation of possible meanings and possible life experiences, depending on how we choose to understand it. "I don't know" can open up either a clearing of paralyzing insecurity or a clearing of adventuresome discovery.

Socrates, who was widely regarded as one of the wisest men in ancient Greece, claimed that his so-called wisdom consisted simply of knowing that he did not know. Because he knew that he did not know, he was able to entertain possibilities that others often found strange and threatening. Socrates' contemporaries eventually condemned him to death, ultimately because they refused to face the possibility that they might not know either. This is a typical human reaction when faced with the strange. When we assume that the familiar (what we already know) is the whole of reality, encountering something beyond the familiar threatens our world — threatens it because we have implicitly denied that there is any "beyond" at all. Typical self-defensive responses to a strange idea include ignoring it, ridiculing it, or attacking it. In doing so, we may preserve the seeming security and validity of our familiar view, but it will be at the expense of any real growth and creativity. As you read the following chapters, I encourage you to maintain an "I don't know" attitude. This is more than merely acknowledging that you don't know certain facts or information. The deeper meaning of "I don't know" is remembering that ultimately I don't know and I can't know "what the picture really looks like." When I remember that I don't know the whole of what is possible, I can remain more open whenever I encounter what seem at first to be strange ideas and theories — open not in the sense of just blindly accepting them, but rather truly entertaining their possibility. In its deepest sense, remembering that "I don't know" reminds me to always listen to the truth of what is said — to move into its lighted clearing with an open heart and an open mind, in order to discover what possibilities can reveal themselves therein. As Shunryu Suzuki said in his wonderful book, *Zen Mind, Beginner's Mind*, "In the beginner's mind there are many possibilities, but in the expert's there are few."

❖ What Truly Serves You

How can we consciously and deliberately choose those basic belief choices, choose those "light choices" that will define and color the lighted clearing of our life experience? From what we have said so far, it is obvious that this is not simply a matter of choosing the "right" belief over the "wrong" (false) one. According to the Possibility Model, "what is" is an indefinite range of possible life experiences, and my belief choices filter and interpret these possibilities, allowing some of them to become actual life experiences for me. The whole range of possible life experiences is so rich and vast, that it seems to contain many experiences that are contradictory and mutually exclusive of one another. Thus there may be many situations in which two opposite belief choices can be equally valid or "right." This is not to say, however, that all basic life beliefs are therefore equal. Some may reveal more possibilities than others. Perhaps even more important than the quantitative measure of how many possibilities are revealed, is the *qualitative* measure of what kinds of possibilities are revealed — how my belief choices affect the quality of my life experience. Some belief choices may reveal "better" possibilities than others (however I may define "better" for myself). Just as important as the question of which possibilities are revealed by a given belief or worldview, is the question of which ones are concealed by it. Every *definite* belief choice, precisely insofar as it is "definite," is necessarily *partial* — it can reveal only those possibilities that are within the horizon of its definition, and will conceal all of those that are outside of its scope. So, in making any belief choice, we always want to consider not only what it may allow us to experience, but also what it may exclude or shut out from our lives.

So how can I choose my basic life beliefs — the beliefs that will influence and color and define my experiences of myself and my world? What criterion or reference point can I use? I believe in the final analysis you have to ask yourself, "What truly serves me?" "Truly" serves you means serves you in your truth (who and what you are in your deepest unhiddenness) — serves to help you experience and express your truth. Seen in this light, "what truly serves you" is not necessarily an egocentric criterion — in fact, it becomes egocentric only if you (choose to) believe that you are, in your deepest truth, just a separate and self-interested ego. But if you were to think of yourself, for instance, as part of the greater whole of life, or as one unique expression of the deeper spiritual reality of all things, then "what truly serves you" would necessarily include what truly serves the whole.

In order to use "what truly serves me" as my criterion, I have to have some idea of who and what I am in my deepest truth — and my idea of my truth will be the touchstone of all my life choices. My concept of "who I am and why I am here" is what we could call, "my life purpose." My understanding of my life purpose will be *the* fundamental reference point for every other conscious belief choice I make. Moreover, it is a *positive* reference point — I make my choices on the basis of how they can help me to move *toward* fulfilling my purpose, rather than simply how they might help me to avoid or move away from things I don't like.

One way I can think of my life purpose is in terms of three basic components. The first is the component of "who I am" — this is the general "quality of being" I desire to bring to *every* situation and *every* moment of my life. Since this is a way of being that I myself *bring* to life, no external circumstance can prevent me from fulfilling this component of my life purpose. From this perspective, the quality of my life is not wholly determined by what I "do" and what happens "to" me —it is primarily defined by *who* and *how I am* throughout the various doings and happenings of my life. The second component is "how I want to contribute to others and to the whole." This again is to be understood at the most general level — not as a specific action, but as the general way of being-with-others that I wish to bring to *every* interaction and *every* relationship in my life. The third component is what some Native American peoples have called, my "give-away" or my "soul-gift." This is the unique way I can best live and fulfill my contribution to others — the unique gift(s), quality(s) or talent(s) I have been given to "perform for my People." It is how I can best fulfill the sacred promise of my life, how I can best express my unique truth — it is how I live my life truthfully, how I express who I am as fully and unhiddenly as possible. It is important to understand that the third component of one's life purpose is simply a further specification of the second component.

Here are a couple of examples of life purpose statements that come from participants in the workshops my wife and I teach: "My purpose is to be kind and happy in every moment, and to serve others in every interaction by helping them to remember that they can always choose happiness for themselves. My soul-gift is my ability to easily forgive others, and to see the best in everyone." Another one: "My purpose is to appreciate the beauty inherent in every moment (appreciation as a way of being, rather than as a particular doing), and to help others to discover the beauty in their own lives. My soul-gift is my artistic ability as a painter."

This is only one possible way to understand the idea of "life purpose." What is most important is that you, the reader, actually ask yourself the question, "What is my life purpose?" Having some provisional understanding of your own life purpose will help to transform our subsequent discussion of belief choices from a merely interesting intellectual consideration of possible alternatives, into a concrete encounter with *your own life*. If you have not yet formulated your statement of life purpose for yourself, I urge you to stop reading at the end of this section, and write out a provisional version of it. If you're not sure about what it is, then just do your best to specify it now — you can always change it later if you wish. But if you don't deliberately formulate your own life purpose, you will be left with living one that you adopted unconsciously —some hodge-podge combination of your childhood wounds, your fears, your parents' ideas, and general public opinion. I believe that your best effort now will be more authentic and true to yourself than this haphazardly inherited mish-mash. If you're going to seriously consider fundamental belief choices that can affect every aspect of your life, you will want some *authentic* criterion, some reference point that is truly your own. In order to decide what choices will serve your best interests, you have to have some idea of what your best interests are. If you haven't clarified your own life purpose for yourself yet, take some time now to begin thinking about it. Don't worry about getting it completely "right" on the first try. It may be that there is no pre-determined right purpose for you — formulating your purpose may be a creative act, rather than a guessing game. Moreover, even if there is some right purpose for you, perhaps the only way you'll ever come to know it fully is by living your best version now, paying attention to the feedback, and updating your purpose statement as you grow and learn. In the end, only you can determine what your own unique life purpose is, and know whether you are fulfilling it.

Many people, of course, do not deliberately choose their fundamental reference point, nor are they even aware that they have a choice in the matter. Often their unconscious and unexamined reference point is not a single or coherent focus at all, but is a mixture of contradictory and inconsistent ideas. Consciously and deliberately choosing your own life purpose not only allows you to make more authentic belief choices for yourself, but also makes your choices more powerful and effective. What gives a laser beam its phenomenal power is that all of its individual light waves are in synch with one another — it is a *coherent* beam of light. In a non-coherent light beam, the various individual light waves are not in synch, and so they partially cancel each other out. In a laser, however, the energy of each individual wave is added to that of all the others, resulting in a powerful beam of light that can even penetrate steel. Likewise, as you become more clear about your own life purpose, your belief choices tend to become more focused and coherent, resulting in more power — more power to express your truth.

Another important part of your fundamental reference point is what you truly desire — what you truly desire to become, to accomplish, to have, to do, to experience, to contribute. Clarifying your own visions and dreams for yourself allows you to make those belief choices that best enable you to move toward and realize those dreams — belief choices that create a lighted clearing, within which you can discover those possibilities that best support your dreams. What is important here is that you consciously define for yourself your own *authentic* dreams — "truly" desire means that your desire grows out of and expresses your truth and your purpose. The clearer you are about your purpose, the clearer you can be about your true desires.

Your conscious choices of your life purpose and your dreams will generate new kinds of questions in your life. When faced with a seemingly adverse situation, for instance, you will tend to ask such questions as, "How can I fulfill my purpose in this situation? How can I meet this challenge, and still be the kind of person I desire to be, regardless of the eventual outcome? How can I use this situation as a stepping-stone toward realizing my dream?" Such questions open you up to those possible experiences that can help you fulfill your purpose and realize your dreams. Looking for something does not guarantee, of course, that you will find it — but it does open you to the possibility of finding it. The real power of "what truly serves me" is that it puts your life into a positive perspective — a perspective that is defined in terms of what you *are*, and what you are living *toward*.

❖ Fingers Pointing at the Moon

Many years ago, when I was a university professor, I sat by a campfire one evening with one of my colleagues who taught physics. I began talking about how fire was an elemental idea in a particular Eastern cosmology, an archetypal symbol of energy and transformation, of spiritual light and clarity. I also mentioned that many Native American tribes regarded fire as a living presence, which they approached with the deepest reverence and respect — "Grandfather Fire" who helped us interpret our dreams, and who offered us support and guidance on our life journeys. After I had waxed poetic for a while, my friend said that my ideas sounded very inspiring and beautiful, but what was "really happening" was that the energy of the sun's light had somehow been stored in the atomic structure of the wood, and that the oxidation process was now releasing the energy in a form we perceived as heat and light. I don't remember all of the intricate physics of his explanation, but what struck me at the time was his assertion that this was "the one true way" to describe what was "really" happening. He did not say that if we viewed the phenomenon of fire through the interpretive framework and presuppositions of science, then we could experience it and talk about it in a particular way — a way that would be very helpful if we wanted, for instance, to control and use fire for our own ends. Instead, he said that his way of talking about the fire described what was "really" happening, whereas my poetic or mythic way of speaking about fire was *merely* a pleasant fantasy.

In a similar vein, my wife relates a story that happened in her childhood. She and her sister used to observe with wonder the bright sparks of light that seemed to jump from the satin comforter, whenever it was rustled in a dark room. My wife says she was amazed and awestruck by these bright blue flashes. But at one point, her older sister casually remarked, "Oh, that's just static electricity." My wife recalls that at that moment she felt very knowledgeable to learn this bit of scientific information — and yet some of the magic was lost. It was, after all, *just* static electricity. Even though she didn't know what "static electricity" meant, it was enough to know that it was named and known and understood by someone. When her friends came over to her house, she would show them the flashes, and tell them, "That's just static electricity." As the years went by, she took various science courses, and her understanding of static electricity became more sophisticated and mathematical. But she never again fully experienced the wonder and awe of those childhood flashes. It was almost as if all she saw was a reflection of her understanding — almost as if the mysterious flashes themselves now became only a barely perceived event, which triggered her idea of "static electricity" with all of its accumulated associations. The magic and the mystery were somehow gone. (This story makes me wonder to what extent we live in a world of labels — experiencing *just* "a tree," *just* "a deer," *just* "a mountain," *just* "my wife," *just* "the rain.")

In both of these stories, it is not the scientific concepts and theories that are the problem. It could be argued that our scientific understanding of static electricity has allowed us to understand and experience possibilities that have led to valuable technological inventions. Moreover, for some people science itself is the doorway to wonder. Nor is the problem here the fact that the scientific view of the world is only a partial view — for every definite view, precisely insofar as it is "definite," is inherently partial. But when we presume that one way of seeing and talking about something is the only accurate description and the only true way to see it, then we cut ourselves off from all other possibilities of experience. From a certain kind of worldview, poetry and myth are *merely* mental fantasies that fall short of the accuracy and precision of scientific, factual, descriptive language. For our Possibility Model, however, the potential truthfulness of poetry and myth lies precisely in the fact that they *do not pretend to describe* ultimate reality. Whenever our ideas pretend to accurately describe "what's really going on," they become opaque — hiding both their own limitedness, and any appreciation for a deeper and richer field of possibilities that might lie beyond it. In this spirit, I earlier encouraged you to approach my ideas not as an opaque word-painting that pretended to give an accurate copy of the "really real," but rather as a translucent stained glass window — a window which invites you to look through and beyond what I am saying toward the very heart of what I am talking about.

The Mystery

The "beyond" is what I will call "the Mystery" — that generative field of possibilities that can never be completely comprehended and expressed by any particular theory or point of view. As I said, every definite theory, precisely insofar as it is "definite," is necessarily partial — even as it reveals some possibilities, it always conceals others. In this way of thinking about the world, there will always be an irreducible element of Mystery at the heart of all things — an aspect or dimension which is unknown in principle. This is not a mystery in the sense of a puzzle that we haven't yet solved, as if all we needed were a little more information or a little more time to think. The underlying Mystery is not cause for me to think harder, but rather a reminder to approach the world with openness — openness to that dimension which is always beyond everything I can understand. Many of our important belief choices concern what we choose to believe about this underlying Mystery. If, for instance, we choose to understand it as inherently sacred, we might approach it with a sense of reverence, and thus open ourselves to otherwise hidden possibilities of guidance and blessing.

The Mystery at the heart of all things also means that we can never completely understand any particular thing — we can never know "what the picture really looks like." No matter how many meaningful experiences we have of a thing or person or event, we can never know what unactualized potential may still lie beyond all of those partial glimpses.

Inherent to the meaning of Mystery is that we cannot prove its existence. Choosing to believe that there is an irreducible Mystery in the heart of all things is a leap of faith — but so is choosing not to believe. In considering such a choice, we would want to ask, "What possibilities of experience are opened up by a belief in the 'Mystery at the heart of all things'?" Part of the importance of the concept of Mystery is that it recalls us to wonderment — it reminds us to not merely take things for granted, and to not become so lost in our theories about the world that we forget to remain open to the unknown, the new, the strange, the creative, the miraculous.

In the context of the Possibility Model, *the only true value of a belief choice is the quality and depth of life experience it makes possible.* Another way to say this is that *the truth of anything is the clearing it creates in my life now.* The various belief choices we will consider throughout this book are possible ways of *thinking about* the world. The Zen Buddhists talk about language as a "finger pointing at the moon" — the ultimate goal of our words is to direct our attention back to our immediate and direct experience of life. Too often, however, we tend to forget about the direct experience, and become preoccupied with the ideas and theories in themselves — we get lost in debating and comparing the various fingers, and forget to actually experience and appreciate the awesome mysterious beauty of the moon itself.

In the chapters that follow, we will explore some basic belief choices. I call them "basic," inasmuch as each of them involves a choice about the fundamental nature of reality in general, and thus will tend to affect every area of our life experience. I will discuss each choice in terms of two alternatives — but these alternatives should be understood as defining a *spectrum* of possible choices. Depending on how you define the alternatives at either end of a spectrum, you may be faced with an either-or choice, or a range of possible gradations. There are many possible spectrums of belief choices, and many ways to define each spectrum. (To save the Latin scholars an unnecessary trip to their dictionaries, "spectrums" is one accepted variation of the plural of "spectrum.") I have tried to present each spectrum as broadly as possible. For some readers, my alternatives may be too extreme; for others, they may seem too conservative. Ultimately, the true value for you of this whole discussion of these alternatives will be the clearings they help you to create for yourself, and the possibilities of your own life experience that you can discover within those clearings.

I have tried to present these belief choices in an unbiased and neutral way. But I myself do have my own preferences, as I'm sure will show through in what I say and how I say it. But it's not my intention to convince you that my choices are right for you. How you understand each of these alternatives, and how you experience your life through them may be different from my understanding and my experience. Again, I invite you to see through me — to see through my theories and explanations into the truth of *your* own life. If you disagree with me, use that disagreement as a stepping-stone to clarify for yourself what you *do* believe, rather than merely as an excuse to criticize and attack what you don't believe. The real purpose of this journey — not the "destination," but the purpose inherent in every step of the way — is your own self-discovery.

CHAPTER 5

THE SEPARATIVE AND
THE HOLISTIC VIEWS

The first spectrum we will explore is defined by the two belief choices I call the "Separative view" and the "Holistic view." I want to emphasize once again that these two belief possibilities are my own constructions. The purpose of this discussion of the Separative and the Holistic views is to help you to create a lighted clearing for your own exploration and self-discovery.

❖ The Separative View

For the Separative view, reality fundamentally exists as a collection of *separate and independent* beings and things. This essential characteristic of separateness applies not only to physical things, but also to minds — each person's mind or consciousness is considered to be fundamentally separate from every other mind or consciousness. To say that each mind is "separate" means that each has its own private thoughts and its own separate will. Here, "separate will" implies both an independent ability to choose, and a separate individual good — and since "my good" is different from "your good," what I will for my life is different from what you will for yours. Since reality consists entirely of separate things, any concepts that describe collections of things are considered to be mere abstractions. From this perspective, ideas such as "community," "nation," "species," "ecosystem" and even "Reality" are understood to be abstract mental notions that we use to refer to collections of separate individuals.

I am calling this view the "Separative view," rather than something like the "Multiplicity view," because the emphasis here is not so much on the quantitative "many-ness" of things, but on their *separateness* from one another. For the Separative view, each being is thought to be essentially self-contained and independent. In particular, each person is conceived to be self-enclosed and separate — separate from other people, and separate from the rest of the world. I will use the term "ego" to refer to this separate, independent identity (note that this is different from the more Freudian idea of "ego" as a social persona). The most fundamental separation experienced by a self-aware Separative person is the separation between himself and everything else — the separation between "inside" (of me) and "outside" (of me), or between "me" and "not me." For the Separative view, all of the other things and people in the world remain essentially and irrevocably external to oneself.

In terms of the Possibility Model, we could say that the Separative view acts as an interpretive filter which allows me to experience only my separateness from everything else, and excludes any possible experience of interconnectedness. When I experience myself as separate from all other people and things, I will tend to feel cut off and alone. A common theme in modern literature and philosophy is man's alienation from other people and from Nature. Often in these discussions of what to do about this alienation, the "fact" of separateness is never questioned at all — separateness is assumed to be simply a given. In general, the Separative view tends to be so prevalent and so taken for granted in our culture that it is not considered to be a "view" at all — it is presumed to be simply a description of how things are. From the perspective of the Separative view, any experience of interconnectedness is essentially illusory — merely a subjective projection of lonely wishful thinking.

Separative Ethics

The word "ethics" comes from the ancient Greek word "ethos." One of the root meanings of ethos is "true (unhidden) character." In its original sense, to speak or act ethically meant to speak or act *truthfully*. To live an ethical life meant to live in such a way that my inner nature would shine forth unhiddenly through my words and deeds — to live ethically meant to live *authentically*. Since the Separative view focuses exclusively on the separateness of individuals, the corresponding ethics will tend to be egocentric. The term, "egocentric," refers to a way of life whose primary focus and reference point is one's own separate good. For the Separative perspective, the most authentic way I can express my own reality and my own separateness is by "looking out for number one" — for instance, by the acquisition of power and possessions for myself. If I also believe that reality is made up of only a limited number of things, and that there is not enough for everyone, then I will tend to relate to others competitively, since one person's gain will always be another's loss. In general, the Separative view will tend to be reflected in an egocentric ethics of competition, struggle, and acquisition in the dog-eat-dog jungle of separate individuals.[7]

But obviously this is not the only ethical view in our basically Separative culture. Many people who maintain a Separative view also aspire to a morality of altruism, and of cooperation and harmony among individuals. But since the Separative view believes that reality consists of separate individuals, it will tend to regard altruism as self-sacrifice — every noble altruistic gesture essentially requires choosing another's good *instead of* your own. Since this self-sacrifice is inconsistent with the Separative person's authentic egotism, he must find a way to justify it. Typically he does this by appealing to some external authority — for instance, believing that someone or something outside of himself tells him he "has to" or "should" be kind and loving. This outside source may be God's commandments, society's customs, or some arbitrary legal structure — or it may be simply the rational arguments of pragmatism, which contend that one has a better chance of survival if he cooperates with others. If a Separative person believes that altruism is "good," he will try to rein in and control his authentic egotistic instincts in order to *act* kindly, compassionately and lovingly. In the Separative view of the Ten Commandments, for instance, God gives humans a number of "shalts" and "shalt nots," in order to control their basic selfish nature. In one version of Freudian psychology, man is described as having a primal selfish, animal-like core (the id), which is held in check only by the internalized learned constraints of society (the superego).

Thus, for a Separative person, altruistic morality usually involves an inner conflict. Acting compassionately and unselfishly toward others is defined as "good," even though it is artificial and inconsistent with his true selfish nature. Conversely, acting selfishly and exerting his will over others for his own gain is considered "bad," even though this way of acting authentically expresses what he believes to be his true inner nature as a separate being. He is caught in the paradox that what is *truly* good for himself is defined as bad, and what is *truly* bad for himself is defined as good.[8] The Separative person tends to live under the constant threat that if he lets his "real self" out, he will be bad — he will sink into an uncivilized existence of lust, greed, and selfishness. In order to be good, to be morally acceptable to himself and others, he has to pretend to be something he is not. Shame is built into such a morality from the beginning — because even if I can manage to fool others, I am constantly aware that my real inner self is actually bad in its very being.

Social Relationships

A Separative person's ethics of egocentricity and selfishness will tend to influence all of his social relations. Each person is seen as a completely separate, independent individual, and in his true heart of hearts, he is primarily out for himself. The only reasons why a person might act unselfishly would be hypocrisy (he is merely pretending for the sake of some ulterior motive), foolish ignorance (he is not aware of his own separateness), or an artificial morality. Thus friendship and love tend to be on a very tenuous foundation of pretense, deceit, and self-interest. A self-aware Separative person tends to view his friends and loved ones with an undercurrent of suspicion — everyone and everything is a potential enemy or competitor, and every seemingly loving word or deed is ultimately unreal. Conversely, every word or deed that is selfish or inconsiderate is seen as the truth — as the true inner reality shining through, an epiphany of our essential selfishness. The overall emotional tenor of this perspective tends to be one of fear and suspicion. You are always on the lookout to unmask others for their hypocrisy, so that you can condemn them and reject their pretended friendship. Since others will also be on the lookout for your own hypocrisy, you live in constant fear that others will see through your pretense — that they will see that you are truly not good enough, and will either attack or abandon you. In this way, the insecurity and fears of our infancy become embedded in the morality of our adulthood.

Since each person is inherently selfish, moral education becomes a process of discouraging the bad, rather than encouraging the good. We have to use threats, fear, and punishment to compel others to act unselfishly — and often withholding love is the primary way we motivate or "train" someone to be "good." Our penal system is based on the belief that we must punish the criminal so harshly that he will be afraid to commit another crime. Many religions use the threat of divine punishment, eternal damnation, or bad karma to deter immoral or anti-social behavior. A common form of parenting, at least in our culture, is to spank and yell and punish and threaten, until we have frightened the child into acting "civilized." This form of parenting, which continually focuses on and emphasizes the bad and the unworthy in the child, tends to engender low self-esteem. The child grows up believing that he can never possibly be good enough. From this perspective, self-love can only be a pretense.

Because the Separative person believes in the essential selfishness of every person, he will tend to have the greatest difficulty in his most intimate relationships. Even to have such a close relationship at all seems contrary to the fundamental reality of separateness. This contradiction becomes especially apparent in the notion that you can "let your hair down" and "really be yourself" with the people you love the most — with the underlying assumption that your "real self" is essentially selfish and defensive. Consider the following example, which is very typical in our culture. After a long day of trying hard to appear nice and courteous to all of the strangers and business associates in your workplace, you return home exhausted to your spouse or loved one. Now you can finally relax and just "be yourself." You no longer have to hide your so-called "true" feelings, for fear of offending a client or losing your job. No longer making that extra effort to appear patient and understanding, you tend to snap and react, and to vent every petty irritation. Since your loved one is probably also "letting her hair down" or "just being himself," he or she will be acting the same way. Thus, what could be the closest relationship in your life and could offer you a real alternative to the feelings of separateness and alienation, often becomes the arena of your most intense struggle and defensiveness.

I am not arguing, however, that the belief in separateness *necessarily* makes a person egocentric, or necessarily leads to a competitive social structure based on selfishness and greed. Nor am I arguing that every Separative person is necessarily mean or petty or unhappy. But the Separative view inherently tends to engender an ethics of egocentricity and competition, even when these values are buried under a divinely or socially sanctioned morality of altruism. And by emphasizing separateness and isolation, the Separative view also tends to promote a fearful and defensive frame of mind.

The point of this discussion is not to condemn or discredit the Separative view, but to show some of the implications of this one basic belief choice. Often a Separative person will not even question these implications, because he isn't aware of his underlying presupposition of separateness. Thus, a Separative person tends to regard the selfishness and fear and negativity in his life as merely "the way things are," and merely the cost of being "realistic." The purpose of exploring the psychological and social implications of the Separative view is to raise the possibility that this fear and negativity may not be as inevitable as we sometimes think. I am not trying to argue that such a fearful and unhappy view of life is necessarily a "wrong" or "false" belief choice — I am simply emphasizing that it is a *choice*.

❖ The Holistic View

Like the Separative view, the Holistic view is my own construction. My definition of the term "holistic" may differ from how others use the term. I will capitalize it to indicate when I am referring to the Holistic view, according to my definition.

For the Holistic view, the fundamental reality is the whole. Even though the various parts of the whole may be distinguishable from one another, and may even have some *relative* degree of independence or autonomy, they exist as essentially interconnected parts of a greater totality. "*Essentially* interconnected" means that the inner essence or truth of your being (your being in its deepest unhiddenness) *is* that it is a part of a greater whole. Your relationship to any other part of the whole is not somehow "outside" you or "between" you and a separate other — being-related is an *intrinsic* dimension of your own being. For the Holistic perspective, to say that you are "part" of a greater whole does not mean that you are like one separate, interlocking piece in a huge puzzle of many separate interlocking pieces. Here, "part" means that you *are*, in your own being, one unique and distinct expression or manifestation of the greater whole. (Often the analogy of a hologram is used to illustrate this kind of part/whole relationship, since every "part" of a holographic plate contains the information of the whole holographic image.)

From the Holistic perspective, there may be many overlapping levels of wholeness, and each relative whole can itself be an integral part of a still more comprehensive whole. The various "levels" of wholeness represent *possible ways of thinking about and experiencing* the whole of Being. For instance, a holistic doctor would approach the physical body as a whole, rather than trying to treat separate symptoms, separate organs or separate body systems — from this perspective, no part of the body could be truly healthy unless the whole body were healthy. At an even deeper level, he would have to consider the whole individual — treating the whole person, rather than the disease. The whole person would include body, mind and emotions — not as separate parts, somehow stuck together, but rather as interrelated aspects of a whole. In terms of our Possibility Model, we could say that these "aspects" were different possible ways I could experience a whole person, depending on my lighted clearing — seeing the person, for instance, in light of an idea of "the physical" or "the mental" or "the emotional." The whole person, in turn, would be seen as a part of a still greater whole — which could include the levels of the whole family, the whole community, the whole human race, the whole planet, and the whole universe. Although each level may be relatively autonomous with respect to the others (so that as a holistic doctor, I could, for instance, recommend a change in a person's diet, without also having to solve the international crisis in the Middle East), the Holistic view maintains that the various levels are not absolutely separate and independent of each other — ultimately, they are only interdependent distinctions within a greater whole.

In this spectrum of light choices, I am distinguishing between "separateness" and "wholeness," rather than between the "many" and the "One" — again, my primary focus is not the quantitative question of "how many" things exist, but the *qualitative* issues of connectedness and interrelatedness.   The issue is not whether Reality is like some homogeneous blob of Jell-O without any differentiation, but whether there is any greater intrinsic wholeness somehow connecting all of the individual things we perceive.   Wholeness, as I am defining it, does not exclude differentiation and diversity, but rather embraces them

For the Separative view, the self is completely separate and independent from everything else — "inside" (of me, of my mind, etc.) is absolutely separate from "outside."   For the Holistic view, however, inside/outside is only a *relative* distinction within the continuity of a greater whole, as are the distinctions of mind/body (or mind/matter) and subject/object. For the Holistic view, the experience of separateness is only the illusory experience of the absence of wholeness.   In terms of the Possibility Model, the mistaken idea of separateness creates a lighted clearing that actively excludes the experience of wholeness. Thus for the Holistic view, the ego is merely a mental fiction — how you mistakenly conceive your identity within the illusory context of separateness.   An egocentric life, far from truly serving you, would actually prevent you from experiencing your truth.

Holistic Ethics

According to the Separative view, man is separate and apart from other people and from Nature in general. Many modern writers, who speak of man's alienation from other people, search for ways to bridge this chasm of separateness. But for the Holistic view, the experience of feeling separate and cut off is only the emotional reflection of your denial of the truth of wholeness — it is what you experience when you conceal from yourself who you are in your deepest unhiddenness. Trying to "bridge the gap" only makes the gap seem more real, as something that must somehow be bridged. For the Holistic view, man is *already* connected with others and with Nature — he is already a strand in the greater web of life. Man doesn't need to build or create a connection between himself and others, or between himself and Nature — he has only to shift his focus and *remember* the connectedness that always already exists.

Starting from a foundation of wholeness rather than separateness, we also tend to develop a very different understanding of ethics and social relations. If what "I" am is fundamentally a part of a greater whole, then the ethics that would most truly express this wholeness would tend to be an ethics of compassion, love, and cooperation. For the Holistic view, the ethics of love and cooperation would be understood as an authentic expression of my own true nature, rather than a moral obligation — as an essential part of my own true happiness, rather than merely as something I "should" do. From this perspective, love would not be thought of as self-sacrifice — seen in this light, my own good is not in opposition to the good of others or the good of the whole. Whatever I do to serve others and to serve the whole also serves me as an integral part of that whole. Similarly, what I do to care for myself also nourishes the greater whole of which I am a part. To forsake or deny or harm any part of the whole would to some degree harm every other part of the whole as well. From the perspective of a whole-centered ethics, either to forsake myself or to forsake others would be equally partial and one-sided.

❖ Stages of Human Development

For a Holistic person, the Separative view can be understood as a natural stage in the development of self-consciousness. When a child begins to differentiate himself from his environment and from those around him, he begins to see himself as one separate being surrounded by other separate beings. Understanding the partial truth of separateness represents a growth or expansion from the undifferentiated and un-self-aware consciousness of the infant. Becoming aware of the self's dimension of separateness is the foundation of a sense of individual responsibility. As the child strives to fulfill and satisfy his own individual desires and needs, he becomes aware of a power structure — he sees others as having more power, less power, or equal power relative to himself. Within this power hierarchy of separate individuals, he learns to fend for himself, using whatever tools seem to work best in his particular situation — for instance, force, anger, violence, passive aggression, politeness, whining, cajoling, etc. Since many people in our culture never really encounter an alternative way of thinking, they grow into adulthood without ever questioning the Separative view they adopted as children. They may refine their social manipulative and coping skills as they get older, but the basic structure of their worldview remains much the same as it was in their childhood.

In many indigenous cultures, there are specific rituals to initiate a child into adulthood. A common theme running through the various forms of these rituals is that the child is taken away from her familiar role within the family group — taken away from the familiar structures of "me" and "mine." The child is introduced to the idea of the Great Spirit in all things — to the idea that she is not merely, or even primarily, a separate, independent being, but is rather an integral part of the greater family of all life. Often these rituals also include an inner journey, such as a traditional vision quest, to discover one's own unique role in the web of life — to discover one's unique "soul-gift," her way to best express her own unique interconnectedness with all beings. After the initiation rite, the person is no longer merely a child — no longer just a separate special individual, whose responsibilities are limited to herself and her particular group. As an adult, she has discovered her deeper and truer identity as a unique expression of the Spirit in all things — she is now responsible to the whole of creation. (Since the Separative view thinks in either-or terms, it will tend to regard such ideas as "the unity of all things" as a kind of regression back toward the undifferentiated awareness of the infant, and thus it tends to judge such indigenous initiation rituals as "primitive.")

For the Holistic person, the loss of such rituals in our modern culture can leave a person partially blinded. There is no definite transition from being a separate individual within the nuclear family (or, for some children, within the local gang) to being a co-participant in the greater whole of creation. "Adulthood" is often defined in our culture only in terms of certain objective events — for instance, a woman's first menstrual period, a person's first sexual experience, financial independence, or the right to vote or buy alcohol. But these external trappings of modern adulthood all take place within the context of the Separative beliefs of childhood — in other words, a Separative adult is simply a bigger, stronger, more powerful child. In our culture, there is no generally accepted concept of a greater, all-encompassing whole, and therefore no culturally accepted way of introducing a child to the idea of a greater identity or a greater context of responsibility. Thus, from the perspective of the Holistic view, many adults in our modern culture remain stuck in the Separative belief system of childhood, unaware that there is any alternative.

CHAPTER 6

THE TECHNOLOGICAL AND THE SPIRITUAL VIEWS

❖ The Technological View

I call one end of this next spectrum "the Technological view." I am using the term "technology" as it was defined by the twentieth century philosopher Martin Heidegger. The suffix "-ology" means "seeing reality through the concept of." Thus, techn-ology literally means seeing reality through (or relative to) the concept of *techne* (technique, manipulation, use). For the Technological view, things in and of themselves have *no intrinsic value* — they become useful or not useful, good or bad, meaningful or meaningless only relative to the needs, desires, and purposes of human beings. All value is simply human projection, and is defined only in terms of usefulness to humankind. For the Technological view, the primary distinction is between humans (as value-givers) and everything else (as mere "stuff" to be given value and meaning by humans). Thus defined, the Technological view would be an example of a thought-creates-reality approach to the world, at least as regards the reality of meaning, value and significance. (It is very important to emphasize here that "the Technological view," as I am defining it, does not refer to the particular human activity called "technology," nor to "technological" inventions and machines. Rather it refers to the worldview or way-of-thinking that would create the activity of modern technology with its associated inventions and machines *in order to* more efficiently dominate and control the world for man's own purposes. Furthermore, the contrast between the Technological view and the Spiritual view does not imply in any way that the activities of science and technology, with all of their associated products and inventions, are in any way "unspiritual.")

In its simplest form, the Technological view is the belief that nothing outside of me has any inherent value. Everything outside of me is simply "stuff," to be used as I please, for my own pleasure and needs. Variations of the Technological view are defined by how narrowly or broadly I define "me." In the most extreme version of the Technological view, the "me" is defined as my own separate ego. In this version, everyone and everything else becomes mere stuff to be used for my own egocentric pleasure and advancement. There is no real moral issue involved for this view, because the value of anything *is* merely "what's in it for me."

In another version of the Technological view, the "me" is defined in terms of my nation, my religion, or my race and ethnic background. Again, everything outside my circle is regarded as "stuff," which has no intrinsic value, and is to be used as I see fit. In the history of our own country, we see this perspective illustrated in the enslavement of the African peoples, and in the near destruction of the Native American nations. In every war, we have terms that dehumanize the enemy and legitimize the atrocities — we tell ourselves that we are not murdering fellow human beings, but merely killing "krauts" or "gooks."

Often the "me" is identified with the human race, and everything non-human thus becomes stuff to be used by humans. This is most clearly exemplified in the Technological view's approach to Nature. Things in the natural world are seen to have no value in and of themselves — they are given their meaning and value by humans, only insofar as they are somehow useful to us. In itself, Nature is wild ("wild-erness") and untamed. Humankind's role is to tame it, to bend it to our will, to forcibly impose upon it some semblance of order and harmony. For the Technological view, humans are unique in the natural world because of their rational minds, which gives them the ability and the right to dominate and control everything else. Humans are the users, the manipulators, the value-givers — everything else is merely something to be used as they see fit. Within this framework of humans versus everything else, a relative hierarchy of value is often assigned to things on the basis of their similarity to humans. Thus, animals may be considered relatively more important or worthy of respect than plants, because animals can move and communicate in ways similar to humans. Since plants cannot make sounds or gestures, it is usually assumed that they have no consciousness at all. But plants are still more worthy of respect and care than so-called inanimate objects such as rocks, since plants are at least "alive" (according to a certain definition of "life"). There is no moral issue here in using or even destroying these things, since they have no intrinsic value. From this perspective, the only reason to limit our usage of the things and creatures of Nature is the strictly pragmatic consideration that we might otherwise run out of the resources we need. The recent interest in ecology is, for the Technological person, motivated primarily by fear for his own survival, and not by any sense of reverence or love for the Earth and its creatures.

The Technological view tends to interpret primitive man's reverence for the natural world as a childish, mythical belief. It considers primitive man's respect for the Earth to be merely a reflection of his inability to scientifically understand and control nature. Once a civilization has become "advanced" enough to have the technological tools to dominate the natural world, there is no longer any reason to indulge in such childish fantasies as Mother Earth or Father Sky, or to see animals and plants as our brothers and sisters. In fact, a "civilized" Technological culture believes that not only does it have the right to dominate and control the natural resources as it sees fit, but also the right to dominate and use "uncivilized," primitive people, who it believes have not yet evolved to their full humanity.

❖ The Spiritual View

At the other end of this spectrum is a view I call "the Spiritual view." At the outset, it is important to make a few comments about my terminology. For many people, the term "Spirit" is highly charged with emotional associations, both positive and negative. But for now I invite you to temporarily set aside any preconceptions about this idea, and focus on what I intend by this term here. Afterwards you can use whatever terms and symbols work best for you to express your own belief choices. In the context of this discussion, "Spiritual" does not necessarily mean religious, nor does it necessarily entail a belief in a God, although it may. I am calling this view "the" Spiritual view, simply to keep the terminology consistent with "the" Technological view. I do not mean to imply that this is "the one and only" spiritual view — it is simply how I am defining it here. Similarly, I will refer to someone who chooses this Spiritual view as "a Spiritual person" — the capitalization of "Spiritual" indicating that I am using my own definition of this term. I am not in any way suggesting that this is the only way to be a spiritual person, or that anyone who has different beliefs is unspiritual. Remember that the overall point here is not whether you agree with my label — with the finger I use to point at the moon — but that you actually look at the moon for yourself.

(For some readers, the remainder of this chapter will be the slowest and most difficult reading in the book, as it challenges the very limits of conceptual thinking itself. But I encourage you to stay with it, because these ideas lay a foundation for much of what follows. You may also find it helpful to consult the glossary at the end of the book.)

Spirit

As I am using the term, "Spirit" is not a particular "being" or "something" that exists apart from the rest of reality. Spirit is rather *the common essence of everything that is*. (And it is important to once again emphasize that "everything" includes the human activities of science and technology, as well as the products of those activities.) Inasmuch as it is the essence of *everything*, it is not possible to precisely define it in terms of the distinctions we use to differentiate one "thing" or one "quality" from another. Even distinctions such as mind/matter subject/object, and awareness/object-of-awareness ultimately differentiate between one form and another, between one kind of appearance and another — and thus cannot be used to define the common truth or essence of *all* forms and appearances. Spirit is a unique concept in that it is all-inclusive, and has no relative opposite — i.e., it is a *non-dualistic* idea. For the Technological view, this lack of definition implies the unreality of Spirit. For the Spiritual view, however, this lack of definability is a reflection of the intrinsic limitedness of dualistic conceptual thought. For the Spiritual view, words can at best "point toward" Spirit — can help to evoke in us the direct experience of our common identity with all things.

From the perspective of the Spiritual view, the different religious traditions of the world focus on different aspects of Spirit. Zen Buddhism, for instance, emphasizes that aspect of Spirit that is beyond all definition, and tends to use a *via negativa* (negative way) approach — i.e., we can speak of the ultimate only by denying every possible quality or attribute. We find such formulations as, "There is nothing (no-thing) which it is, and nothing which it is not," "it (the ultimate) is not this, not that, not both and not neither." Zen often uses ideas such as "Nothingness" or "the Great Void" to point toward the ultimate. Some critics interpret this as a denial that there is anything real at all, and think that Zen is basically nihilistic. But such a criticism misses the point. In its truth, the Zen idea of Nothingness is not so much a denial, as rather an affirmation that the ultimate lies beyond every possible distinction. In this same vein, other religious traditions speak of "the Mystery" or "the sacred Mystery," to emphasize that aspect of Spirit which, in principle, transcends all distinctions.

Some religious traditions point toward this "beyondness" by stressing the absolute transcendence of Spirit. This may take the form of a doctrine of an absolutely transcendent God or Goddess — an omnipresent separate creator being, that stands above and outside of the whole of creation. Other religious traditions emphasize that aspect of Spirit that is the inner essence of all that is — this can take the form of pantheism, the theory that the divine is immanent "in" all things. But Spirit, as I am defining it here, points toward the wholeness of *all* relative distinctions — including creator/creation, transcendent/immanent, sacred/profane and the-Mystery/the-known. These various terms do not refer to *separate* "pieces" or "parts" of Spirit. They are more like windows, which allow us to experience the various aspects of the wholeness of Spirit, and thus can evoke in us an attitude of reverence and gratitude. This is not to say that God (Goddess, the Mystery, etc.) is in any way unreal, or that the various theological and metaphysical doctrines of our world religions are false. It is rather an affirmation that the full depth and richness of Spirit cannot be completely defined or expressed by any specific concepts or dogma.

Ultimately the term Spirit does not refer to some particular doctrine, but rather points toward a *dimension of our direct living experience.* From this perspective, the "Spiritual truth" of any particular religious or metaphysical idea will be the extent to which it enables us to directly experience this fundamental dimension of our being — the extent to which it creates a lighted clearing within which we can experience our Spirituality. The evocative power of any religious doctrine will be determined in large part by its overall context, as well as by the understanding and the attitude of the person hearing it. But the relativity of our various ways of evoking the experience of Spirituality does not necessarily imply the relativity of the experience itself. The ineffable experience of Spirituality may be identical from one person to the next, even though each individual might use different ideas and symbols to re-create the lighted clearing of that experience.

The Qualitative Dimension of Spirit

So far, I have emphasized the universality and undefinability of Spirit. Spirit is not a "something" that is, but rather points to the very "is-ness" of everything that is. The metaphysical concept of "Being" often indicates the abstract sameness or commonness shared by everything that is. But in referring to the common essence of all things as "Spirit," we are implying that this essence has a *qualitative* dimension. As I am defining Spirit here, this qualitative dimension has two components. First, the common essence of all things has *Presence.* In the context of the Spiritual view, I can encounter each being and each thing in my life as one presence meeting another in mutual recognition and respect, open to possibilities of communication, support, and guidance (as opposed to the Technological user-man encountering mere stuff-to-be-used). In this sense, I will sometimes refer to Spirit as "the living Presence of the world." I use the capitalized form, "Presence," to indicate that Spirit is not merely one presence among many presences — it is the very Being or truth of Presenc-ing itself, which is expressed as your presence and the presence of every being in your world; the very "I-am-ness" of every "I am."

Second, this essence has a positive quality — but here, "positive" is being used in an evocative sense, rather than as a literal description. Although "Spirit" or the dimension of Spirituality cannot be accurately defined or described, it can be directly experienced — not as the experience of an object or a thing apart from oneself, but as the experience of participating in the common sacredness shared by all existence. This experience has been variously called "the religious experience," "the mystical experience," or "the Enlightenment experience." Those who have directly experienced this dimension of Being agree that the experience itself cannot be adequately described or defined. It is beyond all possible distinctions and definitions — it is even beyond the distinction of "beyond all distinctions." But although the experience is utterly ineffable, it nevertheless has an overwhelmingly "positive" character. On the surface, such a claim seems paradoxical, since an experience that is beyond *every* distinction, would also be beyond the positive/negative distinction. The mystics seem to say, however, that even though no words can actually describe the experience, some words can point toward it or evoke it better than others. Thus, the Spiritual view will often use such terms as goodness, wisdom, love, benevolence, awareness, unity, light, joy, peace, holiness, and sacredness when talking about Spirit, insofar as these ideas seem to better evoke the experience of Spirit than do their opposites.

But the potential danger involved when we use any terms at all to point toward Spirit is that we may fall into the trap of thinking that our concepts are descriptive and accurate. Any time we interpret our concepts as descriptive and accurate, they become opaque — we confuse the "finger pointing at the moon" with the moon itself. In the context of the Spiritual view, whenever our ideas become opaque, then no matter how beautiful and inspiring they may seem, they will ultimately block the light, and become stumbling blocks to our deeper Self-realization. When I become attached to the exclusive truth of one particular description, whether it is a particular scientific account of reality or a particular religious doctrine, I will tend to miss that essential part of truth that is beyond every possible description.

Evocative Concepts

The ultimate evocative concept is "Spirit" itself. Although I make statements such as "Spirit is the common essence of everything," and "it is beyond every possible distinction," these are not to be understood as literal descriptions. I do not mean, for instance, that Spirit is the "underlying essence," and *not* the "overlying appearance." Essence/ appearance is but one possible distinction within the totality of Spirit — appearance is just as much an expression of Spirit as is essence. Strictly speaking, Spirit is not (exclusively) one or the other or both or neither. Even the statement that "Spirit is beyond all distinctions" is meant to be evocative rather than descriptive — for the distinctions themselves are as much an expression of Spirit as is the beyondness. In this sense, Spirit is even beyond the distinction, "beyond all distinctions." My so-called "definition" of Spirit is not a definition in the sense of describing the boundary which separates what something is from what it is not — ultimately, Spirit transcends even the conceptual distinction of is/is-not.

From the point of view that sees language as descriptive, all of what I've just said in the last paragraph will seem to be just a meaningless play of words, empty pseudo-philosophical babble. And, of course, all of this discussion becomes even more inconsistent and paradoxical when I talk about the qualitative dimension of this utterly indefinable essence of all things — when we use such "effable" phrases as "sacred living Presence" and "overwhelmingly positive character" to point toward that which is supposedly the most ineffable of all ineffables. But if we understand the idea of Spirit as evocative rather than descriptive, then we can see that its intent is to help us shift our perspective away from our usual preoccupation with separateness, particularity, and difference, and toward the dimension of the wholeness and shared essence of *all* things — a dimension we can point toward only by not pointing toward any particular thing at all. Ultimately, the true value of the idea of Spirit for any given individual will lie solely in its ability to evoke in that person his or her own *direct experience* of the dimension of Spirituality.

Likewise, the term "Mystery" is also evocative — explicitly pointing toward that dimension of experience that lies beyond everything we can know or define. For the Spiritual view, this dimension of unknownness and unknowableness is itself a manifestation of Spirit — thus, from this perspective, we might call this dimension "the *sacred* Mystery" to indicate its fundamental Spiritual character. Again, Mystery in this sense does not mean a puzzle we haven't yet solved; nor does it indicate a temporary failure or shortcoming of our concepts or thought processes. The ultimate

"Mystery of Spirit" or "sacred Mystery" is not cause for me to think harder — it is an evocative concept, reminding me of the limits of conceptual definition and understanding, and calling me forth to an *openness* of mind and heart, to an attitude of reverence, gratitude, and love.

Non-Dualism

"Spirit" is a *non-dualistic* idea — it is not defined relative to something else. Dualistic concepts are defined only relative to their opposites — for instance, "good" and "bad," or "inside" and "outside." The presumption with any dualistically defined concept is that both opposites really exist, because you could not understand or experience either one, except in contrast with the other. From the Spiritual perspective, however, Spirit is the essence of *everything* that is, the essence of "is-ness" itself. That means that there is nothing that is not-Spirit — if Spirit is is-ness, then not-Spirit simply is not at all.

Ultimately, we have to understand the "qualities of Spirit" — the ideas we use to point toward or evoke the experience of Spirit — in a non-dualistic way as well. Thus, for instance, the "goodness" of Spirit is not to be misunderstood as the conditional good of the dualistic good/bad pair of concepts. As we saw above, for the Spiritual perspective, Spirit is the essence of everything that is, and there is no "not-Spirit." And since Spirit is characterized by goodness, there is, in truth, no "not-goodness" or "lack of goodness." (Likewise, there is, in truth, no lack of peace, lack of love, or lack of joy.) You may, of course, experience such lacks if you create a lighted clearing that excludes the experience of Spirit. For the Spiritual perspective, however, the lack of Spirituality you experience in that lighted clearing does not reflect any true lack of Spirit (it does not reflect the reality of not-Spirit), but merely reflects your self-imposed blindness to the truth of Spirit. Furthermore, for the Spiritual perspective, the discomfort involved in experiencing a lack of goodness (or a lack of peace or love or joy) is because you are denying and hiding your Spiritual truth, and thus the experience of suffering can function as a valuable reminder to remember the truth you have forgotten.

The dualistic idea of good (i.e., conditional good) must not be misunderstood as merely a smaller and more limited version of non-dualistic goodness. Dualistic or conditional goodness is defined only relative to dualistic, conditional "not-goodness" (evil, bad, etc.). To affirm the reality of conditional good is to affirm the reality of conditional bad. But for the Spiritual perspective, not-goodness is merely illusory, in the sense that what you experience as not-good is not the real absence of Spirit, but merely your blindness to its presence. (In terms of the Possibility Model, what you experience as not-goodness is not the absence of the possibility of experiencing goodness, but merely your failure to realize that possibility for yourself.) Thus the affirmation of dualistic or conditional good is actually an implicit denial of non-dualistic or unconditional good. In more general terms, any affirmation of dualism and real difference is an implicit denial of non-dualism and the common sacred truth of all things.

Non-dualistic goodness has no true opposite — that is intrinsic to the meaning of "*non*-dualistic." But your unawareness of (your denial and hiding of) the non-dualistic truth of Spirit will appear to you as the experience of a dualistic world — a world of good *and* bad, peace *and* conflict, love *and* hate, joy *and* unhappiness. For the Spiritual view, your belief in a dualistic reality is precisely what prevents you from being aware of the truth of non-dualism. (It may seem that "dualism" and "non-dualism" are themselves dualistic opposites. But from the perspective of non-dualism, there is no truth to dualism — dualism is merely the failure to recognize the truth of non-dualism. So for the non-dualistic perspective, dualism is not a real opposite, but only an illusion caused by thinking about non-dualism in a dualistic way.) Thus, dualistic or conditional goodness, far from being merely a limited version of non-dualistic or unconditional goodness, is actually its denial — a denial that creates a lighted (or, from the Spiritual perspective, a darkened) clearing, which excludes the possibility of experiencing Spiritual truth.

But having said all this, it is important to acknowledge the *relative* value of some dualistic concepts, at least at a certain stage in the journey of Spiritual awakening — at a certain state in the process of moving from forgetting to remembering the truth of non-dualism. The starting point of this journey is dualistic consciousness (because if you were already aware of the truth of non-dualism, there would be no "journey" to take). Within a dualistic context of understanding, you have only dualistic concepts to use for forming your beliefs and creating your lighted clearing. Within this framework, you choose the dualistic concepts that are *relatively* more similar to Spiritual experience than are their opposites — for instance, goodness, peace, love, joy — to begin to orient yourself to the possibility of experiencing the Spiritual dimension of your life. As I have emphasized above, however, it is important to remember that these concepts are ultimately evocative rather than descriptive. Otherwise, you could lapse into thinking that Spirit is goodness, peace, love, and joy, and not-Spirit is evil, conflict, fear and unhappiness. But such an understanding would implicitly affirm that not-Spirit truly "is," and thus would understand "Spirit" itself only as partial, conditional, relative, and dualistic. From the

Spiritual perspective, living in the lighted clearing of this dualistic, relative idea of "spirit" would actually close you off from the possibility of experiencing the true non-dualistic Spiritual dimension of your life. (The reader is referred to the glossary for more on the topics of dualism/ non-dualism, and conditional/unconditional.)

The Ethics of the Spiritual View

For the Technological point of view, the things and creatures man encounters in the world have no intrinsic value in and of themselves — they have only the value that I, as a human perceiver and user, assign to them according to my own changing needs and desires. The value of each thing is thus "external" to it (i.e., is not a part of its own intrinsic make-up), and is limited and relative. From the Spiritual point of view, however, every thing and every creature is ultimately an expression of Spirit, and as such has intrinsic and absolute value. The true value of each thing lies in what it *is* as an expression of Spirit, not merely in what it can do for me, or in how it can be useful to me. A Tibetan proverb says, "When the pickpocket meets the saint, all he sees are the pockets." This expresses the Spiritual view's criticism of the Technological view. To the extent that a Technological person sees the natural world *only* relative to human needs and desires, he will be blinded to whatever else is potentially present to experience and enjoy. (In terms of the proverb, the pickpocket will be blind to the "saintliness" of the saint — arguably the deepest and most valuable experience of meeting a saint.) Moreover, to the extent that he sees himself only in terms of his potential to use and manipulate his world, he will be blind to his other possibilities.

For the Spiritual view, the value of every being is intrinsic and absolute. From that perspective, the attitude that can best create the lighted clearing to discover this Spiritual dimension is reverence — reverence for all beings is our affirmation of their essential Spirituality. This does not mean, however, that we never use things, or even sometimes kill or destroy them, nor does it mean that we simply renounce all of our technological machines and inventions. But for the Spiritual view, our actions are always guided by an overriding sense of reverence and respect for the sacred living Presence of the world. An attitude of reverence is both the way we can discover the Spirituality of the world, and the way we concretely live and express that discovery.

To say that everything has an absolute intrinsic value means that every person does also. From this perspective, a person's value is not contingent on what he does or says, nor does it have to be "earned" — his value resides in what he *is*, as a manifestation of Spirit. In the tradition of Christianity, Christ said, "whatever you do to the least of my brothers, you do to me" (Matthew, 25:40). From the Spiritual point of view, everyone we meet is an expression of Spirit — in the language of Christianity, we could say that everyone we meet is the Christ in disguise. In some cases, the mask of fear and hostility is such a good disguise that it may seem difficult to perceive the intrinsic goodness or Spirituality. In other cases, a person's kind and loving personality transparently expresses his or her Spiritual nature. But from the perspective of the Spiritual view, the inner essential reality of *every* person is Spirit, and therefore deserves our unconditional love

If the essence of every person is Spirit then I, too, am an expression of Spirit — I, too, am an expression of the sacred living Presence of the world, a manifestation of the life force that creates, sustains, and animates all things. My reverence and respect for the Spirit in all things thus extends to include myself as well. The idea of "my soul" (or "Self," with a capital "S") is a way of thinking about my identity that can allow me to experience myself as an expression of Spirit rather than simply as a separate ego. For an ego-based perspective, "self-love" means an egocentric preoccupation with my own separate good — I love myself instead of, or more than, others. For the Spiritual view, however, self-love reflects my reverence for my own deeper sacred essence. Because this deeper essence is the essence of all other things as well, this kind of self-love is not an egocentric love which separates me from others, but rather a way in which I love and celebrate "the Spirit in all things" (i.e., the Spirit that is expressing itself through and as all things) — a way in which the Spirit-as-me acknowledges and expresses its deeper identity with the Spirit-as-you (or the Spirit-as-a-tree or the Spirit-as-the-Earth). In this sense, "Spirit" does not mean some kind of separate soul "thing" riding around "inside" of my body, but rather points toward that deeper common essence which is expressing itself as me.

Unconditional Love

Earlier we said that the word "ethics" originally meant "true character." In this sense, ethics means translucent authenticity — thinking, speaking, and acting truthfully, in such a way that my inner nature shines forth unhiddenly. For the Spiritual view, this means living in such a way as to unhiddenly express my own Spirituality, as well as to express my recognition of the Spirituality of everyone and everything else — living in such a way as to express the intrinsic sacredness of all beings. Ultimately, of course, if Spirit is the underlying essence of *all* reality, then everything that we do or say is an expression of Spirit. But some words and actions express Spirit transparently or unhiddenly, whereas other words and actions hide Spirit in the disguise of fear and separation. In Biblical terminology, I can either bring more light into the world by expressing my own Spirituality, or I can contribute to the darkness by hiding my light under the bushel of fear (cf. Matthew 5:14-16).

The way of living that most unhiddenly expresses the Spirituality of all people is an ethics of unconditional love. Conditional love is always a kind of barter — I will love you only insofar as you and your actions somehow conform to my needs and desires. Thus, conditional love is basically an expression of a Technological and manipulative approach to the world. From the Spiritual point of view, however, *everyone* is an expression of Spirit. At this level, to love some people and not others is to somehow miss what is common to *all* — and if you are blind to Spirit in one person, you cannot be fully open to it in anyone.

On the one hand, when you are actually experiencing the Spirituality of yourself and your world, unconditional love is simply a spontaneous expression of who you are. From this perspective, the various codes of ethics such as the Noble Eight-fold Path of Buddhism or the Ten Commandments of the Judeo-Christian tradition are not arbitrary collections of rules imposed by some external authority — they simply outline how a Spiritually realized person would *naturally* act. The Golden Rule, "to love my neighbor as myself," would not be understood as a moral imperative, but would simply express the reality that I and my neighbor are one in Spirit. From this perspective, the ethics of unconditional love is not self-denial, but Spiritual Self-affirmation. Once again, this ethics of unconditional love is not to be confused with mere passivity. It may, for instance, be necessary to restrain a person who is being harmful or destructive to others or to the environment, or to act to halt economic exploitation, or injustice or cruelty. But for a truly Spiritual ethics, such action always arises out of a foundation of compassion and love, and its intent is fundamentally positive and constructive. I heard one Native American teacher say that our very day-to-day survival necessarily involves taking the lives of other creatures — for instance, plants and/or animals must die in order for us to eat. But we have the choice of whether to take those lives in the spirit of reverence and gratitude, or merely to kill them without a second thought, and with no appreciation for the gift they are giving us. What is important in all of this is not so much whether we are active or passive, but whether we live with reverence and love.

On the other hand, the ethics of unconditional love is also a way to become more Spiritually aware. By deliberately acting *as if* I am already experiencing the Spirituality of all things — by deliberately living a life of unconditional love — I open myself to the possibility of more fully experiencing that dimension of existence. If our Spiritual education is the unlearning of fear, the ethics of unconditional love is the curriculum. The ethics of unconditional love is thus both an expression of full Spiritual Self-realization, and a way toward that realization — it is a means as well as an end, the path as well as the destination.

For the Spiritual view, even though every individual may be distinct and unique, we all share a common sacred essence. Any belief or action that makes me feel fundamentally separate and essentially different from others will tend to blind me to my own truth as an expression of Spirit. Many of the "sins" of traditional religion, such as lust or greed, are based on viewing the other person as someone who is separate and different from me, someone I can cheat or rob or use or abuse in some way. Likewise, the "sin" of pride or arrogance arises from my belief that I am essentially different from, and somehow "above," everything and everyone else. Any time I focus on getting something for me alone at the expense of others, I express and reinforce the illusion of my difference and separateness. From the Spiritual point of view, these so-called sins are not evidence of any real lack of Spirituality, but are merely reflections of my ignorance — I mis-take myself and the other person as being somehow fundamentally separate and different from each other.

The Spiritual view starts from the belief that all beings share a *common* Spiritual truth, and this shared inner essence is good. Thus, when I or another say or do something selfish or harmful, it is considered to be simply a mis-take made out of our ignorance or forgetfulness of the Spiritual nature of all things, rather than a reflection of any kind of inner sinfulness or wickedness. For the Spiritual view, most, if not all, of the suffering we cause ourselves and others is due to forgetting that everything in our world (including ourselves) is a face of Spirit. The only antidote to this hiddenness of Spirit is truth — somehow allowing or enabling Spirit to emerge into unhiddenness. From this perspective, the most appropriate response to a mistake is compassion and love, and the most appropriate way to correct such a mistake would be to lovingly and compassionately help the person who made the mistake to more truthfully experience the Spirituality of himself and the world — to help him remember who he truly is. Rather than trying to discourage our mistakes through punishment, fear, and coercion, the Spiritual view tries to encourage our potential to be loving and compassionate beings who fully express our Spirituality.

After reading a draft of this book, a friend of mine wrote to me, "To be honest, there are some things on which we just don't agree ... e.g., the reality and role of evil...." His comment caused me to seriously question whether I was simply putting my head in the sand — guilty of a New Age smiley-faced optimism that cheerfully denied the "real reality" of evil. If evil really does exist, such a denial would be foolish and dangerous. But for the Possibility Model, the pertinent question here would not be "does evil really exist?" (a variation of "what does the photo really look like?"), but rather "what is the value of the lighted clearing created by (my understanding of) the idea of evil?" From this perspective, "evil" would not be a label that corresponded to some thing or power that "really existed" in the world, but would rather represent a specific light choice that allowed and enabled the emergence of certain possibilities of experience, and concealed others. Moreover, to affirm the reality of (the dualistic pair of) both good and evil is to implicitly deny yourself the possibility of experiencing non-dualistic goodness — which is one possible interpretation of the expulsion from the Garden of Eden.

Forgiveness

For the Spiritual view, a key to healing our perception of separateness from other people is forgiveness. In our culture, we typically believe that when someone does something "wrong" or "bad," we have every right to condemn him and to hold a grievance. From that perspective, to forgive someone is to make an arbitrary choice to let go of my justified grievance against him — it is, in effect, to be untrue to myself. But the Spiritual view sees forgiveness in a very different light. From this clearing, the seemingly wrong words or actions we judge and condemn are really only mistakes grounded in ignorance and forgetfulness. When someone perceives reality only through the filter of fear and manipulation, he will speak and act in ways that do not truly (unhiddenly) express love and kindness, in ways that do not truly express Spirit. The mistake of his perception is reflected in the mistake of his words and actions. According to the Spiritual view, if I judge and condemn the person making the mistake, then I am also making a mistake — the mistake of thinking that the other person really is "bad," rather than simply ignorant or afraid. Moreover, when I condemn the other person, I ultimately misperceive myself as well as him. By thinking of him as "bad" and separate, I implicitly deny his Spiritual essence. But inasmuch as Spirit, by definition, is common to *all* things, whenever I deny Spirit in anyone, I deny some aspect of it in everything else as well — if I cannot see the Spirit in my brother or sister, then I will be blind to some aspect of it in myself as well. Thus, any form of bearing a grudge or holding a grievance — including guilt, anger, bitterness, and hatred — will blind me to the true nature not only of that person, but of everything else as well. Forgiveness of the other person is not arbitrarily "letting him off the hook," when he really deserves to be judged and punished. It is rather my own realization that my initial belief in his sinfulness was a mis-take on my part — in this sense, forgiveness is a way to heal the mis-take of my initial condemnation and judgment. For the Spiritual view, forgiveness is simply letting go of what is not true, and affirming what is true. In affirming the Spirituality of the other, I also affirm my own — in healing my perception of the world, I also heal my perception of myself. For the Spiritual view, I forgive and love in order to heal my perception, and I heal my perception in order that I may more truly forgive and love. My forgiveness of the other is my forgiveness of my own fear and blindness — my forgiveness of the other is a gift to myself, a gift of truth and freedom. And to be consistent, I would also have to extend forgiveness and unconditional love to myself, inasmuch as I, too, am an expression of Spirit. To whatever extent I am blind to my own Spirituality, — to the unique form in which Spirit expresses itself as "me" — I will be blind to some aspect of it in everything else as well.

Thus, for the Spiritual view, forgiveness is ultimately the undoing of my own mistake — the mistake I made when I judged the other person. "Doing forgiveness" really means undoing unforgiveness. In this sense, forgiveness is how I come to realize that there was truly nothing to forgive in the first place. The positive choice that carries me beyond the mistake, and most fully expresses and affirms our Spiritual reality, is unconditional love. By living unconditional love, I proactively affirm my own truth as well as the truth of the other — I love the other as an expression of the Spirituality we both share in common. This love has no strings attached — it is not contingent on the other person speaking or acting in any particular way. It does not depend on whether he is a transparent expression of Spirit and goodness, or has disguised himself in fear and ignorance. It is not reactive at all, but is rather a shining-forth of my own truth as a be-ing of Spirit, a be-ing of love. Not being reactive does not imply mere passivity. I can act in an appropriate way to restrain someone who is being harmful and destructive. I do not act with the aloofness and arrogance of a separate and self-righteous judge, but rather more as one face of Spirit lovingly helping another through his mistake. All of this also applies when I judge and condemn a person who never "really" made a mistake in the first place — for instance, when I, out of my own ignorance and fear, misinterpret another's kind and loving gesture as an attack. The point here is that, from the Spiritual perspective, when I judge and condemn another, I blind myself to both his and my own deeper truth — regardless of whether my grievance is based on a mistake he actually made or not. In either case, forgiveness is the antidote that heals my self-imposed blindness.

Living the Spiritual View

For the Spiritual view, Spirit is not "something" separate and apart from the rest of reality. Spirit is the inner essence of all reality, of every single thing. Living in such a way as to love and honor the Spirit in all things is therefore the truest and most authentic way to live every moment of one's life. Spirituality is not a separate category of one's life, nor is it expressed as some particular activity restricted to certain times and certain places. From this perspective, we are always "in church," everywhere we are. Every meal is a holy communion, received in gratitude and reverence. Everything we do is an act of worship. Everyone we meet is the Christ (or the Buddha, etc.) in disguise. Life is an on-going celebration of the holy.

The Spiritual view, as I am defining it, does not specifically endorse nor does it exclude any particular conception of the divine, or any particular religion. Since Spirit in its own nature is indescribable, no particular system of religious beliefs can be wholly or exclusively accurate. From this perspective, the ultimate "truth" of any religion is evocative rather than descriptive — it is true for us to the extent that it evokes in us an openness to *directly experience* the holiness of everything in our lives. For different people in different cultural-historical contexts, different symbols and ideas will be appropriate to evoke the loving surrender of their fearful separateness, and guide them toward a direct experience of Spirit. The possible ways to point toward this holy awakening can range from the abstract No-thing of Zen Buddhism, to the highly personal, loving Christ of Christianity. The Spiritual person will choose his or her religious beliefs and sacred stories according to the innermost promptings of his or her own heart, and will honor and respect the choices of others. Again, this ecumenical religious tolerance is not to be confused with mere passivity — sometimes it may be necessary to intervene when another's fearful "religious" beliefs promote prejudice, hatred, and violence. But for the Spiritual view, this intervention would be guided by love and compassion (as opposed to the zealous and self-righteous conquest of the "infidels" that most of the world's religions have indulged in from time to time.). The real issue is not "us" versus "them," or "our religion" versus "their religion." It is not a question of particular labels and doctrines at all, but rather of the life we actually live — a life characterized by unconditional love, unconditional forgiveness, and unconditional reverence for the Spirit in all things.[9]

CHAPTER 7

COMPARING THE VIEWS

❖ The Larger Spectrum

Although it was helpful to introduce the four views in terms of two separate spectrums, we will now combine those two spectrums into one larger spectrum. At one end of this "super spectrum" would be the Spiritual-Holistic view, and at the other, the Separative-Technological view. The Spiritual-Holistic view is a way of thinking about and experiencing reality that combines the Spiritual and the Holistic views. It sees the "wholeness" of the Holistic view as an essentially Spiritual wholeness. That means that the wholeness or relatedness of all beings is their common Spiritual source, essence, and truth — all beings are interconnected in that they are all expressions or manifestations of *one* Spiritual source. The Separative-Technological view, on the other hand, is a way of thinking about and experiencing reality that combines the Separative and the Technological views. It sees reality as a collection of fundamentally separate and independent beings that have no intrinsic value in and of themselves, apart from that which is given to them by humans.[10] (You may find it helpful to refer to the glossary, especially Table 1, for a summary of the main differences between the Separative-Technological and the Spiritual-Holistic views.)

The Separative-Technological view tends to be the prevalent view of our culture. (The fact that many people in our culture believe in a God does not invalidate this point. Within our culture, God tends to be understood as a separate creator-being presiding over His/Her/Its creation. "Creation," in turn, tends to be understood as a collection of separate, independent beings, and the non-human things are often understood as having been created only for man's use and pleasure. A belief in the existence of God does not necessarily imply a belief in the wholeness or the

Spirituality of creation. In fact, some religions explicitly deny these qualities.) The Separative-Technological view is so prevalent in our culture that often it does not seem like a "view" or "choice" at all — it seems to be merely the ways things are. Most people who live the Separative-Technological view — who experience their lives from the lighted clearing of the Separative-Technological view — are completely unaware of that view and of its influence on every area of their lives.

❖ How Each View Sees the Other

An "illusion" involves confusing the true and the not-true — confusing the "really true" with the "merely seeming." This means mistaking the not-true as the true, and/or the true as the not-true. In terms of the Possibility Model, this means mistaking your perception of the absence of something (that is indeed present as a possible perception, and could be experienced from within a different lighted clearing) as the absolute absence of its possibility altogether. And typically your perception of "the absence of something" takes the form not of a "hole" in your world, but rather as the illusory perception of the presence of its opposite. Your choice of a worldview is a choice that determines which experiences you will judge to be true and which experiences you will judge to be illusory (illusory insofar as they either hide what is truly present, and/or falsely present the appearance of what is not truly present). For example, from the Spiritual-Holistic perspective, the experience of separateness and valuelessness can only be an unreal or illusory experience: you misinterpret the seeming absence of wholeness and Spirit (which are absent from your experience only because you created a lighted clearing which excludes them) as the real presence of separateness and valuelessness.

From the Spiritual-Holistic perspective, the Separative-Technological view is essentially a denial — a denial that there is any greater whole connecting all things, and a denial that things have any intrinsic value. The lighted clearing of this denial excludes the possibility of experiencing the truth of wholeness and Spirituality. For those who have consciously reflected on, and deliberately chosen, the Separative-Technological view, these denials are explicit. But for those who have simply "inherited" this view from their culture without actually thinking about it, these denials are only implicit. An implicit denial has an even more powerful effect on your experience than an explicit one — since you are unaware of its limiting and blinding influence, you will be unaware that there are other possibilities.

Evidence, Proof, and Simplicity

In its own defense, the Separative-Technological view typically offers two arguments to justify the denial of wholeness and intrinsic value. First, it claims that we don't perceive (through the five senses) any greater whole, or any intrinsic value to things — and since we can't see, hear, taste, touch or smell wholeness or Spirituality, they must not really exist. Second, it points out that there is also no way to logically prove that there is a greater wholeness connecting all things, or that they have any inner Spiritual value. It concludes that this lack of perceptual evidence and logical proof would lead any thinking person to choose the Separative-Technological view. From that perspective, anyone who believes in wholeness or in Spirituality must be merely "projecting" meaning and value onto the world. Insofar as such people are blinded by their own imaginary ideas, they are unaware of the "real truth" underneath all of their projections — they are unaware of the *real lack* of connectedness and *real lack* of intrinsic value.

But similar arguments could just as well be used against the Separative-Technological view. It could be argued that connectedness and value are not the kinds of things we can perceive through the five senses — we can perceive neither the existence nor the non-existence of such things. And we cannot logically prove the non-existence of them, any more than we can prove their existence. Furthermore, it could be argued that a belief in the non-existence of these kinds of things is just a projection — a projection that actually blinds the Separative-Technological view to any possible experience of them.

The Separative-Technological view will argue that it wishes to avoid mere pretense and projection at all costs — it wants to avoid any possibility of "merely making things up," and merely imagining that things have any inherent value. To protect itself against any such pretense, it denies all intrinsic value. What it fails to realize, however, is that "no value" is itself one possible and very specific kind of valuing. In your denial of value, you will *actively* screen out any possible awareness of it in your life. Regardless of what metaphysical view we adopt — the thought-creates-reality model, the Possibility Model, or some other model — we want to remember that a denial has just as much of a creative (or filtering or projective) effect as an affirmation. The denial of something is, after all, only the affirmation of its non-existence.

The Separative-Technological view also appeals to the principle of simplicity — i.e., if there is no conclusive concrete evidence to the contrary, we always want to choose the simplest belief possible. But we have already seen that the argument about "lack of evidence" is spurious here, since the kind of evidence being invoked is irrelevant. Even more important, however, is that the Separative-Technological view is not necessarily any "simpler" than the alternative. As we said above, the Separative view does more than merely "not affirm" wholeness and intrinsic value — it actually denies these things, which serves to effectively screen them out of possible awareness. As such, it could be seen as the addition of something to our experiential landscape — the addition of an active block to possible awareness. Earlier I referred to the Tibetan proverb, "When the pickpocket meets the saint, all he sees are the pockets." The pickpocket, in his active and *exclusive* preoccupation with the pockets, blinds himself to the possibility of experiencing the saintliness or sacredness of the saint. The real goal of any simplification is presumably to be more aware, rather than less aware. It may indeed be the case that some metaphysical theories can become so elaborate and complex that they can actually cut us off from our direct life experience. But the other side of the coin is that being overly simplistic may impoverish our experience, and rob it of some of its potential beauty and depth. We do not want to unnecessarily clutter and distort our experience with all sorts of mere "make-believe" affirmations. But neither do we want to limit and impoverish our experience with mere make-believe denials.

It is worth seriously considering that everyone who claims to have directly experienced the unity and sacredness of life — what is often referred to as "the mystical experience" — unanimously claims that that experience is the most real and true experience of his or her life. The Separative-Technological view might claim that these are merely subjective experiences that have nothing to do with the "real world." But the mystics themselves claim that these experiences transcend any subject/object distinction. It could be argued that only the mystics are in a position to actually compare these various kinds of experience, since only they have tasted both possibilities firsthand. This doesn't mean that we should simply accept whatever they say. But, on the other hand, neither can a Separative-Technological person logically and reasonably discount the possible truth of that experience, merely because he has not had such an experience himself — especially since he has chosen a worldview that excludes the very possibility of any such experience from the outset.

Inclusive and Exclusive Views

From the perspective of the Possibility Model, the question is not which view is right and which is wrong, but rather which view creates the lighted clearing that best serves you? As I said, from a strictly logical point of view, the Separative-Technological view tends to be primarily negative — it is a denial of connectedness, and a denial of any intrinsic value to things and events. As a denial, it excludes the possibility of these kinds of experiences. The Spiritual-Holistic view, on the other hand, does not so much exclude the beliefs of the Separative-Technological view, as rather incorporate them into a larger perspective. The Holistic view, for instance, acknowledges the relative truth and value of the distinctions we make within the whole. But it adds that there is also another possible dimension of experience, a dimension of wholeness and connectedness — and that it is only from the perspective of this dimension of wholeness, that we can see the fundamental relativity of all of our distinctions, and the true place each part has within the whole. Likewise, the Spiritual view maintains that the use-possibilities of any being are only part of a wider range of possible experiences, which includes the experience of the sacredness of all things. Moreover, from the Spiritual perspective, this experience of Spirituality is not merely one more possibility that we may or may not experience, on an equal footing with all other possibilities— it maintains that the Spiritual dimension of a being is its deepest truth. (And again it must be emphasized that the Spiritual view is not a rejection of the human activities of science and technology, nor of all of the various technological products and inventions. Far from claiming that science and technology are "unspiritual," the Spiritual view affirms that the truth of *everything* — including science and technology — is Spirit. The Spiritual view does not exclude science and technology, but understands and embraces them within a higher truth or a deeper unhiddenness.)

Thus, a Spiritual-Holistic person would consider the Separative-Technological view to be relatively less true — since it is primarily a denial of possibilities, it opens us to a relatively narrower range of possible experience. In contrast, the Spiritual-Holistic view opens us to a relatively wider range, since it is inclusive rather than exclusive. Of course, the Separative-Technological view will argue that its beliefs exactly match the whole range of truly possible experiences, and that there really aren't any more possible experiences beyond this range. In the final analysis, the only way to find out if there truly is a wider range of possible experience is to choose a belief that opens you to its possibility, rather than one which precludes it from the outset. Being open to an experience is no guarantee that you will have that experience — but being closed off from a possibility virtually insures that you won't experience it.

The Useful Fiction of "Equally Valid"

When I discussed the Possibility Model and the various spectrums of light choices, I introduced all of the possibilities as "equally valid." This meant that either the Separative view or the Holistic view, and either the Technological view or the Spiritual view, would open you to an equally valid experience. For the Spiritual-Holistic view, however, the notion that all of these possible belief choices and experiences are "equally valid" is ultimately a fiction — but paradoxically it is useful, and perhaps even necessary, to believe this idea of equal validity, in order to experientially discover that it is not true. For the Spiritual-Holistic view, you start your Spiritual journey in a Separative-Technological framework. From within the Separative-Technological view, separateness and valuelessness do not seem to be "beliefs" or "choices" at all — they seem to be simply "how things are in themselves." The first step in altering this view is to see it *as* "a view," as one possible way of thinking about and experiencing the world. You do this by considering the possibility that there is another way of thinking about and experiencing the world (for instance, the Spiritual-Holistic view), which is equally valid. This step opens you to the possibility of a different kind of experience. The Spiritual-Holistic view claims that as you begin to actually *experience* the truth (unhiddenness) of Spiritual wholeness, you realize that the Separative-Technological view itself is not an equally valid possibility at all, but is merely the denial of Spiritual wholeness. From the perspective of that experience, it is not really a choice between two equally valid possibilities, or between two equally valid truths, but is rather a choice between truth and the denial of truth, between unhiddenness and hiddenness. But, starting from a belief in the truth of the Separative-Technological view, the only way you can come to this *experiential* realization is to first entertain the possibility that there is an alternative view that is equally valid. So for the Spiritual-Holistic view, any theory of "equally valid possibilities" (for instance, the Possibility Model) is ultimately only a useful fiction, whose purpose is to allow and enable you to directly experience the universal and non-dualistic truth of Spirit.

For the Spiritual-Holistic view, you start your Spiritual journey from within a dualistic frame of consciousness. From within that thought framework, you understand "dualism" and "non-dualism" only as a dualistic pair of ideas — and you consider each one to be equally valid and equally real. This opens the door for you to begin thinking about and exploring non-dualism. But with the direct *experience* of non-dualism, you realize that dualism itself is not a real alternative at all, but is only the denial of (and hiding of) the truth of non-dualism. From the perspective of that experience, the ideas of "non-dualism" and "dualism" no longer represent two equally valid truths — they now represent respectively truth and the denial of truth (truth and illusion, unhiddenness and hiddenness, Being and nothingness). But, according to the Spiritual-Holistic view, until this is an *experiential* truth for you, the best you can do is to consider that the dualism and non-dualism are equally valid possibilities. And, according to the Spiritual-Holistic view, if you openly explore the non-dualistic Spiritual-Holistic alternative, such ideas as separateness, valuelessness, and dualism will be revealed as mere illusions and mistakes. You will not have to deny them, or disprove them, or somehow overcome them — when these ideas are unmasked as illusory, they will simply cease to have any power or reality in your experience. Ultimately truth cannot attack or battle illusion, because illusion *is not*; illusion does not truly exist. In fact, the very attempt to battle and overcome illusions only makes them seem more real to you. From the Spiritual-Holistic perspective, the key is to become aware of, and directly experience, the Spiritual wholeness of your life (for instance, through living in the lighted clearing of the Spiritual-Holistic view) — and it is only from *within* that experience that you will see the nothingness of illusions. And for the Spiritual-Holistic view, illusions would include any experience that is not characterized by perfect peace, love, and joy.

❖ Choosing a Way of Life

Earlier, I said that your fundamental reference point is, "what truly serves you." How you define your "self" will be the basis for your belief about what truly serves you, and will determine all of your other life choices.

The Separative-Technological view defines your identity or your "self" as a separate, independent ego, with its own agenda, and living in a world populated by other separate, independent egos with their own agendas, which do not always match yours. You have no *intrinsic* connection to anyone or anything else — they are all "outside" of you, and separate from you. The meaning and value of each being in your world is only what you give it, relative to your own needs and values and desires — nothing has any *intrinsic* value in and of itself.

Thus, for the Separative-Technological view, the fundamental reference point for every life decision will be the separate ego, and the way of life that follows from such a view will tend to be essentially egocentric.

This does not mean that everyone who (consciously or unconsciously) chooses and lives the Separative-Technological view is necessarily selfish and manipulative. Indeed, many people who believe in a Separative-Technological worldview are sincerely altruistic, and are consciously committed to a path of selfless service — they are genuinely kind and loving people, who put the good of others ahead of their own. But for the Separative-Technological view, any altruistic value, and any act of kindness or loving service, always involves some form of self-sacrifice (denying your own good), and overcoming your truth and reality as a fundamentally separate being (for instance, overcoming your "animal nature," for the sake of some higher ideals — whether these ideals are dictated by some higher divine source, or are simply the moral tenets of a rational humanism.) But since the truth and essence of reality is separateness (lack of wholeness, lack of essential relatedness), your on-going life experience will always include some sense of separateness and defensiveness, even if you are able to successfully suppress or hold in check all of your "natural" defensive and aggressive inclinations. For this view, selfless service always means giving something up, even if you believe that the reward for your sacrifice is more than worth it — whether this reward is simply the good feeling you have when you do a good deed, or some heavenly reward you believe you will receive in the future.

The Spiritual-Holistic view, on the other hand, starts from the belief that the truth of Being is essentially whole and holy. The way of life that would best express this view would be one of reverence and unconditional love for all beings. In this view, unconditional love is not seen as self-sacrifice, but simply as true self-expression — far from being a form of self-denial, unconditional love is the source of true happiness. "What truly serves you" (or what serves your truth) *is* what serves the Spiritual truth of all beings. For the Spiritual-Holistic view, the goodness you perceive in the world is not understood as merely your own projection of value, and does not depend on your on-going effort to "make" positive judgments. Unconditional or non-dualistic goodness is simply the truth of Being — Being experienced in its deepest unhiddenness. Your role is to not choose values and ideas that would block your awareness of the Spiritual truth of the world — in terms of the Possibility Model, to not create a lighted clearing for yourself that would actually exclude the experience of Spirit. From this perspective, any experience of "not-goodness" (badness, evil) would be an illusory artifact arising from your hiding the truth of Spirit from yourself.

In choosing your own fundamental beliefs and your own lighted clearing, there are two questions for you to ask and answer for yourself.

The first question is, what lighted clearing are you already creating for yourself — what lighted clearing are you already living in? Only when you are aware of your current lighted clearing do you have any real choice at all — until then, you are simply living on automatic pilot. The first step in answering this question is to examine your beliefs. But sometimes the belief choices you consciously think you have chosen are not necessarily the ones you are actually living. For instance, some people who are living the Separative-Technological view believe and would claim that they are choosing and living an alternative view, such as the Spiritual-Holistic view. In addition to examining your beliefs, you will also want to look at the emotional tone of your life, and the kinds of experiences that fill your days. The lighted clearing of the Separative-Technological view tends to be characterized by a more negative emotional tone — for instance, unhappiness, fear, anger, and lack of peace. I am not claiming that every Separative-Technological person feels unhappy and miserable all the time — but the separateness, alienation, and competitiveness inherent to that view are typically reflected in a generally more negative emotional tone. In addition, the Separative-Technological view tends to generate such feelings as weariness and a sense of weighty responsibility — the belief that it's somehow all up to you to "make" yourself good, and to "create" your own happiness, and that as soon as you stop this on-going effort, your life will be empty, if not actually negative. We often see this kind of emotional burnout several weeks after someone has taken an ego-empowerment workshop — the on-going pressure and effort to continually "make" oneself positive and happy becomes increasingly desperate and draining.

Once again it is important to note that the Separative-Technological view tends to have a great capacity for self-deception. Often a Separative-Technological person will claim and believe that she feels happy, peaceful, and loving, even while her words and her actions betray a deeper sense of desperation, fear, and insecurity. In contrast to the emotional negativity of the Separative-Technological view, the Spiritual-Holistic view is emotionally reflected as a feeling of perfect peace, perfect love, and perfect joy — when you are aware of your truth as a be-ing of Spirit, you experience the non-dualistic qualities that characterize Spiritual truth. Moreover, for the Spiritual-Holistic view, your experience of perfect peace and love and joy is not dependent on your actively "making" your own happiness — that experience is the emotional reflection of your awareness of your Spiritual truth. Your role in this is simply to not block that awareness — to not "make" yourself unhappy.

The second question you want to ask yourself is whether the choices you are currently living truly serve you — serve you not in the sense of some possible future rewards, but truly serve you *now* on a moment-to-moment basis.

Asking and answering these questions for yourself is not something you do just once and for all. Even when you have consciously chosen an alternative belief, you typically find yourself repeatedly slipping back into forgetfulness — back into unconsciously assuming the prevalent beliefs of your culture. If you wish to deliberately choose the quality of your life on a moment-to-moment basis, you have to ask these questions daily — not in the sense of a merely intellectual analysis of your life, but rather in the sense of being mindful of the on-going quality of your life, which reflects the specific lighted clearing you are creating for yourself.

PART THREE

LIVING YOUR CHOICES

CHAPTER 8

CHANGING YOUR BELIEFS

❖ The *Quality* of Your Life Experience

In Parts One and Two above, we explored the Possibility Model, and we looked at two possible spectrums of basic belief choices. In the metaphor of the lighted clearing, our beliefs determine the size, location, and coloring of the clearing, within which we can realize meaningful possibilities of ourselves and our world. In this context, the true value of any idea or belief is the *quality of life experience* that it makes possible.

Parts One and Two are relatively more theoretical in their focus. Now we begin a transition to the relatively more practical — how we can actually change the quality of our own life experience. At any given moment, the quality of my life experience is reflected in how I *feel*. How I feel about myself and my world is determined by what the things and events in my life *mean* to me. When confronted with the same facts, one person may feel joy or peace, another anger, and a third merely boredom — it is a matter of how each person *interprets* the given circumstances. In our Possibility Model, any situation is a constellation of possible life experiences, and my specific beliefs open me to experience some of these possibilities and not others. As I change my focus and my interpretation, I can change what that situation means to me — not in the sense that I merely "make" it mean anything I want, but rather in the sense that I become receptive to other possible experiences of it. The Actuality Model of reality claims that there is only one actual reality out there — it is fixed, and my only choice is to see it as it is (be realistic) or not. The practical value of the Possibility Model is to remind us that we are free to intentionally choose the kind and quality of life experience we will be receptive to. This is not necessarily a guarantee that we will always receive exactly what we desire — no more than tuning a radio to a given station guarantees that we will hear a particular song. But if I want to hear a particular piece of classical music, I will probably not find it by tuning my radio to the local country-western station. Changing the focus and intent of our receptivity can play a decisive role in changing the quality of our life experience. In Parts Three and Four, I will share some real life examples of this as well as some practical exercises that I have found valuable in changing the quality of my own life experience.

In Part Two above, we saw how the Separative-Technological view tends to open us to life experiences characterized by feelings of alienation, fear, and defensiveness. But from the perspective of the Possibility Model, these negative feelings are not inevitable, since the Separative-Technological view is *only one possible way of thinking about the world.* There may well be other equally valid ways to think about the world — "equally valid" insofar as these other possibilities would have just as much objective evidence and internal logical consistency as the Separative-Technological view. In particular, we explored the Spiritual-Holistic view — a way of thinking about the world that can open us to life experiences characterized by such qualities as peace, joy, trust, hope, and unconditional love. Just because this alternative view leads to more positive feelings does not necessarily mean that it is "right." You would first have to find out if this view is true for you at all — if it actually unhides, and allows you to experience, new possibilities. And if this view is true for you, how does its truth (unhiddenness) compare with that of the Separative-Technological view for you? The standard is always your own experience. The point here is that we may have a great deal more choice about the quality of our life experience than we previously thought. We may be able to choose to experience the world and live our lives in a way that brings more peace, love, and joy to ourselves and others — moreover, a way that is just as valid as a more negative and cynical approach.

Improving the Quality of Your Life Experience

In what follows, I will use the lighted clearing created by the ideas of "wholeness" and "Spirit" as the overall context for my concrete examples and suggestions. My basic assumption in this discussion is that the reason anyone would choose to change the quality of his life experience is in order to experience more peace, joy, and love in his life. All of the examples and suggestions will be oriented toward this kind of change — and these qualities will define what I mean by "improving" the quality of our life experience. It is important to remember that even though different belief choices may be equally valid relative to opening us up to possible experiences, they may not be equal relative to the quality of experience they enable us to have.

Again, I am not arguing that you should adopt my own basic belief choices. In the first place, the unique clearing defined for me by a belief is determined by the subtle shades of meaning and association that its words have for me. The "same" belief expressed in the "same" words will create a different lighted clearing for each individual. Second, I believe that what is revealed in the clearing is not wholly determined by the ideas which define that clearing. The Mystery itself, that infinite range of possible life experiences, reveals itself within the clearing — the clearing simply provides a horizon of possible discovery. The "same" clearing may reveal different experiences, depending on the individual's personal history and needs at the time. Finally, what ultimately makes a belief appropriate for an individual is the extent to which the experiences made possible by that belief truly serve her own life purpose and dreams. Given all of these considerations, I don't think it is possible for any person to argue or prove that his belief choices are the best belief choices for someone else.

But the relativity of individual beliefs and values does not mean that it is a waste of time to share our beliefs and experiences with one another. I know that I certainly have learned a great deal from (my interpretation of) what others have said and written of their own beliefs and experiences. I find that when another shares his or her own deepest truth — shares his or her own being in its deepest unhiddenness — it somehow illuminates my own truth. I have found that as I discover or remember my own truth, I tend to have more compassion for myself and others. I also tend to create less suffering in my own life and to contribute less to the suffering of others. So it is my hope that sharing my experiences and discoveries may help to empower your own process of self-discovery and self-creation. I believe that remembering one's truth is always a healing process — healing for the individual who remembers, healing for all those whose lives he or she touches, and healing for the planet on which we live together.

Living Your Beliefs

Although I am speaking here of "discovering" and "remembering" our truth, it is important to note that creating a new clearing in our lives involves much more than just being "mentally" aware of a new idea — it involves *living* a belief choice in everything we think and say and do. The living of a belief is what transforms it from a merely mental notion into a *living truth* — a living opening of discovery and creation. The ethics of the Spiritual-Holistic view, for example, is not simply an optional code of behavior, which we may or may not adopt as we "observe" the world in a Spiritual-Holistic way. On the one hand, from within the context of experiencing the world in this manner, we could not live another way — for instance, when we truly experience the Spirituality of something, we spontaneously feel reverence and respect for it and treat it accordingly. On the other hand, we cannot come to fully experience the world this way unless we are living our lives accordingly — in this sense, the ethics is an intrinsic part of coming to discover the truth of these views. The choice to believe the Spiritual view is at the same time a choice to embrace all things in reverence, gratitude, and love. According to the Spiritual view, unless we fully live with reverence, we can never fully discover that which is worthy of our reverence. Ethics in this sense is more than merely the things we say and do — it also includes the attitude that underlies and motivates our words and deeds. It is the way of *being*, out of which the appropriate actions and words naturally flow. This approach to ethics is radically different from that of the Techno-logical view, which sees everything in terms of "technique" — i.e., in terms of the technical knowledge and skills necessary to successfully manipulate the world.

Living an idea means *living toward* its openness — a process that involves both discovery and creation. As I explore how my own belief choices affect the quality of my life experience, I realize that I don't have to be a victim of a supposedly "external" reality, and I discover new possibilities of myself and my world. And by asking such questions as "What is *my* life purpose" and "What are *my own* authentic values and priorities?", I open myself to discover new possibilities of my life. But the process is not over when I have just discovered these various possibilities as possibilities. For these possibilities to become actual or real in my life, I must act to realize them. In actively realizing these possibilities, I help *co-create* my experience of myself and my world. For example, the Holistic and Spiritual views may reveal new possibilities of relating to my spouse or to my co-workers, or even new possibilities of somehow communicating with a tree or a stone. But unless I act on this discovery, the possibilities would remain as merely abstract possibilities, and not as concrete life experiences. Thus, the process of personal growth is an on-going balance of the receptive and the active — of opening myself to discover authentic priorities and possibilities, and then acting to co-create my life experience accordingly.

Transition to Spiritual-Holistic *Experience*

The ideas and practical suggestions of Parts Three and Four of this book are geared toward making the transition from the Separative-Technological view to the Spiritual-Holistic view — or, more to the point, the transition from a Separative-Technological kind of *experience* to a Spiritual-Holistic kind of *experience*. Parts Three and Four are intended primarily for two categories of readers. First, there are those who are already familiar with and have already chosen some version of these alternative views, and who are looking for suggestions of how to live these ideas more fully. For these readers, my suggestions may be helpful in making those theoretical convictions more of a direct living experience. Secondly, there are those readers for whom the ideas presented in Part Two may seem new and strange, yet still intriguing and appealing. For these readers, these exercises and suggestions can provide an avenue to explore an alternative way of living in the world and experiencing reality. It is only from the perspective of having actually *experienced* your life from within the clearings of these various views, that you can best choose which alternatives are most satisfying and fulfilling for yourself — which alternatives truly serve you. In our culture, virtually all of us have experienced the Separative-Technological view by the time we reach early adulthood. But we have no generally accepted way to explore the Spiritual-Holistic perspective — and many of the available avenues of exploration are so enmeshed with tradition and dogmatism, that they do not seem to be living options for modern "sophisticated" thinkers. As a result, many people in our culture believe there is simply no realistic alternative to the Separative-Technological worldview. The purpose of this book is to introduce some viable alternatives, and to provide concrete suggestions and examples for how one can further explore them in his or her own life.

But Parts Three and Four are not to be understood as a "How To" manual of technological skills, which enables you to manipulate and control your perception of reality — for instance, in order to "make" Spirit reveal itself to you. The purpose of these suggestions is to help you discover, affirm, and more fully express the inner truth of yourself and your world. These are tools of discovery rather than of domination — ways to open yourself to a different kind of experience. Opening ourselves to new experience always involves a dynamic balance of undoing and doing. We want to "undo" those ways of thinking and speaking and acting that would close us off from the possibility of the new experiences. At the same time, we want to actively cultivate or "do" those practices and attitudes that could help to open us to the possibility of these new experiences.

The various suggestions in the coming chapters can best be understood as signposts and maps to help you in your process of self-discovery and self-creation. They do not describe the living openness itself, nor are they a substitute for it — no more than a map of the Grand Canyon could possibly be a substitute for the actual experience of its grandeur. We need such signposts only when we have lost our way or have forgotten ourselves, or when we are choosing to venture into new territory. In our moments of forgetfulness and confusion, maps and trailmarkers can be very helpful in reminding us how to recreate a clearing of discovery for ourselves. Some of our signposts may be ones we have received from other teachers, and some we may create for ourselves. As fellow travelers on this life journey, we can share with each other the reminders that we have discovered, in the hope that this sharing will allow more ease and joy in the journey for all of us. This is more than just a matter of telling others our favorite theories. Ultimately, everything we think and say and do expresses our truth — it expresses the openness we ourselves are living, and in doing so, it helps create a clearing for others. For instance, how do you respond to a "rude" clerk, or an "argumentative" spouse, or a "fussy" child, or an "unreasonable" employer? Do your thoughts, words, and deeds tend to create a context of separation, judgment, and fear for yourself and the other, or help to open a clearing of connection and love? In our day-to-day living, we are all both teachers and students for each other all of the time.

❖ Feelings: Your Guidance System

Positive and Negative Emotions

In our Possibility Model, the real truth (unhiddenness) of our belief choices lies in the quality of life experience they make possible. I am motivated to reconsider and rechoose my belief choices only when I do not like the meaning and quality of my current life experience. When I experience my life as joyful, peaceful, and deeply satisfying, I have no reason to explore other belief alternatives.

I can think of my feelings as a feedback mechanism that tells me whether the lighted clearing I am creating is opening me to a positive quality of life or not — a quality of experience characterized by feelings of peace, love, and joy. A positive quality of life, however, does not necessarily mean that I am always cheerful. Several years ago, for instance, I felt a deep grief when one of my friends died — but at the same time, I felt that my grief was somehow "good," and was a healthy expression of my love for this friend. At that time, I didn't want to be cheered up; I didn't want any helpful advice, such as "It's all for the best" or "Death is only an illusion." I didn't want to indulge in my grief, but neither did I want to disown it, or to dishonor the love that was at its heart. Even in the midst of my tears, I felt a deep sense of peace and joy. Sometimes the process of healing — whether physical, mental or emotional — seems to involve discomfort. But this is a different kind of discomfort from the discomfort of disease. Ultimately each person has to learn to distinguish between these two kinds of discomfort for herself.

When the lighted clearing I am creating closes me off from experiencing a positive quality of life, this closed-off-ness is emotionally reflected as "negative" feelings (feelings which are unpeaceful, unloving, and unjoyful). Typically such negative feelings tend to involve blame — in the midst of a negative emotion, I will tend to think that someone else or something outside of me caused me to feel depressed or angry.

Some people seem to deliberately choose a life path whose emotional tone is predominantly negative. (It is important to emphasize here that calling these emotions "negative" does not imply that they are wrong or bad — peace, love, and joy are not necessarily "better" than unhappiness in any moral sense.) They seem to have become accustomed to feeling miserable most of the time —they even seem to almost enjoy griping and complaining their way through each day. At some level, it is as if they are content with being discontented. Perhaps they find security in the familiar identity of whining and grumbling (although they might object to this characterization of their behavior). Perhaps they receive sympathy and support from others for being so unhappy all of the time — what psychologists would call "secondary gain." But whatever the reason, some people seem to be comfortable with their on-going misery. For them, a negative emotion is not an occasion to re-think basic beliefs and to make new life choices — it's just the status quo. We cannot say that these people are making a "wrong" choice in any absolute sense — but they are certainly choosing a more negative and unhappy approach to life than I desire for myself. (In terms of the Possibility Model, we could say that their way of looking at life allows them to see many possibilities for misery, anger, and self-pity, which may be concealed by my more positive orientation. Thus I may miss many opportunities to be unhappy, while they may be blind to many opportunities for growth and joy. Every clearing has its price tag.)

Then there are others who are not especially content with their unhappiness, but who don't realize that they have any choice in the matter.

They don't realize the role their basic life beliefs play in filtering and interpreting their life experience. They don't see their own view as a "view" at all, but simply assume that it is a clear perception of reality. They think that their feelings are dictated by the "given" facts of their lives and that they are merely passive observers and victims of the way things are. They think that their misery is simply an accurate reflection of a miserable world — merely the cost of being realistic. They do not know that they are currently making a specific choice, nor are they aware of any possible alternatives.

As I said, I think of my feelings as an internal guidance system that tells me how I am doing now, based on the choices I have *already* made. My current feelings reflect how I am *now* experiencing the world, and thus they are based on belief choices I have made in the past. Even when I am worrying about the future, my worry reflects belief choices I have *already* made as I looked forward toward what I interpreted as a "threatening" future.

Moreover, by the time you are aware of a feeling, you are *already* feeling it — in that moment, you have no choice about how you are feeling. So when you find yourself already feeling a negative emotion, the real question is, how do you want to respond? One possible choice is to try to deny or disown the negative feeling. But a negative emotion is a valuable feedback mechanism that can alert me to the fact that I am closing myself off from a truer (more unhidden) and more desirable field of possibilities. It can let me know that it is time to refocus my attention and re-think my belief choices. To simply repress the warning signal without heeding its underlying message is like taking the battery out of a screeching smoke alarm — even as you are enjoying the peaceful quietude, your home may be burning to the ground. Or to use a medical example, when you take drugs to merely mask or hide your symptoms, without bothering to correct their underlying cause, you are only dying more comfortably.

Another possible response to a negative emotion is that I might choose to continue to feel it — I might choose to indulge in my anger, my resentment, my self-pity or my worry. Some people choose to indulge like this much of the time. There is nothing intrinsically wrong with this alternative, although I personally believe such indulgence is ultimately a waste of my time. I find that negative emotions tend to rob my life of its power and presence and joy. They tend to keep me narrowly focused on what's wrong, without helping me to move toward anything better. I prefer to look at these negative reactive emotions as a wake-up call, reminding me that I have another opportunity to examine the light choices I am currently living — another opportunity to re-choose my beliefs, and to re-focus my energy and attention. I don't think of my negative feelings as the "enemy." Quite the contrary, they are most valuable friends — friends that signal me that I am beginning to live my life and see the world in a way that does not truly serve me. These friends remind me that it is once again time to ask who I truly am and what I truly desire — and then to make those belief choices that support and express my deepest truth.

At this point, a more cynical reader might ask, "What if it's not merely a matter of changing my beliefs? What if the world truly is an awful, hostile, tragic place, and no amount of positive, wishful thinking can change the essential negativity of reality?" I don't think that there is any way to prove that the cynic is wrong. In any given circumstance, it is always possible that no amount of re-choosing and re-interpreting the world will change my experience and my negative emotions. But, on the other hand, there is also no way to prove that the cynic is right — for it is always possible that a new belief choice could reveal my situation in a whole new light, that would offer growth and hope and joy.

Authentic and Inauthentic Desires

We live in an economy that depends on creating desires and needs in the consumer. Most advertising is designed to convince me that I need a certain product or service in order to be happy. Clearly, most of these so-called "needs" are artificial, and do not arise from my own truth. But I can become so preoccupied with chasing after these artificial needs that I am blinded to who I truly am and what I truly desire. In fact, some ads and products are designed to actively suppress my true desires and needs — one current television ad for an indigestion medication implies that if we use those tablets, we can eat all the junk food we want. The medication is able to suppress symptoms such as heartburn and indigestion, regardless of what we eat — to suppress the body's healthy response to unhealthy food. So instead of listening to your body's own feedback system, which could guide you to health and well-being, you take a pill which numbs your body's responses, thus allowing you to consume junk food (which itself is advertised as a source of pleasure and happiness) — and thus, even though you may get sicker and sicker, you don't have to suffer any annoying symptoms in the process.

But my intent is not to indulge in Madison Avenue bashing, or to complain about any particular products and services whose advertisements bombard us daily. The point here is that our culture encourages and stimulates desires that aren't necessarily authentic. Some of them are created by mere commercialism, and others simply by general social agreements about the desires of a "normal" person, which may or may not be my own authentic desires. It is important to first ask the question, "What do I *truly* desire?" If the negative emotion I am experiencing is only relative to an artificial desire — if it does not reflect my own authentic desires, and/or it is inconsistent with my own life purpose — then I will want to clarify what I truly desire, before proceeding to make any changes based on that negative emotion. In other words, if my emotional feedback system is calibrated with inauthentic standards, it cannot lead me to true happiness.

As we saw earlier, the lighted clearing of the Separative-Technological view tends to exclude experiences of Spirituality and wholeness. From the Spiritual-Holistic perspective, to whatever extent I am cut off from the wholeness and Spirituality of my life, I will feel a lack — a lack of peace, love, and joy in my life. If I do not attend to this sense of uneasiness or dis-ease, it can eventually manifest itself as actual physical or psychological disease. Moreover, from the Spiritual perspective, it is precisely this sense of lack that modern advertising exploits. From the lighted clearing of the Separative-Technological view, the only way I can resolve this feeling of lack is through such things as possessions, sensory pleasures, social power and prestige. Advertising keeps us locked in this perspective, since it promises us that we will find happiness and fulfillment by buying some product or service. Of course, this all works out beautifully for the advertisers — inasmuch as each product you buy does not actually satisfy the underlying lack of peace, they can always sell you something else tomorrow. Again, this is not to say that such things as luxury items or sensory pleasures are bad or wrong — but they cannot satisfy the feeling of lack that arises from Spiritual disconnectedness. To whatever extent you attempt to satisfy a lack of Spiritual attunement by means of acquiring more things, you will be caught in a self-reinforcing cycle — the more your current purchases fail to fulfill your need, the more desperately you rush to purchase more. This brings to mind the lyrics of a popular song, "Looking for love in all the wrong places."

Again, however, the intention here is not to criticize Madison Avenue or to belabor the cliché that advertising creates artificial desires. But from the Spiritual perspective, the artificial desires created by advertising and socialization are more than merely counterfeit versions of my true desires. To the extent that they keep my attention exclusively focused on pleasures and things, they can actually serve to deprive me of any deeper form of Self-realization. From the Spiritual perspective, the real issue here is not choosing the "right" pleasures and things over the "wrong" ones — it is a matter of discovering and living your truth as fully as possible. From this perspective, my feelings can be understood as a guidance system that leads me toward a fuller awareness of my own truth. Seen in this way, re-lighting is more than simply a tool to make my life more pleasant. When my re-lighting is guided by the question, "What do I *truly* desire?", it becomes a vehicle for Self-discovery and Self-realization. Not every re-lighting choice made on this basis will be easy or fun — in some instances, pursuing what I truly desire may involve effort and even inconvenience or discomfort, although this may be experienced with the overriding sense of peace and joy that come from living in attunement with my deepest truth. There is, of course, nothing wrong with having fun, or with taking it easy, or with frivolous pleasures and diversions — and in some situations, fun and frivolity may be an essential part of my Self-discovery and Self-realization. But if I do not identify and realize what I *truly* desire, not only will I continue to feel frustrated, but I will in effect be living a lie.

Emotions in Light of the Spiritual-Holistic View

For the Spiritual-Holistic view, your experience of your truth is your experience of yourself in your deepest unhiddenness as an expression of Spirit — your experience of your truth *is* your experience of Spirit. This experience is emotionally reflected as feelings of perfect peace, love, and joy — and here, "perfect" means universal, unconditional, and non-dualistic. For the Spiritual-Holistic view, negative emotions reflect your unawareness of Spirit. They reflect that you are creating and living a lighted clearing that actively denies and hides Spiritual awareness — you believe that you are separate and cut off, and living in a world which is meaningless and valueless (i.e., you are living in the lighted clearing of the Separative-Technological view). The *experience* of the illusory absence of wholeness and Spirit is characterized by feelings of lack of peace (feelings of conflict and threat), lack of love (feelings of fear, anger, hatred), and lack of joy (feelings of depression or unhappiness). From the Spiritual-Holistic perspective, this seeming absence of wholeness and Spirit is only illusory, since the possibility of experiencing wholeness and Spirit is never truly absent or non-existent, even though your denial of this possibility may hide it from your own awareness. Thus, for the Spiritual-Holistic view, only the positive emotions of peace, love, and joy are true, in that only these kinds of feelings reflect your being in its unhiddenness. The so-called negative emotions (lack of peace, lack of love, lack of joy) are untrue, since they emotionally reflect your unawareness of your truth. Your negative emotions reflect your experience of the absence of the true (i.e., wholeness and Spirituality), which you misinterpret as the presence and reality of the untrue (i.e., separateness and valuelessness).

The Separative-Technological person makes value in his world by judging things as "good" or "bad" relative to his own needs and desires. This view is intrinsically dualistic, in the sense that it sees "good" things *and* "bad" things, positive emotions *and* negative emotions, as equally real and valid. The goal of a Separative-Technological person is to "make" good things happen, and to "make" himself feel positive emotions. To this end, there are numerous ego-empowerment workshops that teach you how to control your emotions, influence other people to do what you want, and mentally or physically manipulate the world to conform to your desires.

But for the Spiritual-Holistic perspective, you do not create your positive emotions, nor do you make yourself happy or peaceful. You only create the lighted clearing that allows you to be aware of your truth, and this awareness is emotionally reflected as feelings of perfect peace, love, and joy. Any negative emotions you feel, however, are wholly your own doing, because they are a reflection of the fact that you are actively creating a lighted clearing that denies and excludes the experience of your truth.

The Spiritual perspective is non-dualistic, since it maintains that *only Spirit "is"* at all. In experiential terms, this means that only Spiritual experiences (which are emotionally reflected as perfect peace, love, and joy) are truly valid. Seemingly "non-Spiritual" experiences (which are reflected as negative emotions) are merely illusory experiences created by your denial of, and blindness to, the truth of Spirit. From that perspective, your negative emotions are the feedback system that reminds you that you are actively refusing to experience truth. The way back to the experience of truth is not so much something that you have to do or accomplish, but is more of an "undoing" of your denial of your truth — the undoing of your active hiding-of-your-truth.

For the Spiritual perspective, this process of ceasing-to-hide-your-truth is the essence of forgiveness. Forgiveness means releasing all dualistic judgments that express and reinforce the belief that you are separate and different from what you are judging — this includes both condemnation-judgments (grudges, grievances, anger, hatred, etc.), and judgments that see another merely as something to be used for your own benefit or pleasure. To whatever extent you believe you are somehow essentially different from another, you will be blind to the common Spiritual truth you both share. In this sense, you don't so much do forgiveness, as rather you cease doing unforgiveness — you cease making dualistic judgments that separate you from others (i.e., that give rise to the illusory experience of being separate from others). You don't so much give forgiveness to another — rather, you stop withholding it. The motive for forgiveness is to become aware of your truth. This awareness of Spiritual truth will be experienced as perfect peace, love, and joy. Understood in this way, forgiveness is never a form of self-sacrifice (giving up something of truth or value), but is rather a means to true Self-realization and Self-expression. For the Spiritual-Holistic view, forgiveness is your active letting go of the illusion of separateness and conditional value, in order to remember the truth of wholeness and Spirituality — essentially giving up nothing in order to gain everything.

Since the Spiritual-Holistic view is non-dualistic, true forgiveness is an all-or-nothing proposition. Any unforgiveness at all is implicitly an active denial and hiding of your shared Spiritual truth — and even the seemingly most trivial unforgiveness and the smallest judgment of any real difference is an affirmation of your separateness, and thus an implicit denial of the common sacred truth you share with the other.

Earlier when we discussed non-dualistic truth, I said that any affirmation of dualism was an implicit denial of the non-dualistic truth of Spirit. But we also saw that, from within a dualistic framework, some dualistic ideas (goodness, peace, love, joy, etc.) could have a *relative* value in helping us move beyond dualism, as long as we understood these ideas as evocative rather than descriptive. Similarly, positive dualistic judgments can have a *relative* value in the process of coming to release all dualistic judgments (i.e., unconditional forgiveness). In the beginning of our journey of Spiritual awakening or remembering, we typically understand forgiveness to mean releasing all negative judgments, all grievances and grudges — releasing every judgment of ourselves or others as "bad" or "un-Spiritual" in any way. At that stage in our journey, our positive judgments can have a relative value for us — our choice to see everyone and everything as "good" (even in a dualistic and conditional sense) is one way we can begin to proactively open ourselves to experience our shared Spiritual truth. Ultimately, however, we have to release all dualistic judgments — the judgments of (dualistic) "goodness" as well as those of (dualistic) "badness" — in order to experience the non-dualistic truth of Spirit. (See the glossary for entries on "Conditional/unconditional" and "Dualism/non-dualism.")

Another way to say this is that *forgiveness means releasing every judgment that limits your expression of unconditional love.* It is obvious that to see someone as "bad" or "unlovable" would limit your expression of unconditional love. But even to see someone as good in a dualistic, conditional, and limited way would mean that you see him as only limitedly worthy of love — and limitedly worthy only insofar as, and as long as, he fulfills the specific conditions of "goodness" as you define it. For the Separative-Technological view, releasing all dualistic human projections would leave you with only a vast collection of meaningless and valueless separate things. This would be a life experience that was directionless, devoid of joy, and empty of all significance — it would, in effect, be the sacrifice of everything that makes life good and happy and worth living. For the Spiritual-Holistic view, however, releasing all dualistic and conditional human projections would allow you to become aware of Spiritual truth — would allow you to become aware of, and fully express, your truth as a be-ing of unconditional love. And for the Spiritual-Holistic perspective, this *is* the source of true happiness. In exchange for giving up a life experience of an on-going roller coaster of limited, conditional happiness alternating with limited, conditional unhappiness, you would discover and experience your truth as perfect, unconditional, and unlimited joy. Far from being any kind of sacrifice, unconditional forgiveness enables you to exchange illusion for truth, to exchange nothing for everything.

For the Separative-Technological view, negative emotions are often regarded as merely the cost of being realistic. They are the cost of being aware of the truth of separateness and valuelessness — being aware of the truth of conflict and threat. For the Spiritual-Holistic perspective, however, negative emotions can serve to remind you that you are actively maintaining some form of belief or judgment that is hiding your Spiritual truth from yourself. Negative emotions remind you to release those judgments that are blinding you to your truth as a be-ing of unconditional love — *negative emotions remind you to forgive.*

❖ Mindfulness

Self-awareness or mindfulness is the foundation of any process of change or personal growth. Before I can responsibly choose to change the quality and meaning of my life experience, I have to be aware of what I am currently experiencing and how I feel. Before I can begin to change my current basic belief choices, I have to be aware of what they are and their effect on my life. Before I can make new choices that better serve me, I have to be aware of my life purpose and my vision, of my own authentic values and priorities.

Becoming self-aware involves two interrelated processes. On the one hand, I want to actively do those things that help to cultivate and strengthen mindfulness — for instance, the practice of meditation. On the other hand, I want to undo those things that tend to make me less mindful — to recognize and disrupt those mind-numbing routines and habits that seem to operate on automatic pilot, without any real self-awareness or deliberate choice involved.[11]

Meditation

There are many kinds of exercises and practices that can help us to actively cultivate mindfulness and become more aware of ourselves and our world. One of the most powerful practices is mindfulness meditation. There are many methods and techniques of meditation — some focus primarily on mindfulness, and others focus on promoting other qualities. Of the various methods of meditation that are designed to cultivate mindfulness, each person must discover which ones work best for herself. But doing some form of mindfulness meditation on a consistent basis can be extremely helpful in becoming more aware of yourself and your world. I strongly recommend that you choose a meditation method and begin to practice it on a regular daily basis. Which method you choose is not nearly as important as that you actually *practice* some method on a regular basis.

At the outset of our discussion, I invite you to try an experiment. First, read the instructions in the following paragraph. When you are finished, put this book aside for a few minutes and actually do the exercise. This will make the discussion that follows much more concrete and relevant to *your own* experience.

Find some way you can sit upright, and yet be comfortable and relaxed — for instance, either sitting up straight in your chair, or sitting or kneeling on a cushion on the floor. Close your eyes and just notice your breath going in and out. As you breathe out the first time, silently say to yourself, "One." Then "Two" with the next out-breath. Then "Three" with the next out-breath. Then "Four" with the next out-breath. With the fifth out-breath, say "One" again. Continue breathing quietly and naturally, counting each out-breath. Each time you get to "Four," start over again at "One." If you happen to lose count, simply start again at "One." This is *all* you will do for the next ten minutes: be aware of every breath and every number. You may find it helpful to set a timer, so you don't have to keep looking at the clock. I invite you to put down this book now and try this exercise.

What happened when you did this simple exercise? Most people, especially if they haven't had any prior experience with meditation, find that their minds wander from time to time during an exercise such as this. You might have experienced that you either lost count entirely, or else you started counting automatically and suddenly discovered that you had gone past "Four." When a thought came into your mind, it didn't simply drift by like a cloud in the sky, while you continued to peacefully and mindfully count your breaths. Instead, it seemed to hit you like a freight train, and the next thing you knew you were lost in thought and no longer consciously watching and counting your breaths. It is almost as if your thoughts were thinking you, instead of you thinking them. Or, you may have found that you were distracted by sensations — an itch or an ache or a noise. Again, these sensations did not simply drift by like clouds in the sky — they seemed to grab your attention and somehow cause you to forget that you were watching and counting your breaths. Or, you may have found yourself distracted by your emotions.

It's not that watching and counting your breath is such a special and important activity in itself. The point is that *you decided* to spend those ten minutes simply sitting, and watching and counting your breaths. Moreover, during that time you never actually decided to stop doing this. But the ever-shifting contents of your mind seemed to derail you again and again from your intention — they seemed to grab your attention and "make" you forget what you were doing. In these moments when you were "lost" in your thoughts, it was almost as if you were a sleepwalker — someone who seems to be awake and in control here and now, but whose mind is not really present. You usually do not notice this sleepwalking in your daily life, because as soon as you or someone else asks you if you are present and awake, you momentarily focus on the here and now and answer, "Yes!" Since every time you ask and answer this question, you are momentarily awake, you tend to believe that you are awake all of the time. But a few minutes of meditation exercise can clearly show you to what extent and degree you are distracted and unaware — if you cannot stay centered and aware for even ten minutes without drifting in and out of distracted sleepwalking (and this is when you are trying your very best to stay focused), then how much of your whole day is spent being actually present and awake?

It is important to note that the purpose of this breath-counting meditation is not to develop a blank mind, devoid of all thoughts, sensations, and feelings. The goal of this exercise is to continue to be aware and present, whether or not there are any thoughts, sensations, or feelings in your mind. The purpose is not to become aloof and distant from your actual experience, but to be more fully present and aware of your world and your responses to it — it is not a retreat from the world into isolation and nothingness, but rather a return to the world with full awareness. Meditation is one very powerful way to practice *mindfulness* — being awake, being here now, doing what you're doing with full awareness. Even when you are remembering yesterday's events or planning tomorrow's schedule, you can still be fully awake and present in the here and now *as* the person looking "backwards" or "forwards."

But, strictly speaking, it is misleading to talk about the "purpose" or "goal" of meditation at all. Ultimately, there is no purpose to the sitting and breathing, apart from the sitting and breathing itself. To sit in meditation with the purpose of *achieving* something — for instance, to "achieve enlightenment" — is to sit with a distracted mind. Insofar as your mind is directed to some goal besides being here now, it is not completely here and now. The many benefits that can come from meditation are almost like side effects that occur only when the meditator is no longer sitting-in-order-to-achieve these benefits — they occur only when the meditator is sitting simply to sit. The sitting is not a means to some separate end — the only purpose of the practice of mindfulness is mindfulness itself. Most of our daily activities are done in order to get something, achieve something, produce something. Meditation can be a time in our day when we are practicing doing something simply for the sake of the doing itself. It is an opportunity to simply be aware of being yourself. Ultimately, the mindfulness we practice in our meditation will extend to other parts of our lives as well — if we are able to sit when we sit, then we will be more able to talk when we talk, eat when we eat, work when we work, and play when we play.

The tradition of Zen Buddhism strongly emphasizes the importance of mindfulness, even in the most ordinary and mundane moments of our lives. A story from the Zen literature illustrates this theme. A young man had come to a monastery to study Zen. His daily routine consisted of meditating, sweeping the temple floor, and washing the dishes. As he did these activities day after day, he became more and more frustrated and impatient. Finally, he went to the Zen master and complained, "I didn't join the monastery to sweep floors and wash dishes!" The master gently asked the novice why then had he come to the monastery. The novice replied, "So I could become more mindful, peaceful, and aware in every moment and every activity of my life." In the midst of his answer, the novice realized that the enlightenment he sought was not some special condition apart from the rest of his life, but an on-going awareness in the midst of everyday living — mindfully sweeping the floor was just as much a part of his spiritual practice as was mindfully sitting in formal meditation, or mindfully studying the topic of mindfulness.

Being a Conscious Co-creator of Your Life Experience

Meditation can help me discover within myself that quiet center of awareness, that peaceful inner space, from which I can observe the contents of my mind. When I am distracted by my thoughts and sensations, by the ever-shifting contents of my mind, I am literally pulled apart (dis-tracted) from myself. But as I become disentangled from my thoughts and feelings, I am able to notice them more clearly — I am able to discover the contents and rhythms of my mind, not merely theoretically, but concretely in my moment-to-moment life. Only to the extent that I am aware of the contents of my mind do I have a choice as to whether I want to change them or not— I cannot evaluate the view I live, nor choose an alternative, unless I am first aware of what and how I currently think and feel. The more I practice this self-awareness in my meditation, the more I can bring it to my daily life.

Often it seems as if I do not actually "decide" to have a particular thought or feeling. They seem to arise "behind the scenes," and I merely discover them as already present in my mind. But regardless of how or where the thought or feeling originated, as soon as I become aware of it, I have a choice as to how I will respond to it. I can choose to continue to invest my energy and attention in it, or I can let it go, or I can modify it, or I can replace it with another thought or feeling. It is important to emphasize that the issue here is not repression, but positive choice. The more mindfully I am living each moment of my life, the sooner I am able to recognize the thoughts and feelings that are not serving me, and respond accordingly. When I am mindful, I waste less of my time thinking and doing and feeling things that are not consistent with my truth.

As I begin making choices about what to think and believe, I become a conscious co-creator in my perception and understanding of the meaning of my world. The "sleepwalker," of course, is also a co-creator of his perception of the world. But he is not aware of this fact, nor does he deliberately choose his own contribution to his experience — he tends to simply live out the beliefs and thoughts he has inherited from his culture and his personal history. Since he does not play a conscious role in the perception of his world, it seems to him as if the world is simply "out there" happening "to" him. This illusion of his lack of choice is further reinforced by the pervasive cultural belief that the world is "objective" and that he is merely a passive perceiver. An on-going awareness of our own thoughts and beliefs and feelings is the starting point and foundation of our ability to consciously choose our role as active co-creators of the meaning of our world. Meditation is one of the best practices to discover and develop our ability to be more fully aware of ourselves, to be "awake." Meditation can also be a good barometer of how awake we currently are — the more difficult it is for us to remain mindful during our focused practice period, the more we need the practice.

Mindfulness and Spiritual Awakening

From the perspective of the Spiritual view, there is yet an even more important benefit of meditation. To the extent that we are completely preoccupied with all of the definite contents of our minds — with all of the particular things and perceptions and thoughts and feelings — we will not be able to experience the common sacred essence of *every* particular "this" and "that." When you focus exclusively on the distinctions, differences, and comparisons of the various physical and mental objects of awareness, you cannot see the dimension of the common or shared essence of *all* things — in our metaphor, we could say that the lighted clearing of difference and comparison does not allow that-which-transcends-all-difference to show itself. Strictly speaking, since Spirit is the essence or the truth of everything, every dimension of experience is Spiritual — including the dimension of the definable and the particular, as well as the dimension of the undefinable shared commonness of all things. Often, spiritual teachers will refer to the experience of the shared common essence as "the Spiritual experience," since it is this dimension of possible experience that lifts us out of our lostness in particular things. But ultimately, this is but the first step in the process of discovering an even deeper dimension of Spirituality, which embraces and transcends both the particular and the universal, both the describable and the ineffable. The term, "Spiritual," is essentially evocative rather than descriptive — its purpose is to point us toward an experience that is beyond every possible pointing-toward. Insofar as meditation disentangles me from the particular contents of my mind, it can be valuable in creating an openness to the dimension of the universal and the common. But ultimately, meditation enables me to disentangle myself even from the experience of the oneness itself, and helps to create the clearing within which the sacred Mystery, which is "neither this, nor that, nor both, nor neither," can emerge as itself.

In this context, "Spiritual truth" means direct and unhidden experience of the Spiritual dimension of Being. Although I will sometimes use the shorthand phrase, "experience of Spirit," it must be remembered that Spirit is not an object apart from yourself that you can have an experience "of." In the way I have defined Spirit, it is the truth or essence of Being Itself, and not merely one particular being among many. Thus, "Spiritual truth" or "the experience of Spirit" or "Spiritual experience" means the direct and unhidden experience of the Spiritual *dimension* of *all* things, including yourself. In this definition of Spiritual truth, it is important to specify the *unhidden* experience of Spirit. Every experience of any being is ultimately an experience of Spirit, since Spirit is the essence or truth of everything. But sometimes the lighted clearing you create hides (from your own awareness) the Spiritual dimension of what you are experiencing — and thus, you do not experience that being as an expression of Spirit, but only as one separate, different thing "in itself." (Here, "in itself" means "has a truth and an essence somehow apart from Spirit.") The "unhidden" experience of Spirit, however, means that you are *aware* of the Spiritual dimension of what you are experiencing — or more precisely, aware of the Spiritual dimension of the whole process of experience, which includes the experiencer, the experiencing, and the experienced.

A Personal Meditation Experience

We had been meditating for several days, interspersed with talks by Thich Nhat Hanh. That afternoon we did a long walking meditation, being aware of every step and every breath. It was a fall day in the Hudson Valley, and I was aware of each step through the wet autumn leaves. I stopped on a little footbridge and watched a small stream cascading over the stones. Suddenly I was aware of a sense of deep peace and joy, and I was moved to tears by the beauty of the stream. But I realized in that moment that the peace and joy and beauty I was experiencing were not "in" the stream — they were somehow qualities of the here-and-now itself. At that moment, I knew that the unhiddenness of the here-and-now was not merely an emptiness, a nothingness into which thoughts and sensations could come and go. The unhiddenness itself, the very here-and-nowness of my life, had an overwhelmingly positive quality. Its positivity was far beyond any possible description, and could not be captured by any of the words I normally used to distinguish one thing from another in my world. But words such as "Peace," "Joy," "Sacred," and "Beauty" helped me to re-mind myself of this ineffable experience. For me, "the truth of meditation" (i.e., what the "doing nothing" of meditation is in its deepest unhiddenness) is the *unhiddenness of unhiddenness itself.* There is no way to "think" my way to this experience — it simply *is*, when I am no longer distracted by my own preoccupation with, and attachment to, anything I find "in" the unhiddenness. Becoming aware of the unhiddenness itself felt like remembering or waking up to what was always already present. In this sense, it didn't feel like a "special" experience, but rather a possibility that was available in every moment, including even the most "ordinary" moments — a possibility that could transform everything in my world.

I realized also in that moment, that whenever I perceived beauty or goodness "in" my world, it was a reflection of the Beauty and Goodness of the unhiddenness. This did not mean that everything good and beautiful was simply a reflection of my own subjectivity — it was a reflection of the Goodness and the Beauty of Truth itself, the very unhiddenness within which I and everything else "existed" at all. This was further underscored for me later that evening. Since it was a silent retreat, my wife and I had to share our small tent without talking to each other. Sometimes that was difficult, when we both needed the same bag at the same time or when we somehow interfered with one another. That evening, I found myself feeling irritable and frustrated at my wife as we got ready for bed — she moved too slowly, she was in my way, etc., etc. But then I suddenly realized that the source of my irritation was not my wife, but was my own distractedness. As I lost touch with the Love and Beauty and Goodness of the unhiddenness itself, the things in my world were experienced as less lovable, less beautiful, and less good — as I lost track of the Peacefulness of the unhiddenness, my life experience became less peaceful. It was not "what" I encountered in my world that determined the tone of my experience, but the quality and openness of the encountering itself.

In terms of my understanding of Spirit, I realized that Spirit was not some "thing" that I could discover "in" the clearing of the unhiddenness. The unhiddenness itself was sacred and holy, and evoked in me a sense of awe and deep reverence — the unhiddenness itself was a *qualitative* openness. The sacredness of the here-and-now permeated everything "in" the clearing — it seemed to shine through each thing as an inner light, a holy essence. In this experience, it wasn't just that everything "deserved" my reverence — there was no other way I could feel. From this perspective, everything was Beautiful, even those things that I would normally judge as ugly. This Beauty transcended the relativity of my usual distinction between beautiful and ugly — the Beauty of the unhiddenness had no relative opposite. From within this experience, Beauty was an absolute, and any judgment of ugliness arose only insofar as I forgot or lost sight of Beauty itself. Likewise with the other words that "pointed toward" this experience — words such as "Good," "Sacred," "Peace," and "Joy." I was reminded of an aphorism of Heraclitus, the pre-Socratic philosopher: "On the one hand, for the gods everything is beautiful and good and just — but on the other hand, humans assume that on the one hand, some things are just and on the other hand, some things are unjust." (The irony of this aphorism, which is especially obvious in the grammar of the original

Greek, is that the distinction between the divine and the human is itself a human distinction.)

As I said, my experience far transcended any possible description. Thus, there is no way to argue or prove that it is true, since it is not within the horizon of argument or proof. The words I have used to talk about it are not an accurate representation of this transformative personal experience. They are merely the words that I use to help turn my attention in the general direction of this experience — that help me to re-open myself to its possibility. But to be able to re-experience this, I have to let go of even these words, for every word is defined relative to other words, and this experience is beyond relativity — including even the relative distinctions of relative and absolute, definable and indefinable, words and silence.

CHAPTER 9

LOVE AND FEAR

Part of being human is having dreams and goals, and living toward them. As a self-aware being, part of your "being here now" is being-underway toward realizing a goal or vision — including the whole range of goals from sweeping the kitchen floor today, to becoming the president of your company, to fully realizing your Spiritual truth. (For the purposes of this chapter, I will use the terms "goals," "dreams," and "visions" interchangeably). An important part of the lighted clearing you create for your life will be how you choose to understand both the role of goals in your life, and the process of living-toward them. That understanding will affect the quality of your life much more than which particular goals you happen to have and/or realize. From the Separative-Technological perspective, for instance, goals are typically thought of as achievements that make your life successful and worthwhile, and make you feel happy and fulfilled. For the Spiritual-Holistic view, however, the feelings of self-worth, happiness, and fulfillment are reflections of the truth of your very being, and do not depend on any specific achievements or accomplishments. From that perspective, to believe that your worth and happiness are somehow dependent on specific circumstances and achievements will blind you to experiencing the truth of your being — and thus, such a belief will actually be the cause of your feelings of unhappiness, unworthiness, and not-enough-ness.

❖ A Vision Orientation to Life

Any time I am trying to effect changes in myself or my world, there are two fundamentally different approaches I can take: a "vision orientation" or a "pathology orientation." (This distinction comes from the work of David Gershon and Gail Straub, although I have developed the ideas in my own way.) My choice of a vision orientation or a pathology orientation profoundly affects the quality and tone of my life. It is a choice between two fundamentally different lighted clearings — a choice that defines what I can experience and how I can respond.

A "pathology orientation" to life is an approach that focuses on what is wrong, on what I can't do, on my problems, on how reality has failed (or is failing, or might fail) to meet my hopes and expectations. In a pathology orientation, I define my life journey in terms of what I am moving *away from*. My goal is simply to fix the problem, deal with the adverse situation, overcome the crisis — my highest aspiration is to cope, to get by. Typically if you ask a pathology-oriented person how he is feeling, he will reply, "Not bad" — as if "not bad" is as good as it gets. For a pathology-oriented person, "better" is defined solely in terms of *less* suffering and *fewer* problems — there is no positive vision above and beyond overcoming adversity. One good example of this approach is the superhero mentality of many comic books and children's shows. When I asked my five-year-old son what the Power Rangers did — those juvenile superheroes who were all the rage with the kindergarten boys — he answered with great gusto, "Fight the bad guys!" But when there aren't any bad guys around, the Power Rangers have nothing to do — they have no positive, constructive aspirations. One of the liabilities of a pathology orientation is that you have to continually have problems to give purpose and direction to your life. When I define my life only in terms of struggle, I will feel lost and meaningless without a crisis. One example of a pathology-oriented person is a friend I've known for several years, who always seems to be endlessly involved in psychological introspection. Whenever I ask her how she's doing, she invariably answers, "I'm working on my stuff" — which means she is trying to sort out and resolve the various hang-ups, defenses, and neuroses from her childhood and adolescence. But I've never yet been able to get a sense of what she is moving *toward* in all of this — she always seems to be just "fighting the bad guys." Some professional counselors and therapists take a similar approach — constantly uncovering and dealing with hidden fears and conflicts, but without an overall guiding vision, without a *positive* definition of mental health and well-being offered for the patient to move toward.

In a "vision orientation," on the other hand, my focus and my reference point in every situation is what is right about it, what I *can* do, and possible positive solutions. I am looking at every situation in terms of how it can be a step *toward* realizing my vision. When confronted with a seemingly negative situation, I ask myself, "How can I use this *constructively?*" — where "constructively" is defined in terms of moving toward fulfilling my purpose and my vision.

As with all basic belief choices, there is no way to prove that a vision orientation is the "right" choice, although there are several obvious practical advantages. With a vision orientation I am always on the lookout for opportunities, and so I tend to be more sensitive to them and more likely to see them when they do present themselves. Even when I encounter seemingly adverse situations, I am on the lookout for any possible hidden opportunities or lessons. I will tend to approach such situations as challenges and stepping stones, rather than as stumbling blocks. This does not mean simply denying the seemingly negative things in my life. A vision orientation is a way of actively remaining open to their positive and constructive potential — a way of creating a lighted clearing that highlights the opportunity-possibilities of my life. Emotionally it is a more positive approach — since I am constantly moving *toward* what I desire, the journey itself tends to be more exhilarating and regenerative. The pathology orientation, on the other hand, tends to lead to weariness and burnout, since I am always fighting against or running away from what I don't want. Lastly, a vision orientation takes me beyond mere problem solving, into a realm of creative intelligence. Instead of merely reacting against what I don't want, I proactively pursue growth and self-discovery — instead of merely coping, I can actually add something to my world.

The choice between a vision orientation and a pathology orientation is not a choice I make once and for all — it is an on-going choice that I must choose anew in every moment. Again, my feelings can serve as my feedback system. When I am focused on and moving toward what I desire, I will tend to experience positive emotions — even in times of great effort, I will feel the exhilaration of meeting the challenge and rising to the occasion.

We can more clearly see the differences between these two life orientations by looking at several examples. For instance, the way a pathology-oriented person tries to "quit" smoking typically starts with *hating* himself for being a smoker in the first place — he judges himself as weak, inadequate, a failure. He then proceeds to *deprive* himself of something he thinks he needs or desires (his cigarettes). He does all of this self-hating and self-deprivation in order to *avoid* suffering, disease, and a possible early death. In addition, he tells himself that he cannot be completely happy until *after* he achieves his goal, since he believes that his current unhappiness will spur him on to even greater effort — and thus the lack of happiness in the present becomes one more thing he is running away from. This entire process of change is permeated with negativity — running away from what he doesn't like, depriving himself of what he does like, and motivating himself with self-condemnation, fear, and unhappiness. Many people take a similar approach to "losing" weight through the personal sacrifices involved in a diet. It is no surprise that such negative approaches usually fail. The fear, self-loathing, and unhappiness in such an approach can exacerbate the very addiction you are trying to overcome. Moreover, when you define your sense of direction only in terms of what you are running away from, you have to constantly keep it in mind as your reference point — and the more you constantly keep something in mind, the more it remains a part of your life.

A pathology orientation is such a prevalent orientation in our culture that you may not always recognize it operating in your life. My examples of the pathology orientation (dieting, quitting smoking) were presented in a somewhat oversimplified way for the purpose of illustration — but a pathology orientation is not always so obvious to the person who is living it. The key to recognizing a pathology orientation is the emotional tone of your life — not just the overall tone in general, but the moment-to-moment tone as well. A pathology orientation will always be emotionally reflected as a negative tone — a lack of peace, a lack of love, and a lack of joy. These feelings are a tip-off that you are orienting your life in terms of running away from or escaping something — and this "away-from-ness" will be emotionally reflected as "negative" feelings.

Some people also take a pathology approach when they are trying to change their beliefs from the Separative-Technological view to an alternative view. Upon first encountering the Spiritual view, for instance, they may judge themselves as being somehow inadequate and deficient because they have believed in their cultural view up until then. They envision the coming change as a process of struggle and deprivation — giving up their defenses and their safety, giving up their right to hold grievances and grudges, giving up their critical judgments of themselves and others, and giving up their sensual and worldly pleasures for some lofty, abstract ideals. They motivate themselves with fear — they may tell themselves, for instance, that until they are "enlightened," their lives will be unfulfilled. To spur themselves on to even greater effort, they tell themselves that they cannot be truly happy or experience peace of mind until *after* they have completed the whole process of change and growth — and they may regard any happiness along the way as premature and a sign of spiritual irresponsibility. Ironically, all of this negativity can tend to block the very Spiritual growth they desire, since self-condemnation, fear, and unhappiness are incompatible with the unconditional love intrinsic to a journey of Spiritual Self-discovery.

In a vision orientation, on the other hand, a smoker would begin by loving himself — by recognizing, for instance, that his previous habit of smoking had been one way he had taken care of himself, and now he was ready to choose a different way. He would think of what he was doing, not in terms of "quitting" smoking, but rather in terms of "beginning" to breathe more freely; not in terms of "depriving" himself of cigarettes, but rather in terms of "giving himself the gifts" of clean air, healthy lungs, and more energy. His focus would not be on avoiding disease and death, but rather on moving toward a better quality of life. Finally, he would not need to spur himself on with unhappiness; he could be happy throughout the process, knowing that he was moving toward what he truly desired.

This example highlights how it can be not only more pleasant, but also much more effective to focus on the positive. That is especially true for the process of moving toward a more Spiritual-Holistic worldview. In this process, a vision-oriented person would begin by loving and accepting herself and her situation just as it is — with all of her imperfections and longings. She would conceive this journey in terms of moving *toward*, rather than running *from* — her goal would be projected as a positive goal (e.g., becoming more Spiritually aware), rather than a negative goal (e.g., becoming less Separative and Technological). Her focus throughout the process would be on giving herself more of what she truly desired in her life, rather than on battling against what she didn't desire. Finally, since she would be going toward what she desired and doing this out of love and respect for herself, she would not have to motivate herself with unhappiness. She would not have to wait until she arrived at some destination to feel happiness and satisfaction — her journey itself could be a joyful expression of her heart. The entire process would be motivated by love rather than by fear — and as we have seen, love plays a crucial role in creating the lighted clearing of Spiritual discovery.

❖ The *Process* of Being Under Way

It is important to remember that as I am moving toward what I desire (whether this is moving toward a different way of looking at the world, moving toward what I desire to become, or moving toward achieving some personal accomplishment), I myself can change in the process. I can discover previously unimagined possibilities of myself — new possibilities of understanding, new possibilities of feeling, new possibilities of responding to my world. This expansion of my possibilities is part of the process of personal growth. In this process, my understanding of my life purpose and my vision may change. Therefore, it is important to remain flexible, for yesterday's vision may not be appropriate to who I am today.

Often people tend to lock on to their first formulation of a goal, and continue to pursue it no matter what, even when it no longer truly serves them — especially if they have identified that particular goal as the source of their happiness. Some people believe that they have to see every project through to the end, if for no other reason than to justify all of the time and energy they have already invested in it. But just because you may have spent the last five years pursuing a goal, it does not necessarily follow that it is appropriate for you to continue to pursue it now. Maybe the five years of striving were a necessary part of your growth process, which enabled you to discover a completely different, but ultimately much better goal for yourself. Obviously, persistence and consistency can be very important. But dogmatic persistence toward a fixed goal, without an appreciation for your own growth, can lead to frustration and to hollow, unsatisfying "victories." The essence of a vision orientation is to be continually moving toward fulfilling your purpose and your dreams as you *now* best understand them. This involves being flexible, and letting your vision evolve as you yourself grow and evolve.

The Continuum of Living Toward a Vision

There are two fundamentally different ways to think about the realization of a vision. Some people understand a vision or goal as a discrete event at the end of the whole process — as a destination separate from the journey. From that perspective, I would think of my goal in terms of some separate future "then," when I will be or have or experience what I desire. Relative to that "then" in the future, "now" is defined as *not* being or having or experiencing what I desire. This approach tends to postpone happiness and satisfaction until I reach that "then" — and now, in the meantime, I am relatively unhappy, unfulfilled, and unsatisfied.

For me, it makes more sense to think of the entire process as a continuum, from the first thought I have of my vision through to its full actualization in its final form. Another way to say this is that the very *being* (be-ing) of something *is* its process of *becoming*. An apple is not separate from the process that proceeds from seed to sprout to sapling to tree to bud to blossom to fruit. We may "think" of an ideal apple apart from such a process — but a real apple, an apple I can fully experience with all of my senses, an apple I can eat and enjoy, exists as one aspect of a continuum of organic growth.

What this approach means concretely is that "now" is not defined in terms of "not having or being what I desire" — not defined solely relative to some imagined future "then," in which I will have or be what I desire.

"Now," as a moment in the continuum of realizing my goal, is the specific way I am currently having or being what I desire — my on-going *living-toward* my vision *is* how I live my vision. (Many who teach the practice of writing and saying affirmations stress putting the affirmations in the present tense. From our perspective of the continuum of the process of realization, this use of the present tense is not merely wishful thinking for something I don't yet have — it is the acknowledgment that, insofar as I am under way, I already have what I desire in its current stage of becoming. We will more fully explore the topic of affirmations in a later section.) Thus the vision orientation is not a process of being unhappy now, while I move toward some future moment of happiness. It is rather a process of "joyful becoming."[12] My focus is not on passively receiving some prize at the end of all of my efforts, but rather on the joy of the *on-going process of co-creating* the life experience I desire — not merely a destination, but a *path with heart.*[13]

This idea of a continuum can also be applied to the process of personal growth. Formulating our vision and our ideals is an important reference point for choosing our beliefs and actions — for instance, I may use my vision of what it means to be an ideal spouse or parent as one of my reference points. But for many people, these ideals become more reasons to judge and condemn themselves in the present for "not being good enough." Relative to some imagined perfection in the future, they judge that they are "imperfect" now. But if we understand personal growth as a continuum, the very being of a perfection is the process of its coming to be — *the perfect be-ing of a perfection is the becoming of the perfection through all of its relatively "imperfect" stages.* An apple blossom can be seen either as an imperfect apple or as a perfect flower — it is a matter of our perspective. But the more I see the blossom only in terms of how it falls short of being something else, the less I am able to appreciate it for what it is. In the process of personal growth, this difference of perspective is especially important. It is often (perhaps always) the case that until I have completely accepted and affirmed one stage of my life, I am not able to grow and evolve to the next stage. If I remain focused only on rejecting parts or aspects of myself that seem to fall short of some imagined ideal, I may never fully understand their deeper lessons. If I am not fully present here and now, I will have no foundation to be able to move from this here toward my vision. A person who throws away all of the blossoms because they are not yet apples may never get to enjoy actually eating the fruit he desires.

Again, we want to find a balance. On the one hand, I want to celebrate my present moment, my present state of being in its own perfection — to evaluate it relative to itself, rather than only insofar as it falls short of some imagined ideal. On the other hand, I want to be aware of the vision I am moving toward, so that I am open to opportunities for further development and growth. But to take either approach to the exclusion of the other will both rob my present moment of much of its joy and fulfillment, and cripple my further growth. If I understand the process of change as a continuum, I see the present moment not as an isolated "point" in time, which is *either* complete *or* incomplete, but rather as dynamic, open-ended, and multi-dimensional. (We will explore the topics of time and temporality further in Chapter 10.)

❖ Living from Love

Earlier, we discussed how a vision orientation is a healthier, happier, and more effective way to live than a pathology orientation. We also explored how seeing your journey and its destination as aspects of a continuum allows you to enjoy the *process* of moving toward your goal, as well as its final attainment — to enjoy the very process of living, as well as the "accomplishments" and "victories." As one bumper sticker expressed it, "Success is the journey, not the destination." But ultimately, this whole discussion of goals and visions is but an introduction to an even more fundamental issue: whether you are living your life out of love, or out of fear.

Our contemporary culture places a strong emphasis on achieving goals — there are numerous books and workshops on goal-setting and "going for your dreams." They teach you tools that can help you to more effectively achieve the outcomes you desire, including techniques of visualization and affirmation, influencing others to do what you want, managing action steps and daily planners, dressing for success, etc. — in short, how to become the empowered, unstoppable you, who can "make" your dreams happen. But despite the passion and excitement of these workshops, they often fail to address the very critical question of the true nature and meaning of goals in our lives.

Most goal-setting books and workshops start from the assumption that in order for you to be able to experience happiness, success, and satisfaction in your life, something has to change in your world — something has to change in your external situation and circumstances. They claim that the answer to your unhappy and unfulfilled life is to clarify your dreams, make an action plan, do daily visualizations and affirmations, and act with power and focus and self-confidence, so that you finally achieve the outcome you desire — and *then* you can feel happy, fulfilled and complete. These workshops promote their techniques of goal-setting and goal-achievement as the way to "attain" happiness. But any approach that makes peace and happiness dependent on a particular outcome or particular circumstances is implicitly saying that you are not enough just as you are — that to experience a truly happy and successful life, you must "achieve" and "earn" and "attain" and "acquire" (fame, power, wealth, accomplishments, etc.). This not-enoughness is the foundation of a fear-based life, since every attempt to change your life will be essentially motivated by the threat of failure — if you don't succeed in attaining your outcome, you will continue to feel not-enough.

A pathology orientation is always a fear-based approach to life, because it is explicitly focused on battling or running away from what you do not want. A vision orientation, however, may be either fear-based or love-based, depending on how you define your vision or dream for yourself. If you believe that you will be truly happy only if and when you attain your goal, then you are implicitly affirming for yourself both that you are not truly happy now, and that if you fail to attain your goal you will continue to be unhappy (In fact, you would be even unhappier, since then you would feel that you had tried and "failed." Not only would your life in general be not-enough, but you would have shown yourself to be incapable and/or unworthy of having it any better — thus piling even more not-enough-ness onto your self-concept.) Thus, even though you are living in the lighted clearing of a vision orientation, and are seeing everything in the light of moving-toward-a-goal, you are still living an essentially fear-based life. In a sense, this kind of vision orientation can be seen as merely a pathology orientation in disguise — although you may seem to be moving toward a goal, what you are really doing is desperately trying to move away from your supposed not-enough-ness.

Any time you see your happiness as dependent on circumstances, you are living an essentially fear-based life. On the one hand, the journey toward your goal will tend to be desperate, since you believe that your happiness is riding on the outcome. For some people, this underlying fear may be covered over with an ambitious, driven, go-go-go attitude. The real issue, here, however, is not the energy level or ambition of one's personality and lifestyle, but whether it is fueled by love or fear. On the other hand, since circumstances are always changing, any circumstance-dependent happiness will be temporary and tentative at best. That means that even if you succeed at achieving your fear-based goal, you will still live under the threat that things could change.

In the Four Noble Truths of Buddhism, the first Truth is, "Life is suffering," and the second is, "The cause of suffering is attachment to desire." "Attachment to desire" implies a fear-based desire — the belief that things have to be a certain way in order for you to be happy. When that is your starting point — when that belief fundamentally defines the lighted clearing of your life — then your life will be suffering. You suffer because you don't have what you want; because you have it and lose it; because you had it and lost it; because you have it and fear losing it; because you have what you don't want; because you had what you didn't want (regret, guilt, wounds); or because you fear getting what you don't want. According to Buddhism, your unhappiness is never really caused by circumstances — *the real cause of unhappiness is your belief that your happiness is caused by circumstances.*

The Separative-Technological view tends to be intrinsically fear-based, since it believes that nothing has any intrinsic value besides what you give it. This means that you have to "make" the quality of your life — it is up to you and your on-going "doing." This puts a continual pressure on you, because without your on-going effort, your life is simply nothing, has no quality, is merely empty. And in the dog-eat-dog world of this view, you will end up being used by someone else.

The alternative to a fear-based approach is a love-based approach. The Spiritual view provides a good theoretical foundation for understanding and experiencing a love-based life. According to the Spiritual view, you *are* an expression or manifestation of Spirit. Spirit *is* the very be-ing of Peace, Love, and Joy — Spirit is the very peac-ing of Peace, the lov-ing of Love, and the joy-ing of Joy. Thus you *are*, in your very being, an expression of peace, love, and joy. You do not have to accomplish or acquire or earn anything to experience peace, love, and joy now. You do not have to "make" your own happiness — all you have to do is to stop making yourself unhappy and to remember your own deepest truth as a be-ing of Spirit.

Earlier, I said that you might believe at a conscious level that you were living a vision orientation, and be unaware of the subconscious pathology-oriented thoughts and beliefs that were dominating your life. Likewise, you can believe at a conscious level that you are choosing and living a love-based approach to life, when in truth you are subconsciously motivated by fear. Again, the key to recognizing that you are living a fear-based approach to life is its negative emotional tone. For the Spiritual-Holistic view, negative emotions are *always* a reflection of fear and ignorance, and serve as a reminder to shift your focus back to your Spiritual truth. From the perspective of your awareness of your Spiritual truth, there is nothing to fear, and nothing you "need" to strive for — there is only the truth and wholeness of Spirit in all of its many forms and manifestations. Whereas the Separative-Technological view often tends to be expressed as a fear-based approach to life, the Spiritual-Holistic view is intrinsically and necessarily a love-based approach to life, which is emotionally reflected as the experience of perfect peace, love, and joy.

Does this mean that we simply give up all of our desires and dreams? No, because it's not the goals and dreams that are the problem, but rather how we understand and live toward them. Going for your dreams can be an intrinsic part of the joy and passion of your life — can be how you concretely express the love and joy that are your truth. But as soon as you (choose to) believe that your happiness is dependent on a certain outcome, or that "things" have to change for you to be happy, then you are living in fear. You are no longer expressing your joy, but are desperately trying to achieve or earn it. The *Bhagavad Gita* defines the path of "karma yoga" (the way we can live Spiritually in our day-to-day world) in terms of "doing what you will, without attachment to the fruits of your labor." In other words, you live toward your dreams with passion and joy, but without any emotional attachment to the outcome of your efforts. It's fun and exciting to have a dream to live toward —whether your dream is skydiving, building a new house, or establishing a soup kitchen for the homeless. What is important is whether your dream grows out of and expresses your deepest truth, and whether you live toward it in love or in fear. But from within the Spiritual-Holistic perspective, the actual outcome of your efforts is ultimately irrelevant to the quality and worth of your life. The quality of your life is simply "given" as your truth — this is one meaning of the term, "grace." And everything that you "do" in your life is simply your joyful expression of that truth.

CHAPTER 10

THE TIME OF YOUR LIFE

❖ The Dynamic Now

The re-interpretation or re-lighting of the events and situations of your life can apply not only to what you are presently experiencing in your life, but also to what you remember about your past and what you anticipate about your future. For the purposes of this discussion, I am not interested in the "metaphysics" of time — that is, what time "really" is in some absolute sense, or in how the past, present and future exist "objectively." Here I am only concerned with your *experience* of time, your experience of your past, present, and future. In this context, I will focus on the past, present, and future only insofar as they *exist now in your present experience* as "the past," "the present," and "the future."[14]

As a self-aware human being, I am always under way, always in the midst of realizing and living some possibility of myself and my world. I am always in the midst of living the choices I have already made, and actively choosing what I will believe, think, say, and do next. How I choose to interpret and respond to the things I encounter in my world determines which of their possibilities of myself I realize or do not realize in my life. My choices also determine which possibilities I realize or do not realize in my life. The "now," or "the present," exists in my experience as this on-going moment of choosing, this moment of ever-emerging possibility. I am always in mid-step, choosing where to place my foot next. I may forget that I have a choice, but even this forgetting is ultimately a choice, a choice to temporarily abdicate my responsibility to choose. Since the present is the on-going process of being in mid-step or mid-choice, it necessarily includes both past and future dimensions as part of its own intrinsic dynamic structure. Again, I want to emphasize that my focus here is our actual *experience* of temporality — I am explicitly not addressing the abstract question as to how the past, present, and future exist in any objective or absolute sense.

In the living experience of my now, my future exists for me as the dimension of the "toward-which" of my action; the dimension of my purpose, my intent, my goal; the dimension I pro-ject ahead of myself, which helps give meaning and direction to my current endeavors. In this perspective, my future is not so much a separate piece of time "ahead" of me, as rather an intrinsic part of the openness of my now. Insofar as I am a being who is under way, who is in the midst of "going somewhere" or "doing something," *my very process of be-ing here now is a moving-toward the purpose I am projecting.* As the toward-which of my intention, my future is the dimension of my present which allows me to realize the dynamic possibilities I am choosing now. Even if I occasionally choose to do nothing at all, and simply "be here now" without going anywhere, this choosing to "not go anywhere" is possible only within the framework of a life which could go somewhere — a life that has a future dimension as part of its being.

The future is also the dimension from which new possibilities reveal themselves, new possibilities of myself and my world. As new events and situations and possibilities emerge or come out of hiddenness into my life, my perspective can grow — I become more aware of "the big picture," and come to more fully understand the true meaning of the events of my past and present. Ultimately, what any event or thing means in my life also includes what it eventually leads to, and "how it all turns out in the end" — and often a subsequent event can cast everything that went before in a whole new light. The future is the dimension of the ever-emerging larger perspective, the dimension of the possibility of discovering deeper meaning, the dimension of the on-going emergence of truth or unhiddenness. This on-going revelation of new possibilities for deeper meaning and more complete truth is an essential intrinsic dimension of my living experience of the now.

As the dimension of ever-emerging new possibilities, the future exists for me as the dynamic presence of the Mystery in my life. I do not know with certainty what will happen next — in fact, in the unknownness of my own death, I do not even know if there will be a next moment at all. My future exists only as possibility — not merely the possibility of what will happen next, but ultimately even the possibility of whether or not there will be any more possibilities for me at all. In contrast to the Mystery of the future, we tend to think that we already know all about the past and the present. But insofar as the on-going revelation of the deeper meaning or the bigger picture can affect and change my understanding of the meaning of the past and the present, the Mystery inherent in my future also permeates my past and my present. As I become more fully aware of the ever-emerging Mystery of the future as Mystery, I recognize that my interpretation of my past and my present is always only provisional, always subject to further re-vision — since the picture can always get bigger, I cannot say with certainty or finality at any given moment what any event or thing truly means, or how it ultimately fits into the whole of my life and my world.

My past exists for me now as the dimension of the choices I have already made — the choices whose effects and consequences form the basis of my experience and understanding. I use my experience and understanding to make sense of the choices and possibilities I am facing now. Thus, in terms of my actual experience, my past is not just a collection of events that exists "behind" me — it is instead a dynamic horizon that I project ahead of myself (into my future) to help myself shape and define my openness to new possibilities. As we have mentioned before, every definite way of interpreting a field of possibilities illuminates or reveals some possibilities, and hides or conceals others. The dimension of your past experience is one way to filter, interpret, and understand your future possibilities. As such, your past can illuminate and reveal certain possibilities that you might have otherwise overlooked — this is the advantage of "experience" (as in, "she was an 'experienced' camper"). But, your past can also conceal or distort those possibilities that are radically new or different. A person who believes that his past and his personal history constitute the "whole story" will not only be unaware of any radically new possibilities, but will also be unaware that he is unaware of them. Thus, his past becomes a closed and rigid way to interpret the future, a kind of prison which constrains him to live within the same limited field of possibilities day after day — for example, the person from a "dysfunctional" family who blindly repeats the same dysfunctional behavior toward his own children.

The solution to this kind of closed-mindedness is not, however, to simply forget or deny my past, even if that were possible. My past is the framework of the familiar and the known, which allows me to make sense out of, and more fully realize, the new possibilities that are presenting themselves to me every moment. Even to appreciate a new possibility *as* "new" or "different" is to understand it relative to what is already known. The familiar and the strange, the known and the unknown co-define each other. A person with total amnesia would be virtually paralyzed — nothing would make any sense at all, and he would have no basis to choose one alternative over another. What we want to strive for is the balance we spoke of earlier as "beginner's mind" — a dynamic balance between honoring the truth of what I already know, and also remaining intentionally open to those unknown possibilities which stand silently in the shadows beyond my lighted clearing.

What is significant about the past and the future for me *now* is not so much the so-called "facts" which have already happened or which may yet occur, but rather what they *mean to me here and now* — which I define by how I filter and interpret their possibilities now. In this sense, my past is not "fixed" or "cut and dried" — as it actually exists for me now, it is but one possible interpretation of one possible set of data, an interpretation that determines which events are significant and what these events mean to me now. The dynamic possibility of the past and the dynamic possibility of the future constantly affect and co-define each other. On the one hand, my interpretation of the past affects how I project and understand my future possibilities. On the other hand, as new events and possibilities unfold in my life, they can affect how I understand and interpret my past. For instance, I might come to realize that, in the light of a larger perspective, some events in my past had a much different meaning for me than I had previously thought. This change of meaning of my past would, in turn, affect how I approached and understood my future possibilities. In this whole process, the present is not a separate and closed off "moment" or "piece" of time. The present is the on-going dialogue of past and future possibilities — a dynamic reciprocity, wherein my understanding of the familiar affects my interpretation of the strange, and what I perceive of the emergence of the strange affects my understanding of the familiar.

My now is the on-going process of making my next choice within the framework of my memory of choices already made. My future and my past, as they actually and effectively exist in my on-going experience of my life, exist as dynamic dimensions of the very process of the be-ing of my now. This is not to claim that time is merely subjective — that, for instance, the past never really happened at all, but only exists as a collection of memories "in my head." The focus of this section is rather on my actual *experience* of time — how my "past" and my "present" and my "future" actually exist in my on-going living experience. Nor is this discussion meant to be a complete explanation of the temporality of our experience — here we are discussing time only in the context of exploring the possibility of re-lighting our lives. Within the framework of my actual experience, the past exists as possibility just as much as does the future, insofar as the *meaning* of my past and the *meaning* of the future for myself are defined by my interpretation of them. The possibility of re-interpreting my life therefore can include not only re-lighting the present "reality" I am experiencing now, but also re-lighting the reality that currently exists now *as* "having-already-happened" or *as* "about-to-happen." But it is important to remember that *any re-lighting of my past, my present, or my future always takes place in the present and for the sake of the present — the truth of any interpretation is the clearing it creates in my life <u>now</u>.* In any process of re-choosing and re-lighting, my real question is, "How can I live and understand my life in the way that truly serves me and my own deepest values *now?*"

The following stories illustrate how the various temporal dimensions of my life can affect one another. They are examples of how re-lighting the past also re-lights the future — how re-lighting the past can help to heal its "scars" in the present and open our lives to a fuller and less wounded future. I am not suggesting that healing emotional scars is a simple or easy process. But neither do I believe that childhood traumas have to cripple us for our entire lives, or that the healing of these old wounds necessarily has to be a long, drawn-out process involving years of hard work and suffering. Each person's journey of healing is unique — each person has his or her own lessons to learn, own challenges to overcome, and own truths to discover. Some parts of this journey may involve many small steps over months or years; at other times, we seem to take giant steps in a matter of minutes or hours. Appreciate each of these stories for the lighted clearing it creates for you.

The Distant Father

This story comes from a personal growth workshop I attended several years ago. During one of the group exercises, a woman who was in her thirties began to cry. It started softly, and gradually grew into heart-wrenching sobs. She was remembering her father, who had never really shown her any outward love or affection. She did not have a single childhood memory of being held or rocked or hugged by her father, nor could she ever remember him telling her that he loved her. She remembered the deep pain of that small child who couldn't understand why her daddy was so distant. She had been loving, trusting and open — but she felt she had received no love in return. In her childhood perception, she interpreted all of this as rejection, as a judgment that she was not good enough. Throughout her adolescence and adulthood, she was unaware of the deep hidden pain of not being able to fully give or receive love — she simply felt it was not safe to open her heart in childlike innocence. Thus, her past not only limited and crippled her present, but also narrowly circumscribed the horizon of future possibilities she could envision for herself. Moreover, because her sense of fear and defensiveness was reinforced by our culture, she thought it was simply "normal." But, in the context of the workshop, she realized that these feelings of inadequacy and fear had originated in her childhood reaction to her father. This is the point of discovery where some people, and even some professional counselors and therapists, stop — merely discovering the "why" of the hidden pain, but never healing the cause. But it is to the credit of the two people who presented that workshop that they did not let the woman simply stop at this discovery. They urged her to once again become that little girl and to look deeply into the eyes of her father — they urged her to look more and more deeply, with the ultimate focus and purpose of discovering the love within him and forgiving him for his distance and coldness. Through her sobs, she spoke of this journey into the deeper truth of her father. She saw him as a newly married man, full of ambition and fun — still as much a child as an adult. She experienced how the unexpected pregnancy of his new wife suddenly made his life feel like a struggle of endless pressure and obligation. She spoke of how her father himself had grown up in a family with very little expression of love or affection — how he had himself, as a child, decided that it was not safe to love or be loved. She saw deep within him the terror that he might hurt his own children as he had been hurt by his father — and the painful frightened decision he made to "keep his distance" so that he would not harm his little child whom he loved so much. She saw beyond the mask and the pain of the adult, to the lonely frightened child within her father — the child who was afraid to love or be loved, the one who did not know how to show love except by working hard and providing for his family. Within the context of this compassionate vision of her father's spirit, she was able to forgive him for his distance, and love him for doing his best in his own fear and confusion. In healing the pain of the little girl within herself, she healed her own history and thus healed herself in the present as well. Months later when I spoke with her, she said that her childhood memories were now very different. Now she remembered the love and acceptance in the heart of her father, even though those feelings were never openly or clearly expressed. Because of these changes in the *meaning* of her childhood memories, she was now able to be more loving and open herself, and to trust the love of those around her. She said her whole life felt "lighter" — both less heavy and less dark.

What is important to note here is that she did not re-write her history in the sense of making up a new set of "facts." Nor did she pretend that her father had been an "ideal parent." Instead, she chose to reinterpret the history that she remembered in light of her current understanding. Her initial interpretation of the events of her childhood had been formed by the immediate and unreflective reactions of a small, frightened child, who had decided that it was unsafe and painful to love or be loved. This childhood interpretation of her father and its consequences had continued to stunt her emotional life well into her adulthood. But when she finally relived the past through her more mature adult level of understanding, she saw that her father's distance was not a reflection of her unworthiness, but only an expression of his own fear. By changing the *meaning* of her past, she changed its impact on her present and thus changed the meaning of her present for herself. In doing this, she also opened up a new horizon of future possibilities for herself. By discovering the deeper truth of her past, she was able to discover the deeper truth of her present, and to open herself up to a fuller range of future possibilities — the deeper truth of her future. This story reminds me of a bumper sticker I once saw: "It's never too late to have a happy childhood." At one level, this means that a person is never too old to be childlike, or to approach life with an innocent, playful beginner's mind — no matter what a person's age, his or her inner-child-possibility has never disappeared, but has only been covered over with more and more layers of experience. At another level, it means that by re-lighting and re-understanding our past, we may discover possibilities of joy that we had overlooked at the time. The point here is not to merely gloss over childhood traumas with a superficial covering of cheerfulness. Nor is it to pretend that every seeming cruelty from our childhood was merely our own childish misinterpretation — physical and emotional abuse does happen. But no matter what the circumstances may have been, it is always possible to re-light the past — I can choose what those memories will *mean for me now*, and how they will either open up or close down my horizon of present and future possibilities.

The Little Girl in the Hospital

The second story comes from a person I met several years ago. This woman had been born with multiple congenital "defects," including very obvious facial "deformities." (Note that calling them "defects" and "deformities" already puts them in a negative light.) Throughout her years as a young girl, she underwent many reconstructive operations and extensive plastic surgery. In addition to the emotional pain of being socially rejected as a "freak," she also suffered intense physical pain. She spent many lonely, frightened childhood days lying in a hospital bed. For that child, life was full of ugliness, pain, and rejection. By the time I met her, she was an attractive young woman in her twenties. But she still carried all of her childhood pain in her heart, and deep inside herself, she still believed that she was defective, ugly, unworthy, and unlovable — no amount of plastic surgery could ever hide this. Her frightened childhood reactions to all of the physical and emotional pains of her early life had hardened into absolute convictions in her adult subconscious — she would never be good enough; no one could ever really love her; it was unsafe to open herself to love and inner feelings; and there was no hope that the future would ever be any better. Because she was largely unaware of these self-undermining and despairing beliefs, they effectively ruled her present life, and they also formed the horizon of her future possibilities for self-esteem, for love, and for relationship.

I suggested that she sit down by herself and mentally take a journey back to talk with this frightened child in her memory — that she visit that little girl lying frightened and hopeless in her hospital bed, convinced that her life could never possibly become anything good or beautiful. I asked her to imagine for herself as vividly as possible that she was taking this little girl into her arms, holding her and loving her, comforting her. As she embraced her little girl, she told her that she was the future self of the frightened child — she told her that everything had turned out well, that the operations had been successful, that both the pain and the social rejection had eventually come to an end. She also told that little child that she was never really ugly or unlovable in the first place — that other people's reactions to the little girl merely reflected their own fears and insecurities. She reassured this little girl that soon she would become a healthy, competent, wonderful young woman, and that other people would some day see the truth of her beauty, the beauty which had always been present, but which had been hidden — hidden beneath her own and others' reactions to those physical characteristics which had been judged to be defects and deformities.

Her private sessions with her little girl were difficult and very emotional at first. But as she continued, the little girl in her memory became calmer, more peaceful, more self-assured, and more hopeful. The little girl in her memory decided that she was lovable, and that it was safe to love and to allow herself to be loved. The woman said that as the child in her memory was healed, the meaning of her past changed — as a result, her past, as it existed for her *now*, contained strong elements of hope, self-confidence, and trust. As her past became healthier and more positive, the meaning of the present, which had grown out of this past, also changed. As she rediscovered her self-confidence and her sense of trust and hope, the horizon of her future possibilities opened up — she could now allow herself to consider a wider range of choices and alternatives than she had ever dreamed possible before. By reinterpreting her past, she also reinterpreted her present and her future. It is important to note that she did not deny or repress the pain of her childhood memories, nor did she "pretend" that those experiences had been wonderful or pleasant. Her reinterpretation of the past was actually a matter of choosing to see it more truthfully — to see it from the truer and deeper perspective of her mature understanding, instead of merely from the limited vision of a frightened child. And as she uncovered the deeper truth of her past, she also uncovered the deeper truth of her present and her future.

❖ The So-Called "Illusion" of Time

Mystics speak of a level of experience that somehow transcends our normal, everyday kind of experience — in the mystical literature, we often find evocative references to some kind of pure, non-temporal awareness. This is the awareness within which and relative to which we can experience the dynamic of time at all — the dimension of experience that allows us to experience temporality as temporality. This would be analogous to the silence, within which and relative to which we are able to hear music — the silence out of which each note emerges, against which each note stands defined as what it is, and into which each note disappears as it ends. Based on the experience of this timeless dimension, some mystics have said that time is "illusory." This has led many students and followers of the mystics to dogmatically proclaim that the non-temporal alone is real and true, and that the temporal is unreal and false. (Although I once heard one of these dogmatic followers get tripped up by a shrewd interviewer: "And just when did you come to this realization that time was merely an illusion?" "Oh, about five years ago.")

I believe, however, that such dogmatic and dualistic claims are a fundamental misinterpretation of what the mystics mean by "illusory." If we read further into the mystical literature, we find that the mystics also speak of a still deeper level of reality that transcends both the temporal and the non-temporal. This deeper level of experience, which grasps the correlativity of the temporal and the non-temporal, and honors the partial and relative truth of both. To merely reject the truth of the temporal would at the same time make the non-temporal meaningless. For the mystic, what is illusory about our everyday conception of time is the belief that time is somehow absolute. For the mystic, *temporality is just one possible way of thinking about and experiencing your life* — a way that makes possible your conception of yourself as a distinct individual with free will, as a person who chooses how he sees the world and where he is going. The very truth of this kind of experience, the very openness that it creates and inhabits, is temporal in its being. The clearing which allows you to experience the meaning of your life now (present tense) is defined by what you have already (past tense) pro-jected ahead of yourself (into your future) — that is to say, the lighted clearing, within which choosing and doing are possible, is inherently temporal.

But for the mystic, there is also another possible way to experience life — a way that is non-personal and non-temporal. This is sometimes characterized as a way in which no one does anything and nothing happens (or the non-happening of the no-thing, relative to which every happening of a something can reveal itself as such). To live as truthfully or unhiddenly as possible involves appreciating the correlativity of the temporal and the non-temporal possibilities. To say that time is "illusory" does not mean that temporal experience is false or wrong, but merely that it is only a partial unhiddenness — that it is not the whole truth. But from this perspective, the non-temporal is equally illusory. Presumably the reason that most mystics stress that the temporal is illusory is that they are addressing an audience who tends to believe that temporal experience is absolute. In order to introduce the strange, the mystic first has to disillusion us of the belief that the familiar is all that there is, the belief that what we already know is the whole truth. But the mystic's ultimate goal is to help us directly experience that no particular way of thinking about reality can be the whole truth.

There is more at issue here than merely whether we are making the logical *faux pas* of mistaking the part for the whole. When we say that time is a partial truth, we mean that the concept of temporality reveals some possibilities, even while concealing others. In particular, temporality defines the very openness that allows me to discover myself and my world, to creatively interact with my world, and to realize my own most authentic possibilities. Note that "discover," "realize," and "create" all imply a temporal process. Perhaps even more to the point, the very concept of "possibility" implies a temporal dimension, within which a possibility can either be realized or not. Even the "process" of "transcending" the limited perspective of the temporal framework, and "coming" to be aware of and fully appreciate the deeper unity of the temporal and the non-temporal, is itself made possible by the temporal clearing which allows every becoming to become. So it is not just a matter of begrudgingly admitting the logical necessity of the temporal in order to define and validate some "higher" concept of the non-temporal. I believe that we also want to honor and celebrate the great gift of time itself, as the very possibility of the clearing within which we can discover and become ourselves — the lighted clearing that allows our deepest truth to emerge.

Earlier, in my discussion of the vision and pathology orientations, I said that the very be-ing of perfection is its process of becoming — a process which involves a series of seemingly "imperfect" stages. The very idea of "becoming" implies a movement from the not yet perfect toward the more perfect (or the more perfectly realized). But since the be-ing of perfection *is* its process of becoming, then there is at the same time, an aspect of perfection to each of the stages of the becoming. Often, if we are only focused on the final goal of the process, we tend to be very critical of the interim stages en route, especially in retrospect. I remember one person telling me, "I thought I knew it all yesterday, but today I realize what an idiot I was then." (Or the dogmatic followers of the mystic, who rush to criticize all of the superficial fools who still believe that time is real.) The problem is that when we simply reject whole-cloth any stage in the becoming, we throw out its gift along with its limitations — as the saying goes, the baby with the bath water. In doing that, we often end up just moving from one dogmatic position to another, rather than expanding and deepening our truth. We tend to mistakenly think that we are somehow being loyal and committed to our ideal of perfection by judging and rejecting everything that is relatively "imperfect." But I believe that we do not honor the whole by dishonoring the parts, nor do we honor our destination by dishonoring our journey. From this perspective, finding a way to celebrate the truth and the gift of each partial understanding in our lives not only makes the journey itself more joyful, but is essential to the process of fully realizing our deepest truth.

❖ Eternal Truth

In the discussion above, "temporal" and "non-temporal" can be understood as the dualistic concepts that refer to two different ways I can think about and experience the now — two possible ways that co-define each other. In any experience, I can choose to focus on either the process of change (what-I-am-doing and what-is-happening), or on the implicit dimension of changelessness that allows me to perceive and understand change as "change." It is only the nothingness and darkness of the night sky that allows me to perceive the something-ness and light of a star (even though when I am preoccupied with the stars and their movements, I am usually unaware of the unchanging nothingness that co-defines them). In every case of dualistic, co-defined concepts, both have to be present for me to understand or perceive either one.

"The eternal," as I am defining it, is the non-dualistic idea that transcends the temporal/non-temporal distinction. "Eternal truth" is the essence of every now (or the essence of now-ness itself) seen in its deepest unhiddenness — and thus, the eternal includes the truth of both the temporal and the non-temporal ways of experiencing now. From the perspective of the Spiritual view, Spirit is the source and essence of everything. Thus, Spirit is the essence of every now — it is the truth of every now (i.e., "now" revealed in its deepest and most complete unhiddenness). From the Spiritual perspective, "eternal truth" *is* Spirit.

As we noted earlier, the experience of Spirit is emotionally reflected as feelings of perfect (non-dualistic) peace, love, and joy. In this sense, eternal truth is the Be-ing of perfect peace, love, and joy. Since every individual being is an expression of Spirit, "the eternal truth of yourself" (you experienced in your deepest unhiddenness) would be that you are a be-ing of perfect peace, love, and joy. The way that Spirit (the Be-ing of peace, love, and joy) *exists* is *as* your be-ing, my be-ing, his be-ing, her be-ing, its be-ing, our be-ing, and the be-ing of the world.

Because the content or essence of eternal truth does not change, the eternal is often identified with the non-temporal. But although the eternal is not "the temporal," it would be a mistake to confuse the non-dualistic "eternal" with the dualistic "non-temporal" — in its deepest truth, the eternal is neither the temporal, nor the non-temporal, nor both, nor neither. If the eternal were thought of *only* as the dualistically defined non-temporal, then you would have to deny the temporal in order to be aware of the truth of Spirit (i.e., in order to experience Spirit in its deepest unhiddenness). But Spirit, as I have defined it, is the essence and truth of *everything* — which includes the temporal as well as the non-temporal. For the Spiritual perspective, the temporal and the non-temporal are two possible ways that Spirit can "exist" or manifest itself, two possible modes of appearance of Spirit. The goal is not to reject the temporal, but to experience the truth of the temporal *as* one possible expression of the eternal truth of Spirit. In terms of the emotional quality of our life experience, that means that the eternal Spiritual truth of now — perfect peace, love, joy — is always accessible in *every* now, in the now of the day-to-day temporal life as well as the now of the deep silence of meditation. *Spirit is the truth of the profane as well as of the sacred.*

Eternal, in this sense, does not mean "later, after death" or "lasting forever" — it means "*always, already now.*" In terms of the lighted clearing metaphor, this concept of the eternal can create the lighted clearing which allows you to dis-cover (un-cover) the experience-possibility of absolute peace, love, and joy that is potentially present in every moment, in every now. From this perspective, you never have to wait until you have achieved or earned it, or somehow changed your circumstances, or until you receive some divine reward after you die. It is the very truth of every now waiting only to be uncovered, and it will appear in your experience when you stop covering it. My earlier story of my experience at the meditation retreat was for me an example of this possibility.

In terms of our earlier discussion on goal-setting and attachment to goals, this idea of the eternal means that your experience of peace and happiness is not dependent on whether or not you are striving-toward and/or achieving goals. As I emphasized there, it's not having a goal or living-toward a goal that makes your life fear-based — it is only when you understand and experience your desired outcome as necessary for your happiness, that living-toward-your-goal is experienced as fearful. From the Spiritual perspective, if you are aware of the eternal truth of now, then now is equally peaceful and happy whether or not you have or achieve goals — because peace, love, and joy are the essence of now-ness, the essence of the lighted clearing of your being that makes possible every experience of striving and not striving, doing and not doing, achieving and not achieving. Experiencing the eternal truth of Spirit does not mean giving up anything. It does not mean giving up goals or dreams or temporal experience — it is not a process of self-sacrifice at all. It is rather awakening to and *remembering the truth that always already is.*

CHAPTER 11

RECLAIMING YOUR RESPONSIBILITY

❖ Re-spons-ibility

As many teachers have pointed out, the word responsibility means our ability to respond. But what does it mean to "respond"? The word comes from the Latin, "re-" (back) plus "spondere" (to promise) — and the word pro-mise literally means, "to send forth." Thus, responsibility means "*my ability to send forth something of myself back to the world.*" In other words, there is a creative space between "what happens to me" and "what I do about it" — a space into which I can interject who I am, a space within which my own unique purpose can creatively and proactively express itself. This is what some writers have referred to as "the gap between stimulus and response" — the gap from which I can send forth my own unique essence back to the world. Man is much more than a Pavlovian dog, completely conditioned by his environment — more than a mere machine, completely determined by what happens to him (and, from the Spiritual perspective, Pavlov's dog itself was much more than Pavlov was able to experience in the lighted clearing of his mechanistic presuppositions). I have a choice as to what I will send forth from myself back to the world. To merely "react" to my world is one way to exercise my ability to respond — it is a way in which I respond automatically and unconsciously. What I send forth when I react is merely the conditioning of my past — including both the negative conditioning (my childhood wounds, the fears and prejudices of my parents and my culture), and the positive conditioning (moral values and altruistic ideals). When I react, I am not deliberately choosing to send forth my own most authentic purpose and values, to send forth my very best — instead I am merely on automatic pilot. *To "respond" always means to consciously and deliberately send forth your truth* (your purpose, who you are in your deepest unhiddenness) — anything other than this is mere reaction.

To "reclaim" means to lay claim to what is already yours — to consciously and deliberately make it your own. The foundation of any process of personal growth begins with reclaiming your responsibility — acknowledging and deliberately assuming your co-creative role in your life. This means reclaiming your ability to deliberately choose your values and your beliefs; to deliberately choose where you will focus your energy and attention; to deliberately choose what meaning you give to the things and events in your world; to deliberately live toward the quality of life experience you desire. You exercise your ability to be more than just another link in a deterministic causal chain — a link that merely reflects the unexamined opinions and fears of your personal history and your culture. You choose instead to be what some physicists refer to as a "white hole" — a locus in the space-time continuum that actively adds its own energy and creativity to the whole. You are not, as it were, merely a Spiritual welfare case, passively waiting to receive whatever charity might be doled out by fate. You begin to ask such questions as, "What do I truly desire to add or contribute to the whole? What is the best I can send forth back to the world in this situation? How can I actively and creatively *be* the best and truest me in this circumstance?"

In this context, blaming is always a red flag — if I am blaming other people or circumstances for how I feel, it is a signal that I am abdicating my responsibility. Insofar as I am blaming the world and feeling victimized, I am hiding from myself my own role in interpreting the situation as "bad" or "awful" or "tragic." Moreover, to the extent that I remain focused on blaming, I will not be open to the more positive possibilities of my situation — by failing to take responsibility for my current interpretation, I actively blind myself to the possibility of choosing another interpretation.

This is not to say that blaming the world and abdicating my responsibility are intrinsically bad, or that I am a "failure" when I feel that way. As I said earlier, by the time I am aware of a feeling, I am *already* feeling that feeling. The real question at that moment is how do I want to respond then — for instance, how do I want to respond when I realize I am feeling anger or self-pity? I need to reclaim my responsibility only when I have temporarily lost my claim to it. When I find myself blaming someone or something for how I feel, it is a reminder to me that I have *already* forgotten my responsibility. Once I have been re-minded of this — once it has emerged from the hiddenness of forgetfulness into the unhiddenness of awareness — the relevant question is, "Do I want to continue forgetting my responsibility, or do I want to re-claim and re-member it for myself?" If I choose to reclaim my responsibility, the first step is to assume full responsibility for what my world means to me now — whether I am seeing it, for instance, as a curse or a challenge, as a stumbling block or a stepping stone, as an obstacle or an opportunity. Once I have reclaimed my responsibility for the meaning of my current life experience and for how I am already feeling now, I can further exercise my creative responsibility by choosing to see my situation in a different light if I so desire. This is not a matter of merely ignoring or denying the difficult situations in our lives, or of merely pasting a happy face over a challenging life experience. It involves first becoming fully aware of the difficulty I am facing, as well as fully recognizing what role I am playing in interpreting it as "difficult." From within this awareness and acceptance, I can then explore whether I might be able to see things in a different way — a way that could open me up to possibilities that are more constructive. Once again, the true value of an idea or a belief is the quality of life experience it makes possible. In this context, the true value of such theories as the Spiritual-Holistic view and the vision orientation lies in their ability to open a lighted clearing within which life possibilities can be discovered that are more constructive — possibilities which allow us to move through our lives with more peace, love, and joy; possibilities which allow us to grow from our life experiences, rather than merely suffering through them; possibilities which allow us to thrive, rather than merely survive.

Perhaps the most important way I exercise my responsibility is through the "light" I shine forth from myself. "Where" I shine my light (my focus of attention), as well as the "color" of my light (how I interpret myself and the world) lay the foundation for all of my other possible responses —my light choice defines the horizon of my possible ways of interacting with my world. In this sense, my light choice is my *primary responsibility*, my first active and creative sending-forth — it creates the clearing which enables me to become aware of and realize my possibilities for thinking, feeling, speaking, and acting in the world.

Insofar as I am aware of myself and my life now in some meaningful and coherent fashion, I am *already* exercising my primary responsibility. Re-lighting a situation means to re-choose my primary responsibility. This is a fundamentally different level of response from merely considering a new option within my current lighted clearing — this is a choice to re-create my lighted clearing in a way that will illuminate a different horizon of possibilities of thoughts, feelings, words, and actions. It is a process of re-creating the context of meaning — the context that determines the significance of each thing and event for me. This is what some psychologists call "re-framing" — re-defining the frame or border of the *whole* picture in a way that not only re-defines which elements are included in the picture at all, but also the perceived significance of each of them in relation to the whole. In the story of the light box, we saw how each different light helped to determine a different experience of the picture. One light allowed the woman's face to appear cold and harsh, while another allowed it to appear warm and kind. One light allowed two adjoining colors to appear in stark contrast, while another allowed them to appear as indistinguishable from one another. From the perspective of the Possibility Model, all of these possibilities were inherent in "the photo itself" — the light merely created a clearing that "allowed" certain possibilities to emerge into unhiddenness as actual experiences.

In the coming chapters, we will explore a variety of ways to re-light ourselves and our world. In some situations, it may be as simple as a slight shift in our attitude and focus, so that we emphasize and highlight aspects of our world we had previously ignored. I consider this slight shift of focus and attitude to be a form of re-lighting, since it can transform our experience of the whole picture. In other situations, it may be necessary to fundamentally re-define those core beliefs which determine the meaning and tone of every element of our experience. In this discussion, the guiding principle will be: How can you re-light a situation which has a negative emotional tone for you, so that it becomes a situation which offers possibilities of peace and joy, and constructive possibilities for growth? Your primary intent in this process is not so much to get rid of the difficult and negative emotions in your life, as rather a choice to actively open yourself to the possibility of moving *toward* the quality of your life experience you truly desire. It is important to remember that your ultimate goal is not merely to "see" the constructive possibilities in your life, but to actually realize them — for it is only in actively and creatively living these opportunities that you can fulfill the promise of your truth.

In exercising your primary responsibility, you will want to choose those light choices which best help you fulfill your purpose — best help you create a clearing that enables you to discover those possibilities most consistent with and supportive of your purpose. If, for instance, part of your purpose were to help empower others to assume responsibility for their own lives, then you would want to choose those beliefs that best allow you to experience others as powerful and responsible beings. The more you actually experienced their intrinsic potential for self-directedness, the better you would be able to speak and act in ways to help bring it forth.

The lighted clearing of your life not only illuminates possibilities for yourself, but can also help to reveal (or conceal) possibilities for others as well. We influence and contribute to others not merely by what we say and do, but by our very being — who you are speaks louder than your words. It is as if the lighted clearing of your own being can act as an opening for others — as a window or a mirror that allows them to glimpse their own truth. The more authentically you are living your own life, the clearer your opening becomes for others — in truly fulfilling your own purpose, you help others to discover and fulfill their own. From the Spiritual perspective, we all share a common truth or essence, since we all are manifestations or be-ings of Spirit. Thus, the essence of what you express or shine forth when you are authentically living your truth is the same essence that is shared by others. When you live truthfully, the light that others see shining forth from you is a reminder of the light within themselves, even though their particular authentic form of expressing that light may be different from your own. Your light choices not only create your own clearing for discovering truth, but can also help to illuminate the clearings of others as well.

❖ Exercising Your Responsibility

Just as exercising your body can strengthen your muscles and increase your endurance and flexibility, exercising your "ability to respond" can strengthen your ability to stay on purpose and can increase your endurance and flexibility in remaining true to yourself in whatever circumstances and situations you encounter. One way to exercise your ability to send forth your truth is the practice of the "Best Day" exercise. Ultimately, of course, you desire every day to be your best — this particular exercise is simply one way to concentratedly practice this intent.

On the day you choose to practice this exercise, find some way to catch your attention as soon as you awaken, to remind yourself that this is to be your "Best Day"— your most truthful day; the day you express your truth most clearly and consistently. Today you will give your best to every activity. How do you want to wake up and start your Best Day? With frantic thoughts about the day to come? With prayer? With peaceful thoughts? With affirmations? Let the phrase "Best Day" be almost like a mantra that you repeat in your mind with every breath, calling you back to your intention for this day — a phrase that creates the lighted clearing within which you can discover and be your own unique best. Pay full attention to each detail and each moment — mindfully brush your teeth, mindfully take your shower, mindfully get dressed.

If, during your Best Day, your external circumstances seem to interfere with or be at odds with your desires — for instance, you spill coffee on your new shirt, or you seem to catch every red light on the way to work — then ask yourself, "How would I respond to this circumstance on my Best Day?", or "How would the best me respond to this?" If something happens to you that seems unfair or unjust — for instance, your boss yells at you for something that was not your fault (or even for something that was)— ask yourself, "How would I respond to this on my Best Day?" Often it may seem that you have little or no choice about some of the events and circumstances in your life — but you always have a choice about how you will respond to them. This is the creative gap between stimulus and response — the gap from which you can project your own unique purpose into the world.

Since this is *your* Best Day, your real question is *how do you desire to respond* to these kinds of circumstances and situations? For instance, how important is peace of mind or happiness *to you*? Even if you feel justified in being upset, is that a good enough reason *for you* to give up your peace of mind? If your circumstances don't turn out the way you want them to, is that a good enough reason *for you* to be unhappy? If your project does not proceed according to your expectations, is that a good enough reason *for you* to become embroiled in frustration and anger? You might argue at this point that, "It's 'natural' to become angry and frustrated when these things happen. 'Anyone' (or the ubiquitous, 'Everyone') would feel the same way. 'No one' would remain peaceful or happy under these circumstances (and I most certainly am not no one)." But again remember that this is *your own* Best Day — you are not really concerned with what everyone, anyone, or no one would do in similar circumstances, or with some arbitrary cultural definition of "natural."

Actually paying attention to each moment of your day is perhaps one of the best ways to discover your own priorities. It is, of course, useful to occasionally set aside time to ask yourself what your own real priorities are — to ask yourself, "What is my purpose? What is most important to me? What do I truly desire? Am I living my life in a way that is consistent with my values and goals?" From these theoretical reflections, you might decide to make a list of your priorities to use as a daily reminder or as a basis for personal affirmations. But it is within the context of the moment-to-moment decisions of your daily life that you actually have the opportunity to live your priorities — to try them out and see if they actually work for you, if they truly serve you. According to the Spiritual view, Spirit is always providing you with exactly the lessons and circumstances you most need to grow and to awaken to yourself, to discover your own truth. This perspective can create a lighted clearing within which every event in your life, including even the seemingly "trivial" ones, can be seen as a gift, an opportunity to discover and choose your own deepest truth, an opportunity to actually *be* your best.

What if, on your designated Best Day, you happen to find yourself in a bad mood — irritable, grumpy, impatient, anxious, depressed? Or what if you find that your mind feels dull, foggy, unfocused, or distracted? Or that your body feels sick and weak? You might wonder, "How can I possibly live my Best Day feeling like this?" But in the context of this exercise, your real question would be, "How do I want to respond to this on my Best Day?" Once you discover yourself in a given mental, emotional, or physical state, that state is simply your starting point. Just recognizing it may cause it to improve, or it may not. But your question is still, "How do I want to respond to this condition on my Best Day? How do I want to send forth my truth in this situation?" In every case, by the time you recognize a situation or condition, it *already* exists in your life — to be aware of something as "something" means that it is *already* present for you, and that you have *already* interpreted it. At that point, you simply cannot choose that it never enter your awareness at all — it *already* has. But you can choose how you will *respond* to it. If you choose to see the meaning of these internal and external conditions as "bad luck" that has happened "to" you, then your response will tend to be anger or self-pity. If you choose to see the meaning of these things as challenges to your own creative ability to express your purpose, your response will be to do the best you can. Your question is, "What is *my* best choice on *my* Best Day?" Regardless of the previous choices you have made, every moment is a fresh opportunity to choose anew how you will interpret and respond to your life.

But what of those times when you temporarily forget your resolve to live your Best Day, and then later realize that you are thinking and speaking and acting in ways that fall short of how you want to be? For instance, you suddenly realize that for the last fifteen minutes you have been on automatic pilot, ranting and raving at your teenage son over something he said or did that you found especially irritating or offensive. Or you discover that for the last ten minutes your mind has been on automatic pilot cursing that driver that nearly caused you to have an accident. Or you discover that you have been lost in self-pity for the last two hours over some crisis in your life. Sometimes you are vaguely aware of the fact when you are starting to make a mistake, but choose out of anger or fear to repress this awareness, and to forge ahead anyway. By the time you are fully aware of the mistake as a "mistake," it has *already* happened. At that moment of realization, you no longer have the choice as to whether you will make that particular mistake or not — you already have. What do you do when you discover that you have made or are making a mistake — that you are not living according to your own true values and priorities? Again, in the context of your Best Day, you would ask yourself, "*How do I want to respond* to this mistake on my Best Day? Do *I want* to invest my time and energy into shame, guilt, regret, blame, and self-recrimination? Do *I want* to learn from the mistake, forgive myself, and move on? What do *I choose* to believe is the truer and more real part of myself — the 'I' that made the mistake, or the 'I' that realizes that the mistake is a mistake?" Remember that to see a mistake *as* a "mistake" is possible only from the perspective of a greater vision. As long as you continue to grow and learn, to creatively discover your own true path, you will probably continue to make mistakes — a baby learns to walk only through a trial and error process, a process which involves repeatedly falling down. Mistakes do not invalidate your Best Day — just like the undesirable circumstances or the mistakes of others, your own mistakes can be seen as further opportunities for you to learn and grow, further opportunities to fulfill your purpose and express your truth.

Again, your fundamental reference point here is your own life purpose and your own dreams. On your Best Day, you want to ask yourself, "What do I desire to bring to the world today? What do I desire to creatively send forth from my truth? How do I desire to contribute to others and to the world? "

Another question you might ask yourself is, "What kind of balance do I desire in my Best Day?" There are many things that you might do in the course of your typical day or your typical week — for instance, taking a walk, going to work, taking care of your home, spending time with your family, spending time with your friends, spending time with yourself, contributing to the lives of others, leisure and fun time, personal growth time, exercise time, meal time, quiet time. What kind of balance of these various activities do you desire in your Best Day? Of course you may not be able to do everything on that one particular day. But does the relative proportion of time you spend on your various thoughts and words and actions truly reflect your own priorities? Again, this question of priorities and balance is an individual and personal question. It is not a matter of what you "should" do, but rather of what *you truly desire* to do — what you desire to do from the deepest and truest part of your own heart. How will you choose to use and allot the time of your life today? Remember that "using" time does not necessarily mean being productive every minute — leisure, fun, and recreation can also be joyful expressions of your truth. But you may want to avoid merely "wasting time" — in the context of your life, "killing time" could be seen as a form of suicide (or as one of my friends expressed it, suicide on the installment plan). On your Best Day, you may want to ask yourself, "How can I deliberately and mindfully live each moment?" — including the "trivial" as well as the "important" moments, the "non-productive" as well as the "productive" ones.

Remember throughout this exercise that this is *your* Best Day. You don't have to do anything "special" on this day — simply live *your* best possible everyday day. No one else can tell you exactly what you will discover during your Best Day — this is your own unique creative journey into your own unique truth. How you pursue your various activities, how you choose to respond to the internal and external conditions you encounter, how you choose to creatively express yourself, how you choose to balance the time in your day — all of these are personal choices you make from your own heart. If you're not sure of what to do in a particular situation, then make your best choice and see how it works. If it turns out to be a mistake, then learn and grow from the experience and make a better choice next time. At first, I recommend that you do this exercise for just one day in your week. As you make this focused effort for one day of each week, you will probably find that you become more mindful on the other days as well. Focus your full attention on every minute of your Best Day. At the close of the day, be peaceful with the effort you have made. Ask yourself, "How do I want to end my Best Day?" You may want to spend a few minutes making some notes to yourself — not with the intention of shame or blame, but simply as an honest reflection of how the day went, which things you want to appreciate and celebrate, and which things you might choose to do differently next time. As you drift off to sleep, you may choose to be peaceful or prayerful or to express your gratitude — whatever you choose, pay as much attention to the ending of your day as you did to the beginning and the middle of it.

At first, this exercise may seem to take a tremendous amount of effort. You may find yourself almost frantically repeating your mantra, "Best Day, Best Day, Best Day . . ." in the midst of the whirlwind of thoughts and feelings and sensations that threatens to sweep away your mindfulness and your resolve. Indeed, there will probably be stretches of time throughout the day when you completely forget your commitment to do this exercise. But each time when you discover that you have been on automatic pilot, ask yourself, "How do I want to respond now?" Lapses of awareness in your day do not invalidate this exercise — in fact, for most of us, the lapses are probably inevitable, especially at first. Whether it is due to our cultural programming or is simply typical of the human mind in general, we seem to have a tendency to slip into a sleepwalking kind of existence. The Best

Day exercise can be very useful in helping you to wake up in order to discover and express your own truth. In that sense, the Best Day exercise is an active, living meditation. You don't succeed or fail at this Best Day exercise — you simply do your best. Every time you try this exercise for a day, you are a little more awake and aware. The tremendous effort that seems to be involved in this exercise, especially the first few times you do it, is the effort to wake up, the effort to undo your own habits and routines. As the habits and routines lose their hold on you and the mental chatter becomes quieter and less compelling, you realize that your Best Day is simply a matter of being and doing every minute what *you truly desire* to be and do. The only real effort involved is the effort of joyful self-expression. In time, this will probably involve much less effort than the alternative of living out of sync with yourself. It actually takes an enormous amount of energy to sustain a sleepwalking and inauthentic life — but we are usually unaware of this energy because we are lost in our routines. Those who undertake the journey to move beyond a routine life of inauthenticity report that they enjoy more and more energy as they proceed. They now have all of the energy that was previously bound up in the distracted "doing" of those routines that did not truly serve them. Moreover, they no longer have the constant drain of energy that occurs when they live at odds with their own hearts. They report that the journey to mindfulness and heartfulness becomes easier, more natural, and more joyful with every step.

❖ Affirmation of Spiritual Truth

Many of your basic belief choices were formed when you were very young. They tend to be subconscious, especially if you have not made a deliberate effort as an adult to become aware of those beliefs that create the lighted clearing of your life. The early years of childhood are very egocentric — the child interprets everything that happens in the world as a reflection of his or her own meaning and worth. For instance, if a mother does not know how to express affection and love to her son, the child will tend to interpret the mother's limitation to mean that he himself is somehow unworthy of love. Based on this interpretation, he may form fearful and insecure beliefs about himself and his world — beliefs such as, "I'm not good enough," "I don't deserve success or happiness," "I have to earn love" (i.e. all love is conditional), and "It's not safe to trust others." These kinds of beliefs are often referred to as "limiting beliefs," insofar as they tend to create a lighted clearing which limits one's possible experiences of peace, love, joy, success, self-confidence, self-worth, personal satisfaction, and healthy relationships. As the child grows up, these unquestioned beliefs become internalized, almost like subconscious tape loops, endlessly repeating themselves. These beliefs operate in the background of his awareness and help define his experience of reality — in this example, an experience that would be characterized by difficult and painful relationships, failure, struggle, scarcity and lack. The negativity of these experiences validates the fearful beliefs, so that the belief choices themselves never come into question or emerge into awareness at all. If these beliefs remain subconscious, the adult tends to think that he is simply experiencing "things as they are." Moreover, since such negative beliefs tend to be reinforced at every turn by the Separative culture he lives in, he will be even more certain of the accuracy and validity of his fearful experience.

In addition to our own limiting beliefs, we can also allow (what we perceive as) the limiting beliefs of others to limit our own possibilities. One typical example of this is when someone consciously or subconsciously limits her success (e.g., her social, academic, professional, or financial success) because she thinks that some of her family or friends might reject and abandon her if she became or achieved or acquired "too much" — where "too much" is defined relative to their own fears and limiting beliefs. It should be noted that this is not necessarily just paranoia — there are indeed some people who do resent and reject others' successes. The point here is that her perception and fears about the limiting beliefs of others can serve the same function as her own limiting beliefs — namely, they can function to restrict her own lighted clearing of discovery.

Earlier I said that my primary responsibility is the light I send forth, which creates the lighted clearing of my life experience — the light which defines and colors my experience of the truth of my being. I discover what light-I-have-sent-forth-already by looking at the quality and meaning of my current experience. I can understand my negative emotions as my internal guidance system, reminding me to re-evaluate my underlying belief choices. To whatever extent I become aware of my worldview as my own choice rather than simply a reflection of "how things are," I can begin to reclaim my responsibility as co-creator of my experience — I can rechoose the light I shine forth from myself. But I don't have to just passively wait until I feel a negative emotion to begin to rechoose my light. I can also proactively create and choose those beliefs that I feel would best serve me.

One way to do this is the practice of affirmations, a process of saying or writing positive belief statements. To "af-firm" means to "make firm or strong." Affirming a belief is a way that I make it firm within myself — a way that I give it enough strength and momentum, so that it can begin to actually affect my life experience. Typically this involves saying the belief aloud or writing it down several times — and doing this on a regular daily basis to make it firm in my subconscious. It can take considerable effort to maintain this focus, especially if I have spent many years of my life subconsciously focused on a different clearing. Some critics of this practice claim that affirmations are simply a way of brainwashing or hypnotizing ourselves. But holding on to the limiting beliefs and tape loops from our childhoods is subject to the same criticism. The only thing that can prevent any given belief from deteriorating into mere brainwashing or self-hypnosis is our continuing receptivity — approaching the belief not as an opaque description of "how things are," but rather as a transparent window into a lighted clearing. Affirming a belief is a way of actively maintaining my focus on that belief's lighted clearing.

According to one popular theory of affirmations, they function almost like magical chants that mysteriously change the nature of our outer reality — a metaphysical (thought-creates-reality) form of technological control over our environment. Many popular books encourage people to visualize and affirm what they desire, in order to "create" more money in their lives, a new car, a bigger house, more sex, or a better relationship — to "make" their lives successful and happy. Indeed, people who consistently practice this method sometimes report that they do achieve their desired results — especially if they also make an effort to discover and release any subconscious limiting beliefs that conflict with their new affirmations. There is, of course, nothing intrinsically wrong with these kinds of desires, or with their fulfillment. But in the context of our present discussion, affirmations can play a more important role in my life than simply as a technique to manipulate reality in order to gratify my ego's desires. Affirmations can allow me to more consciously choose my unique receptivity to the Mystery, as well as my unique contribution — can allow me to live more fully as a conscious participant and co-creator in a greater whole.

Affirming, for instance, that "I am a kind and loving parent" is a way to create a lighted clearing for myself, within which I can discover those kinds of parenting-possibilities of myself — as opposed to, for instance, the clearing which allows me to experience only my egocentric and manipulative parenting possibilities. I know that I have all of these possibilities in myself, for I have experienced and lived them over the years. I also know that the kind and loving possibilities serve me and my children much better — they make for both a better journey and a better destination. But given my own childhood fears and insecurities, I sometimes lapse back into the egocentric possibilities, especially when I am tired, or overstressed, or feel under attack. Thus, it is important for me to regularly affirm the possibilities I truly desire, in order to maintain a more consistent focus on the lighted clearing that best serves me and best expresses my truth. Doing affirmations can be a powerful way to deliberately choose what I send forth into the world — to deliberately choose both the openness of my receptivity, and the creative input of my own contribution. Seen from this perspective, an affirmation is not a way to create reality, but rather a way to keep myself open to, and bring my experience into alignment with, what I believe is my deepest truth.[15]

The Form of an Affirmation

Although you must discover for yourself what you want to affirm in order to better fulfill your own purpose and experience your truth, there are a few general guidelines as regards the form of an effective affirmation statement. There are many excellent books on this topic, and what follows here are only a few brief practical suggestions to get you started.

First, you want your affirmation to be stated in positive terms. In your regular repetition of your affirmations, you want to reinforce for yourself the truth or the clearing you are moving toward, rather than the clearing you are moving away from. For instance, you might affirm, "I express unconditional love toward everyone I meet," rather than "I am not judgmental and critical of the people I meet." (According to one psychological theory, the subconscious works with images. Since there are no positive images for words such as "no," "not" and "never," negative statements would be processed into the subconscious as affirmations of the very thing we are trying to replace. If, for instance, I were to affirm that "I am not judgmental," the "not" would be "invisible" — leaving the subconscious content as "I am . . . judgmental.")

Second, you want to state your affirmations in the present tense. At one level, you are affirming the truth of the clearing itself. Since your affirmation creates this openness, the openness already "is" in the very act of affirming it — even if you have not yet had any corresponding or validating experiences. You can think of the whole process of the full realization of your affirmation — which includes all of the stages from the initial formulation of the affirmation to your eventual confirmatory life experience — as a continuum. Seen in this light, the very be-ing of the realization of your affirmation is its becoming through all of its stages of manifestation. In this sense, what you are affirming already exists, at least in its current stage of becoming — for instance, in affirming that "I am a kind and loving parent," I am already under way in the process of becoming/being such a parent, even if I haven't yet realized the full potential of my vision. Another reason to state your affirmation in the present tense is that if you constantly affirm that something *will* happen in the future, you may keep it forever out of the scope of your present experience. You are affirming that it is always around the next corner, but is never actually here and now.

Third, since affirmations are a tool to focus your attention on your truth, you will want to make them simple, concise and specific, so that your focus can be as precise and clear as possible.

Fourth, you want your affirmations to be authentic — to express the truth of your own heart in your own words. Don't merely write down what you think others would like to hear, or what you think you "should" affirm. The purpose of your affirmations is to help you discover and realize your own unique truth. Your affirmations are for your own personal use. It can be helpful to keep them private, especially at first, so that you don't get distracted by concerns about how they might appear to others.

As far as the specific content of your affirmations is concerned, you will have to discover and create the ideas and beliefs that are most appropriate to your own unique life journey. Here are several suggestions as to how to begin. You can start by focusing on the truth or clearing you wish to move toward, relative to your own purpose and values. What kind of a person do you desire to be? What qualities do you desire to cultivate in yourself? What is your deepest truth? How do you desire to contribute to others? How do you desire to contribute to the whole of Nature? Your answers to these kinds of questions can provide you with the basic material for your affirmations. These affirmations are one way of exercising your primary responsibility, in that they help to make firm the values and belief choices you desire to send forth from yourself — deliberately creating the lighted clearing which truly serves you and your world. Simply writing down or reading aloud your statement of purpose on a daily basis can itself be a very powerful affirmation, helping to create the lighted clearing of your own authenticity.

You can also use your negative emotions as a clue in formulating affirmation statements. As we have seen, your negative emotions can be thought of as an internal guidance system, reminding you that your current light choices do not truly serve you. From the Spiritual perspective, your negative feelings reflect underlying limiting beliefs — beliefs which are limiting you from experiencing the peace, love, and joy of your Spiritual truth. If you can identify an underlying limiting belief, you may be able to simply let it go. Or you can create a "turnaround belief." This is an affirmation that reverses the limiting belief that hinders you, so that you are better able to experience and express your truth. (For example, if your limiting belief were something like, "I can't be a good parent, because my own parents were such poor role models," you might create a turnaround belief such as, "Having grown through the challenges of my own childhood, I am now a more sensitive and self-aware parent." Now, what used to limit your experience of your truth is transformed into something that actually helps you to better experience and express it.) From the Spiritual perspective, all limiting beliefs are illusory, in that they claim that you cannot experience perfect peace, love, or joy now. In this context, a turnaround belief is merely the undoing of an untrue belief (a belief that hides possibilities of Spiritual experience from your awareness).

There are many ways of "doing" your affirmations. One effective way is to simply read your list aloud several times — for instance, for a few minutes when you first awaken in the morning, and again just before you retire at night. Read each affirmation with feeling and conviction. In addition, some people like to choose one affirmation to silently repeat to themselves throughout the day as a kind of mantra. This can help you remember your purpose and your truth throughout the various "challenging" situations of your day. Another method of practicing with your affirmations is to write each affirmation several times — writing with focused awareness and intent. You may also find it helpful to say it aloud as you write it down. One very effective variation of this involves also writing down your inner response each time you write down your affirmation. Since your affirmation may be in conflict with some of your subconscious limiting beliefs, it will tend to bring them up to the surface of awareness. For instance, after I write down the affirmation, "It is always safe to love others," I might experience a rebellious voice arising out of my subconscious, bursting into my awareness screaming, "No it isn't! What about that time when I was betrayed by my best friend?" The lighted clearing of your actual experience is created by the sum total of all of your various conscious and subconscious light choices — and contradictory light choices tend to cancel each other out. Once you are aware of these limiting beliefs, you can release them or change them if you choose. You might also use what you learn from these responses to modify and further refine your affirmation statements.[16]

In closing this section, I want to emphasize again that affirmations can serve a deeper purpose than merely being a way to manipulate reality to gratify our egos — than merely being a New Age technique to "materialize" or "manifest" a new car or a bigger house. My primary responsibility, both to myself and to others, is the light I shine forth from myself — this is the active role I play in creating the lighted clearing of my life. This lighted clearing, which is the living truth of my being, illuminates possibilities for myself as well as for others — it is how I contribute to the light of the world. Doing affirmations is one powerful way I can consciously and deliberately choose how I will define the receptivity of my mind and heart, so that my life becomes an opening for the realization of those possibilities that truly serve me and my world.

❖ Receptivity to the Mystery

The thought-creates-reality model is often understood to mean that if we simply think about something hard enough, or passionately enough, or often enough, then that something will somehow "show up" in our lives. The manifestation process is variously explained as either attraction (my thought-form somehow "magnetically attracts" the corresponding material reality into my life) or actual creation (the formless quantum energy of the universe is somehow structured by the energy of my thoughts, causing the objects and circumstances I desire to "materialize" in my life). In another variation of this model, there simply isn't anything else beyond my thoughts — they somehow "materialize" things out of sheer nothingness. In still another version, reality itself is considered to be a merely subjective mental phenomenon — and whatever we believe hard enough becomes our mental experience of the world, including our experiences of sounds and sights and textures, as well as our experiences of feelings and emotions.

In all of these variations, humans alone play the active creative role, and the rest of reality (if there is any "rest of reality" at all) is merely passive — whether you think of it as a world of pre-formed objects that are being pushed around by your thoughts, or some vaguely physical quantum soup being molded into actual objects and things, or some kind of mental energy that is being coalesced into sensations and perceptions. From this perspective, human will is the *sole* active creative force in the universe — the force that gives all form and value to reality. This calls to mind the Technological view, which claims that man is the value-giver, and that the rest of reality consists of meaningless, valueless "stuff," passively waiting for humans to project their needs and desires onto it.

Philosophically, all of these approaches represent an advance over the more naive view of reality, which claimed that man was merely a passive perceiver whose experience of reality was completely determined by factors outside of himself.[17] From that point of view, what you perceive and how you feel is entirely dependent on what happens to you from the outside. The thought-creates-reality model, however, emphasizes man's active role in the process of perception — you are no longer merely a victim of circumstances. This represents a shift from seeing yourself as dependent to seeing yourself as independent — and thus allows you to begin to reclaim your responsibility for your own experience. From the perspective of the thought-creates-reality model, the concept of "reclaiming your own responsibility" means taking over your role as the creator of everything in your life.

From the perspective of the Possibility Model, our primary responsibility is the light we choose to send forth from ourselves — the light that creates the lighted clearing within which we can discover and realize specific possibilities of ourselves and our world. Note that this is a very different idea from that of "creating" reality, or even from that of "projecting" some meaning "onto" reality (as if my projection were an opaque film of meaning that overlays the surface of my experience, so that I can see only what I have projected). When we think in terms of projecting a light and creating a lighted clearing, there is an implicit element of receptivity involved. Although I myself am ultimately the only one who can choose my own light choices, I do not play the only active role in the creation of my experience — the Mysterious field of possibilities (including possibilities of myself as well as of the world) also makes a contribution to my experience. My will and the Mystery *co-create* my life experience. Thus I evolve from an experience of independence to one of *interdependence* — from thinking that I am somehow outside of or apart from the world and acting "on" it, to truly *participating* in a greater whole. I no longer believe that I am imposing my will on some passive, valueless, meaningless "stuff." When I approach the Mystery with a reverent receptivity, I am open to discover possibilities of myself and my world that I never could conceive of "on my own"; I am open to sources of guidance and wisdom beyond my own ability to figure things out; and I am open to possible experiences of joy, beauty, goodness, and value deeper than anything my ego could imagine and project from its current limited understanding.

From the perspective of the Possibility Model, I am not projecting a picture, but rather a light that allows certain kinds of possibilities to reveal themselves — but I do not completely control which particular possibilities, if any, emerge into my experience. In this model, what I am creating with my thoughts is not a reality, but rather a lighted clearing of discovery — a specific horizon of openness and invitation, within which I am able to experience whatever "comes" to light there. Thus, my primary responsibility — my ability to choose and send forth from myself the specific light that will define and color my openness — necessarily involves a balance of both the active and the receptive. We could say that the lighted clearing created by the very idea of "a lighted clearing" opens me to possibilities of receptivity as well as activity.

Whenever we forget that we have an active role in co-creating our experience, we will believe that the world is simply a "given." This is what we earlier referred to as a relatively naive model of reality. Whenever we remember our active role in determining our experience, but forget the element of receptivity, we will believe that we are simply creating reality all by ourselves — i.e., we will tend to adopt some version of the thought-creates-reality model. From the perspective of the lighted clearing model, each of these ways of thinking is a one-sided and partial view of experience. Reclaiming the full truth of your responsibility involves remembering *both* the creative *and* the receptive elements of the process.

The Lighted Clearing of "Mystery"

Previously, I said that the lighted clearing you create for yourself in the process of reading this book is a synthesis of the words and ideas I present, and the unique interpretation and personal experience you bring to them. It is important to keep in mind that what is being created by this synthesis is a lighted clearing, rather than some doctrine which combines my ideas and yours. By keeping the *clearing* of your own experience in mind, rather than getting completely preoccupied with what you discover in the clearing, you remain open to the Mystery itself — that creative no-thing that is always just beyond the horizon of everything you can see or understand. The Mystery is the dimension of the unknown, which defines every known — the inconceivably strange, which defines and lies at the very heart of the seemingly familiar. My on-going awareness of the intrinsic limitedness of every perspective or point of view reminds me not to take myself or the world for granted — and not to take myself or the world too seriously.

The element of receptivity is more than just an awareness of the limitedness of my perspective — it is also an affirmation of, and an active intentional receptivity to, the Mystery itself. "Mystery" is a unique evocative concept, since it does not positively define a specific clearing of discovery, but rather points toward the "beyondness" that borders and defines every clearing. My idea of "the Mystery" is a reminder to me to remain open — open to that which can be present for me only as "that which is always concealed"; open to that which can be unhidden only as "the hiddenness that is the inconceivable ground and source of all possible truth." My active intentional openness to the Mystery can take a variety of forms. For me personally, for instance, an essential component of my own primary responsibility is the Spiritual view — my understanding of "Spirit" is an essential part of the light I send forth from myself to create my own lighted clearing of discovery. From within that clearing, the Mystery — the creative source that allows me to constantly grow beyond the horizon of my familiar, conceivable possibilities — is one manifestation or "face" of Spirit. From this perspective, the Mystery is a *sacred Mystery*. Thus, for me, receptivity to the Mystery is not merely a neutral passivity, but is colored with reverence and wonder — and that particular "flavor" of receptivity opens me to certain possibilities that might otherwise remain hidden. Each person must decide his or her own best way to be intentionally receptive to the Mystery. But it is important that each of us remember to continually cultivate this receptivity — for it is only through one's own unique openness to the source, that truly authentic, origin-al thought and action are possible. I have repeatedly emphasized that the goal of this book is not to convince you that my ideas are "right," but rather to invite and encourage you to use your understanding of the truth of my ideas as a clearing, within which you think for yourself — the clearing within which you open yourself to your own origin-al thoughts, to those thoughts that emerge from the very origin of your thinking.

It is especially important to keep the ideas of "the lighted clearing" and "an intentional receptivity to the Mystery" in mind as we move into Part Four of the book, which focuses on specific examples and suggestions for re-lighting your life — for creating "lighted clearings for the soul." Earlier, I said that the true value of a view or an idea is the quality and depth of life experience it makes possible for you. The same applies to the value of my examples and suggestions for re-lighting your life. It is relatively easy to remember to remain receptive when the topic of discussion is "the lighted clearing" or "the Mystery." But in our Technological culture, we have a tendency to interpret concrete suggestions as mere techniques — as things we can "do" to change ourselves and our world. Indeed, many self-help books and workshops are presented in the form, "Just follow these simple steps, and you will have a happier life." Earlier I stressed that my practical suggestions are not meant as a kind of a Technological "How To" manual, which instructs you how to manipulate and control your perception of reality, or how to "make" your experience be some certain way. Ultimately, I don't believe that there is some special series of techniques and steps that you can apply to your life to "make" yourself joyful and fulfilled. I believe that the real joy and fulfillment we can have in our lives derive from somehow discovering and following the deeper inner guidance of our hearts — it is not merely a matter of our "doing," but also of our receptivity. Therefore, I encourage you to approach the practical suggestions and examples in Part Four in the same spirit with which you approached the earlier "theoretical" suggestions. Just as *how* I think about a concept determines whether it becomes a closed, dogmatic idea or a lighted clearing of discovery, so too, *how* I approach a practical suggestion determines whether it becomes a merely dogmatic technique or a vehicle to further discover my own truth. It is important to remember that these so-called practical suggestions are not intended so much as recommendations of "what to do," but rather as ways to redefine your receptivity.

I can't know which of these suggestions might enable you to re-light your own life in ways that best allow you to fulfill your own unique purpose — ultimately, you are the only one who can discover this. I invite you to actually practice whichever of these suggestions seem right to you, because it is only in actually *living* our ideas that they can creatively affect our lives. But remember that the purpose of any re-lighting is to create a new clearing, within which you are able to open yourself to your own deeper inner teaching that only you can learn.

PART FOUR

LIGHTED CLEARINGS OF SPIRITUAL DISCOVERY

CHAPTER 12

SHIFTING YOUR FOCUS

For the Spiritual-Holistic perspective, positive feelings are the emotional reflection of my awareness of my truth (my awareness of myself and the world in our deepest unhiddenness as expressions of Spirit). Negative feelings are merely the emotional reflection of my unawareness of my truth (which can only mean that I am denying, and hiding from myself, the awareness of wholeness and Spirit). A negative feeling reminds me of the need to re-light my life, not merely in order to feel better, but to remember my truth. The purpose of re-lighting is to experience my life truthfully — and this will be emotionally reflected as positive feelings and a "better" quality of life experience. A "better quality of life experience" does not mean that my life now has more value or is more worthwhile in any absolute sense, but simply that the *quality of my experience* is deeper, richer, and more satisfying. Nor am I a "better person" than someone who feels miserable and unfulfilled — I am simply more aware of my truth.

To change the quality of my experience in order to bring more peace, love, and joy into my life, I can shift my focus of attention to something more positive, and/or re-interpret what currently seems "negative" in order to see it in a more positive light. This does not mean merely overlooking the challenges and difficulties in my life. There is an important difference between actually re-lighting a situation in order to have a different life experience, and just pretending that everything is OK. Several years ago I had a friend who always acted cheerful — even when she was obviously feeling considerable stress or anxiety, she would smile and almost frantically repeat, "Everything is great!" But her tone of desperation belied her words. It often felt as if she was pretending something to herself, in the hope that if she pretended it hard enough and long enough, it would come true. But since she never honestly acknowledged her negative feelings, she was unable to really use the feedback to make the changes in her life that could have helped generate genuine positive feelings. Since the very struggles you are experiencing can signal the emergence of a greater truth into your life, to merely ignore or forcibly deny or repress the seemingly negative parts of your life can actually postpone your Spiritual growth. The first step in re-lighting any situation is to fully acknowledge the negative emotion, and also to understand what role your own projected interpretation has played in defining your experience as "negative" or "bad" or "threatening" in the first place — i.e., to "own" or take responsibility for your negative emotions. It is only from this awareness that you can make changes that will truly improve the quality of your life experience. The intention behind the re-lighting suggestions in this book is not to eliminate negative emotions from your life, but to use their feedback as constructively as possible, and to respond in a way that truly serves you and your world.

Normally when we think of re-lighting a situation, we think of seeing the whole situation in a different light — a light that allows us to better see the more positive possibilities of the seemingly negative elements of the situation. We will consider examples of that kind of re-lighting in the later chapters. But in this chapter we will be looking at variations of a simpler form of re-lighting. This is not so much a matter of trying to reinterpret the negatives, as rather a shift of focus to become more aware of and to more fully appreciate the positives that *already* exist as possible experiences within our current interpretation of the world — possible experiences we may have been overlooking because of our preoccupation with the negatives.

When I am in the midst of feeling negative emotions, I tend to focus even more on the negative things in my life — in this way, a negative emotion has a tendency to be self-reinforcing. In this self-augmenting process, I will come to have a more and more one-sided or partial view of myself and my world, insofar as I will tend to focus *only* on the negative — I will tend to see only the situations and things I don't want or like, and to interpret everything in the most negative light possible. In terms of our metaphor, I am creating a lighted clearing that highlights the negative possibilities, and leaves the positive possibilities hidden in the shadows. From the Spiritual perspective, the negative possibilities are only my misinterpretation of my unawareness of my truth — misinterpreting the illusory absence of wholeness and Spirit as the illusory presence of separateness and valuelessness. The only thing that interrupts this self-reinforcing cycle is that I eventually become so miserable that I am motivated to change my perspective.

One simple way of breaking this cycle is to proactively focus my attention on what is positive in my life. This shift of focus does not necessarily solve my difficulty, nor does it automatically change a seemingly negative situation into a positive one. But such a shift of focus can give me a broader, more balanced, and truer perspective. In some situations, this simple shift of focus will be sufficient to change the emotional tone of my life. In other situations, the truer vision of my whole situation will serve as a foundation for a more truthful re-interpretation. It is important to have as complete a view as possible of my current situation before making changes in my interpretation — to be as aware as possible of my starting point before setting off on my re-lighting journey.

❖ How We Make Ourselves Miserable

For me, one of the best examples of how the seeming negativity of our lives can be created by our focus of attention is a brief conversation I had with one of my patients. During a typical day of greeting many patients, it is inevitable that the topic of the weather comes up occasionally. Often a patient's attitude about the weather will reflect something of his overall approach to life. Some patients are cheerful and positive about the weather, no matter how cold or dreary it may be. For instance, one very gloomy summer day, one of my most cheerful patients told me, "God didn't send this rain out of spite — it was given to us as a gift, so we could go home and relax after work, instead of having to mow the lawn." Other patients, however, seem to find a reason to complain, no matter how beautiful the day. This became very obvious to me one fantastic spring day several years ago. This was our first clear and temperate day after a long period of cold rain and gray skies. This day was absolutely gorgeous: clear, sunny, a slight breeze, and not too hot or too cold. When I enthusiastically remarked about the weather to one of my patients, he sourly replied, "Yeah, but it's been lousy for weeks, and it's probably going to be miserable again tomorrow." Although this person could not find a single thing to criticize in that day's weather, he was nevertheless determined to be unhappy and to complain, even if it meant ignoring the weather that was "right in front of his nose." While many of us enjoyed and celebrated that perfect day, he sought refuge from any possible experience of happiness, refuge in the misery of a darkly remembered past and a darkly imagined future. The sunny reality of his present day was eclipsed by the mental shadows of unhappy memories and gloomy anticipation. This story is an especially good example of how someone can be so committed to misery that he completely ignores all of the possibilities for happiness that are "right before his eyes." This person had to actively screen out the beautiful weather that surrounded him, and actively remain focused on remembered and imagined bad weather in the past and the future, in order to maintain his negative mood.

Another incident illustrates how our focus can magnify the negative or difficult elements of a situation out of proportion. Several years ago, I went with a group of college professors to tour the museums and cultural centers of Japan. As we moved from city to city by train, we carried all of our luggage with us. With each successive week, we acquired more souvenirs, and more luggage to carry the souvenirs. For all our credentials as serious academicians, we did a great job of impersonating a typical bunch of tourists. Near the end of the trip, we looked like a Mount Everest expedition that had lost its baggage carriers. To make matters worse, there were no porters or handcarts to help us at the train stations. A couple of days before leaving one of the last cities on our schedule, a few of us went to the train station to check out our boarding arrangements, including such factors as which track we would be leaving on and what obstacles we would have to negotiate with our mountains of luggage. We discovered to our dismay that we would have to deal with six very long flights of stairs in the course of getting from the train station to the departure track. For the next two days we agonized over the awful ordeal we were facing. When departure day finally came, we woke up dreading the coming endurance test. Then, finally, we all suffered about twenty minutes of arduous physical exertion while we huffed and puffed our luggage up and down the seemingly endless stairs. For the rest of that day and for the next two days, we relived over and over what an awful ordeal it had been. A popular chewing gum claims to "double your pleasure, double your fun." But at this train station, we did much better than merely doubling our misery —all in all, we actually created five days of suffering out of a mere twenty minutes of hard physical labor! To the relatively brief discomfort of the actual effort, we added the dread of the future and the anguished remembering of the past. In fact, even when we were actually on the stairs, we used our immediate past and future to amplify our misery. Instead of focusing simply on the present moment of physical discomfort we were experiencing, we intensified our suffering by reminding each other of how many, many stairs we had already climbed, and how many, many stairs were yet to come. (On reading this story, my wife commented that with a slight shift of focus, we might have remembered that our so-called "burdens" were actually the wonderful treasures and souvenirs we ourselves had chosen.)

Both of these stories are examples of how we can make ourselves miserable, even when our "objective" circumstances are not all that challenging. The antidote to most or all of the negative emotions in both of these incidents would have been to merely focus on the here and now — to celebrate the beautiful day, or to enjoy every minute of the once in a lifetime opportunity to visit Japan. Instead, the people involved (including myself) made themselves miserable by either looking toward a remembered or imagined past, or toward an imagined future.

But from a broader perspective, neither the past nor the future is the problem here or the cause of the misery. As we discussed earlier, the past exists for me now as a range of possible memories. In thinking of the past now, I can choose which possibilities to focus my attention on, and I can choose how I will interpret them. I can choose to remember those times when everything went well, when I fulfilled my purpose or realized my dreams, times of joy and success, times of beauty and strength. These kinds of memories and imaginative reconstructions can bring joy and power to my present moment. Or I can remember or imagine past times of failure, weakness, ugliness, and regret, and can use these thoughts to make myself weaker and more miserable in the present. But the point here is not that we should remember only the "good times," and repress all of our past difficulties and challenges. My past difficulties and perceived "failures" can serve an important role in my on-going personal growth and learning. The issue here is how I am using my remembered or imagined past — to bring more strength and joy into my life, or merely to wallow in misery, regret, and self-condemnation. The guiding question is, "What truly serves me — what helps me best fulfill my purpose *now*?" Likewise, the future also exists for me now as a range of possibilities — possible things that could happen, possible things I could say and do. I can choose what possibilities to focus my attention on, and how to interpret them. Again, this is not merely a matter of looking at everything through rose-colored glasses. To merely look away from possible future challenges does not make them disappear — in fact, to just ignore them can leave me unprepared. But I can focus on the future in a way that truly serves me and brings joy and strength to my present moment, or I can lose myself in worry and fear that rob my present moment of its power.

In this context, I find it helpful to remember our earlier discussion of "the truth of meditation" — my discovery during the meditation retreat that the here-and-now-ness itself has a very positive quality. I discovered that the shift of focus to the here-and-now, not just in terms of its particular contents, but in terms of its very truth or unhiddenness, was the foundation of any experience of inner peace and joy. But this shift of focus does not mean ignoring the past and the future. What is important is my mindfulness, regardless of what I happen to be thinking of. I can, for instance, be fully mindful in the here-and-now as the person remembering the past or anticipating the future, rather than simply getting lost in what I am remembering or anticipating. The inner peace and joy of the here-and-now-ness is not so much dependent on what I am doing or thinking or on what is happening to me — rather the quality of my experience is a reflection of *how* I am doing or thinking, and *how* I am present in the midst of what is happening.

How You Focus on "Change"

Within the context of a temporal perspective, *how* we focus on "change" itself can dramatically affect the quality of our life experience. In the temporal mode of experience, our lives are characterized by constant change. In every moment, some possibilities are disappearing from our lives and new possibilities are coming into being. The opportunities I have today for perceiving, thinking, and acting are different from those I had yesterday. The *process* of living is a process of the continuous dying and birthing of possibilities. Earlier, I said that "things" and "beings" and "situations" can be thought of as constellations of possibilities — now we are considering that these constellations themselves are dynamic and ever-changing. In this on-going process of change, I could choose to focus only on the constant dying of my life possibilities. I could become so preoccupied with the doors that are closing in my life, that I am unaware of those that are silently opening. Such a focus can turn my past into a source of grieving and regret. It will make my present feel anxiously unstable and insecure. My future will tend to loom ahead of me as threatening — threatening me with the loss of whatever minimal stability or contentment I may feel now. Or, I could choose to also focus on the continual birthing of new possibilities — on the on-going freshness and creativity of the Mystery. Notice that I said that I could choose to "also" focus on the birthing of new possibilities in my life — for the purpose of this whole shift of attention is not to deny or repress possibilities in my life (for instance, to deny or ignore those which are dying), but rather to gain a more whole and more truthful perspective. It is important to remember that my awareness of the on-going dying of my possibilities can play a valuable role in my life — it can help awaken me from my sleepwalking lostness in routines to more fully appreciate my life now. In this context, "death" is not a morbid or sad thought — it is my recognition of the change and growth in my life, both moment-to-moment and in my life overall. Without the on-going change, there would be no growth, no discovery, no freshness, no challenge, no excitement. The grief of dying and the celebration of birth are two sides of the same coin. Being truly mindful in the present moment means to be aware that some of the possibilities that define me-here-now are in the process of disappearing. When I realize that dying is a part of every moment of dynamic living, I will want to focus on, embrace, and celebrate my current possibilities. My moment-to-moment dying becomes a wake-up call to be aware of and appreciate and make the most of what is here now — to "seize the day." And since the death of one possibility is simultaneously the birth of another, I also want to remain open to the on-going birthing of possibilities in the ever-emerging Mystery of my life. Fully appreciating the endings in each moment is an important part of awakening to the joy of my beginner's mind.

From the Spiritual perspective, there is an even deeper level of truth or unhiddenness. This level of truth does not involve a shift of focus "within" temporal experience (shifting focus from "dying" to "birthing and dying"), but rather a shift from temporal experience to the eternal (the always already now). For the Spiritual view, the truth of Being itself — and the truth of every now — is Spirit. That means the content or essence of every now, when experienced in its deepest unhiddenness, is perfect peace, love, and joy. The content itself never changes — what we experience as changing, as coming and going, are merely the forms or appearances or manifestations of this underlying Spiritual truth (although, depending on the light we bring to a particular now, we may experience these changing forms as "un-Spiritual" — as un-peaceful, un-loving and un-joyful). From the Spiritual perspective of eternal truth, the content or essence of your experience is always the same — when seen in its deepest and fullest unhiddenness, the content is Spirit. What this means is that the experience of your Spiritual truth is always available. Your experience of Spiritual truth, of perfect peace, love, and joy, is not dependent on any particular circumstances or situation — and that means it is not limited or conditioned by the past or the future. Your experience of Spiritual truth is dependent only on your openness — on your choice to create a lighted clearing of receptivity to the Sacred.

From this perspective, the way that we make ourselves miserable, the ultimate cause of our experience of unhappiness, is our belief that our happiness is dependent on circumstances. When we choose to believe that our happiness is circumstance-dependent, we are always focused on our ever-changing circumstances, and feel a constant alternation of happiness and unhappiness as the forms of Spiritual expression come and go. Within this exclusively temporal perspective, relatively more happiness is possible when you choose to focus on the unity and correlativity of "coming" and "going," so that in the midst of every seeming loss or death, you have faith in and look forward to the corresponding birth. But for the Spiritual view, the real value of understanding the unity of coming and going, and maintaining a positive equanimity in the midst of change, is that it serves as a way of undoing your lostness in temporality; a means of becoming open to a level of truth that transcends time and change.

It is important to note that all this is not meant as a rejection of the temporal world of perception. From the Spiritual perspective, the ever-changing appearances in the temporal realm of experience are, after all, forms *of Spirit*. We have no choice whether or not to have temporal experience — we find ourselves already having it. The problem is not the temporal experience or the many forms that appear to come and go. The cause of our unhappiness is the belief that these forms are separate, independent realities in themselves — and that "Reality" is merely the process of the real birth and real death of these real, independent things. From that perspective, we desperately grasp at these fleeting "realities" — happy when we get what we want, and unhappy when we lose what we want. For the Spiritual view, however, we can enjoy *all* the comings and goings as the ever-changing diversity and richness of Spiritual expression — and in truth, our lives are not less for the going of one appearance, or more for the coming of another. Far from being a rejection of the temporal and the changing, the Spiritual perspective is a celebration of *all that is*, instead of limiting ourselves to some arbitrary decision that some appearances are "good" and will "make" us happy, and others are "bad" and will "make" us unhappy. Ultimately, the Spiritual perspective is not about giving up anything — it is a way of experiencing our lives, in which we re-gain the everything we had never really lost and always already had.

❖ Remembering Your Life Purpose

Several years ago, my family took a vacation to Disneyworld in Florida. We were all so excited as we boarded the plane — anticipating a whole week of fun and play. But a couple of days into our vacation I was already feeling overwhelmed. Getting five people dressed and equipped with full survival gear for a long Disney day was a logistical nightmare — especially for me, the self-appointed commander-in-charge. To get the very most out of each day, we had to start as early as possible. Once we were actually in the park, I rushed around marshaling the troops, trying to make sure that we rode lots of rides and saw lots of attractions — making sure that we got the most out of each day, where "most" was defined in terms of the quantity of our experiences. As the day wore on, we all got hot and tired and hungry, and we all became irritable and snappy with each other. This wasn't just our family either — we saw lots of crying children and cranky parents in this international mecca of fun. But I saw one family vignette that finally woke me up and brought me back to myself. An impatient and haggard mother was kneeling beside her overwrought and screaming child, shaking him by the arm and yelling, "What's the matter with you? We're supposed to be having fun here. Start having fun now, damn it!" I had come to Disneyworld with my wife and children to have some close and loving family time together. In one sense, the rides and attractions were only the stage setting — the substance was the quality of our family time. My purpose in taking this vacation was to express my love for my family and to share close and loving time together. This "vacation purpose" was in turn a part of my larger life purpose, which includes elements of loving and serving others (including my family), as well as celebrating and enjoying life, both individually and with others (and most especially with my family).

To the extent that I got lost in the vacation agenda of doing as many fun things per day as possible no matter what, I tended to sabotage the quality of my life. Instead of feeling relaxed, peaceful, and happy, I spent much of each day feeling pressured and irritable. Instead of feeling a loving closeness and rapport with my family, I tended to be snappy and bossy — "Hurry up! Do this! Do that!" The overall lack of peace and joy in my life could have served me as a warning signal that I needed to somehow re-light my situation — my internal guidance system telling me that I was no longer on purpose. But at first I tended to blame my lack of peace on circumstances and other people — the lines were too long, my children were not cooperative enough, etc., etc. It was only when I saw that mother shaking her distraught child that I realized that what I needed to change was not my children and not Disneyworld, but my own perspective. In that sense, that woman and her child were valuable teachers for me.

The re-lighting that transformed my situation was simply choosing to remember my purpose. Within the perspective of my purpose, each unexpected "setback" now became an opportunity to pull together as a whole family to meet a new challenge. It made little difference how many rides we rode, as long as we were enjoying each minute of our time together. If the only thing this re-lighting accomplished was to make our family vacation more relaxed and fun for all of us, that would have been enough. But for me there was something else at stake besides simply having more fun. To the extent that I focused on my purpose and saw my day-to-day activities in that light, I was able to better fulfill my purpose — I was better able to fully be and become myself. From that perspective, the lack of peace I felt earlier could be thought of as my deeper purpose trying to assert itself — trying to help me remember that I had forgotten it.

Another story illustrates this same point. Last year, a friend of mine told me that she was driving her father down to Florida and back. Her father was determined to make the trip, but given his age and his health, she feared that he was not capable of driving that long distance safely. She told me she was feeling considerable stress about the coming trip — about all of the many preparations involved in leaving her business for a week, making the necessary arrangements to have her house taken care of, her car serviced, etc. I suggested that she focus on *why* she was choosing to go through all of this "inconvenience" — namely, because she loved her father and cared about his safety. She found that when she shifted her focus to her underlying motivation, all of the trip preparations became much less stressful. To the extent that she felt less stressful, she was able to better express her love and concern for her father, which was, after all, the whole reason for taking the trip in the first place.

I learned a similar lesson in my own life many years ago when I completed my time in the Army. When I had received my draft notice, I had had to temporarily interrupt my study of philosophy. Three years later, I excitedly returned to my group of friends, and I looked forward to an intensive summer seminar studying Wilhelm Windelband's *A History of Philosophy.* The seminar was demanding — about two to three hours of class daily, and at least another two to three hours of reading and preparation. Midway through the summer, I felt overwhelmed by the "demands" and "obligations" of this rigorous schedule. One day I complained to one of my friends that this seminar was keeping me from doing what I really wanted to do. He asked me, innocently enough, what I really wanted to do. I thought for a while, and then replied, "If I could do whatever I wanted to this summer, I would like to get together with a group of friends and study Windelband." Somehow what had started off as the opportunity to do exactly what I wanted had turned into an obligation, into something I "had" to do. As an obligation, it became a daily struggle — or more accurately, the more I thought of it as an obligation, the more I experienced it as a struggle, ultimately a struggle against myself.

In the Disneyworld story, we saw how negative emotions can serve to remind us that we are no longer acting on purpose. These last two stories add still another dimension to this theme. In both of these stories, even though the people involved were acting consistently with their purpose, they (or rather, we) had forgotten that purpose. Forgetting the underlying purpose had robbed our actions of their joy and turned them into mere labor and drudgery. Now, whenever I feel victimized by obligations, I remember to ask myself if I am living my own purpose or not. If not, I can rechoose a course of action that better expresses my truth. If I am indeed living my purpose, then I can pursue it deliberately and happily as my own choice, my own path with heart.

Seeing my situation from the lighted clearing of my purpose allows me to focus on and appreciate the actions and attitudes and events that are already contributing to my purpose — and this in itself is often sufficient to make the situation much more positive. This shift of focus can also bring to light those things that are not contributing to, or are actually interfering with, the fulfillment of my purpose, and can provide valuable clues as to how to constructively change them. In this sense, the lighted clearing of my purpose can help me to get "unstuck" from my negative perspective, so that I can once again begin to appreciate and express my own most authentic possibilities.

❖ Gratitude and Spiritual Awakening

In our everyday lives, we often tend to focus predominantly on what is negative. When we are lost in the familiarity of a world we take for granted, we tend to notice only those things that aren't working for us — the things and people and events that momentarily interrupt our sleepwalking routines. The overall result of this interruptive noticing is that our awareness of the world tends to be dominated by what is wrong with it — or at least what we interpret as "wrong" with it. Moreover, from the perspective of the Separative-Technological view in which the world is seen as an on-going conflict of separate self-interests, we have to be ever vigilant lest we be "used" by someone else. In this worldview, the primary question of our lives that functions as our protective mantra, is "What's wrong?" — and this question creates a lighted clearing that highlights every possible threat and attack. (This on-going focus on what is negative and what is not working for us is the underlying reason behind the seeming truth of "Murphy's Law" — the "law" that says that whatever can go wrong will go wrong. Since we are preoccupied with looking for what's wrong, it's no surprise that we would seem to find it everywhere.) Furthermore, to whatever extent that we feel frightened or insecure, we will tend to look for someone or something to blame — we will focus on the "bad" things that have happened to us in the past; the regrets, shames and guilts we carry inside; the things in the present that seem wrong or tragic or threatening; the future possibilities which cause us dread and anxiety; the things about ourselves or others that seem to reflect our failure and inadequacy. This overall tendency to focus on the negative is further aggravated by our news media, which bombard us daily with stories of crime, war, cruelty, and tragedy. All of this sets up a self-reinforcing cycle within ourselves. The more we think about such seemingly negative things, the more we feel frightened and desperate — and the more negative we feel, the more we tend to focus on those things that seem most wrong.

But usually when we stop to reflect, we discover that there are also many good and right things in our lives too, things which we have been ignoring in our preoccupation with the negative. One way to refocus my attention on the positive aspects of my situation is to ask myself, "What am I or what could I be grateful for in my life now?" Asking this question opens up a *lighted clearing of gratitude*, within which I can discover the blessings and gifts that are already present in my life. An example from my own experience illustrates this shift of focus. Several years ago I took a weekend workshop that explored the practical and the psychological aspects of managing your finances. Most of us who took this workshop felt very unpeaceful about our financial situations — the constant pressure and desperation of struggling to catch up, to pay off large debts, and somehow do more than just barely making ends meet each month. In one guided visualization, we were asked, "In what ways is your life prosperous now?" My family came to mind immediately — how we loved each other, the many close times we shared over dinner or playing games or watching a video together. I felt very blessed and very prosperous — and from that perspective, my financial concerns no longer seemed so overwhelmingly important. Of course I still wanted to develop better practical strategies for managing my finances, and to investigate my own fears and limiting beliefs regarding money. But all of this was now in a larger context of feeling already peaceful and happy, rather than thinking that a certain amount of money was the necessary precondition for peace and happiness. I am not minimizing the issue of financial hardship, and I admit that I have never lived on the edge of poverty. But the point of this example is that my simple shift of focus from what was troubling me to what I was grateful for made me more aware of what was already positive in my life, and also allowed me to see the negative from a truer and more balanced perspective.

One concrete exercise you can do to put your life into a larger perspective is to focus on what you are grateful for. As a specific exercise, this could take the form of starting each morning with five minutes of expressing your gratitude — doing this aloud can be even more effective. Simply spend five minutes saying, "I am grateful for...," "I am thankful for...," "I thank God for...," "I thank Mother Earth for...," etc. — whatever forms of expression feel most genuine to your own heart. Don't just go through your items mechanically — try to say each one with a sincere *feeling* of joy and gratitude. What you are grateful for can include the whole spectrum from those things that are obvious blessings and gifts, to those seemingly trivial things that you usually take for granted. By actively searching out what you are grateful for, you may discover many positive and good things in your life, things that had previously been hidden by a fearful focus on the negative. Sometimes it can be helpful to write down what you are grateful for. Later, reviewing your list in the midst of a "bad time" may help you restore your perspective.

Gratitude as a Tool for Spiritual Self-Discovery

From the Spiritual perspective, gratitude is much more than simply a mental technique to make yourself feel better. It is one of your most powerful tools for Self-discovery and Self-remembering. Gratitude — your ability to be grateful and to feel gratitude — is itself one of your most precious gifts, which enables you to awaken to your truth. Gratitude — asking and answering the question, "What am I (or could I be) grateful for now?" — creates a lighted clearing that allows you to more fully experience the peace, love, joy, and abundance that is offered to you by Spirit in every moment. The practice of gratitude typically begins with focusing on particular things in your life that you are grateful for — for all the wonderful things that have happened in your life; for the beauty you have been blessed to behold; for the beings in your life that have helped in your healing, and/or whom you have helped in theirs; for those who have loved you, and those whom you have been privileged to love; for the gifts you have been given to give; for your awareness that you have a choice in how you feel; for the peace of mind that is always available for the asking; for the perfect happiness that is only one thought away. And as you become more aware of the fullness and richness of your life, your focus shifts more to the ultimate source of all the blessings and the good you are receiving — your focus shifts to Spirit. As you become more directly aware of Spirit, you realize and experience it as your own essence and truth. (Earlier I mentioned that "think" and "thank" are etymologically related, and I suggested that truly origin-al thinking involved a thankful openness to the Mystery. From the Spiritual perspective, gratitude is the intentional openness that allows the origin of true thought to speak through you.)

As you live more and more from a source-focus, rather than an appearance-focus (or effect-focus), you are less and less concerned about what happened in the past, or what might happen in the future. You *know* (not hope or think, but know directly and immediately) that the past cannot limit you in any way, nor can the future add or subtract anything from your life. You *are*, in your very being, an on-going creation and expression of Spirit, an out-picturing of the very Being of love. In this awareness, you shift from the realm of experience known as karmic law (a temporal law of worldly cause and effect) to that of grace (an eternal state of being). This is a shift from an "eye for an eye" morality to an ethics of unconditional love — you are aware of your truth as a be-ing of love, and extending and sharing unconditional love is the only way you can authentically be. *A Course in Miracles* says, "Love is the way I walk in gratitude." [W362] The love you extend is unconditional, for there is no reason to make any conditions — the source of *all* your good and your happiness is within you, and external circumstances and events, and other people's words and actions cannot in any way limit your ability to experience and express perfect peace, love, and joy.

Ultimately, gratitude becomes not only a way of Spiritual awakening, but the natural expression of that awakening. As the natural expression of your awakening, it is no longer a "practice" that you "do," but simply the state of mind that reflects your awareness of the perfect grace of Spirit eternally shining through all things.

CHAPTER 13

HEALING

In this chapter on healing, I will be sharing many examples of healing, some of them from my own experience, and some that others have shared with me. I encourage you to use these examples to open yourself to the full depth and richness of your own experience — to approach them in the same way that you would approach a parable or a fable. It is important to re-emphasize this point here, since the format and writing style of the following examples may sometimes seem to be philosophically and psychologically descriptive, rather than overtly symbolic or allegorical. Remember that my words and definitions are only a "finger pointing at the moon" — ideas that help me re-create the lighted clearing of Self-discovery for myself. But whether or not my finger pointing at the moon actually helps to direct your own attention toward the moon depends on where you are relative to me and my finger and the moon. If, from where you are standing, my finger seems to be misdirected, then create your own pointer. How do you do this? Just ask yourself where all of the light is coming from, and then look in that direction.

Remember always that you are responsible for your own learning — or better, for your own openness to learning. An analogy from my experience as a chiropractor may be helpful here. Occasionally one of my patients will say to me something like, "Thank you. You healed my migraines (or my asthma, or my sinus problem, or my blood pressure problem, etc.)." My response to such comments is always, "You're welcome, but I didn't do the healing — it was your body's own healing power." From the perspective of chiropractic, the body's own inherent life force or "innate intelligence" is responsible for the health and healing of the body. A chiropractor's responsibility is simply to remove blockages or obstacles to that innate intelligence — specifically, to address those blockages that are in the form of "subluxations" (spinal misalignments), which interrupt the normal nerve supply to the body. Correcting subluxations allows the body's own intrinsic capacity for health and healing to more fully express itself. Similarly, I am not pretending to be your teacher here — I share these examples in the hope that you can use them to remove those blockages that are interfering with your own Self-remembering. But the true teacher will be the Mystery itself, as it reveals itself to you in the openness of your own heart.

❖ Health, Healing, and Wholeness

The starting point and foundation for our discussion of healing is the Spiritual-Holistic view. To see the world in a Holistic light means to understand it as an integral whole, rather than as a collection of separate parts. Each distinguishable whole can itself be seen as an integral part of a larger whole, right up to the ultimate wholeness (which has been referred to with terms like, The Tao, The Great Void, All That Is, etc.) — these levels of wholeness include the individual cell, the organ, the organ system, the whole body, the whole Self (body, mind and emotions), the whole family, the whole community, the whole of humankind, the whole of Nature, and the ultimate whole of the All-ness of Being.

In the *Spiritual*-Holistic view, the wholeness at each level is fundamentally Spiritual in nature. To see the world in a Spiritual light means to understand everything that exists as sharing a common essence — a common essence that is alive, dynamic, and creative; an essence of presence, with possibilities of love, communication, and guidance; an essence which is unconditionally and non-dualistically positive, and which is experienced as perfect peace, joy, and love. From the Spiritual perspective, everything is understood as a face or a voice of Spirit. To see everything as a "face of Spirit" means to see each thing (including myself) as a unique manifestation of a common Spiritual essence, a unique expression of the sacred living Presence of the world. The Spirit of each being is not some separate part of it, but is rather its *inner dimension of Spirituality*; a dimension of interrelatedness, of common essence, of sacredness. Thus we would not speak of the Spirit "in" me or "in" something, but rather *as* me or *as* something.

Likewise, "my Spirit" is not to be understood as a separate part of my whole Self, in addition to my body, my mind and my emotions. My Spirit *is* my Spirituality — that dimension of myself which is interrelated with and shares a common essence with all things. It is not Spirit "in" me, but Spirit *as* me — including, *as* my body, *as* my mind and *as* my emotions.

This view of Spirit is different from the usual concept of "God" as a separate being or force — for instance, as the "creator," which is separate from His/Her/Its creation. As I am defining the term "Spirit," we could speak of Spirit *as* creator and Spirit *as* creation — understanding creator/creation as one possible distinction within the wholeness of Spirit, one possible way to think about Spirit.

The Self-Revealing Nature of Spiritual Wholeness

Another aspect of this Spiritual wholeness, as I am defining it, is that it is *intrinsically self-revealing*. This means that, in its own nature, the Spiritual wholeness of every level of Being inherently moves toward fuller expression and fuller self-awareness. In the very essence of Being there is an inner impulse toward unhiddenness. This "self-revealing" can be understood as an expression of the perfect love and benevolence of Spirit. A person may be temporarily lost in a negative quality of life experience created by his fears and small ideas — temporarily suffering a lack of peace, love, and joy because he is living in a lighted clearing that denies and hides Spirit. To say that Spirit is self-revealing means that, even in the lighted clearing of the denial and hiding of Spirit, the deeper Spiritual truth intrinsically moves toward coming to light. We are never simply stuck or lost in sleepwalking suffering — our deeper Spiritual wholeness is intrinsically tending to awaken us in every moment.

In this context, health would be defined as the full expression of wholeness and Spirituality in every area of one's life. The very idea of health implies a better quality of life experience — where "better" means more peace, love, and joy in my life experience. Healing is the movement toward health — the movement toward a greater awareness and fuller expression of wholeness and Spirituality in my life. Note that healing is not a movement toward actually becoming more whole and Spiritual — from the Spiritual-Holistic perspective, I am *already* perfectly whole and Spiritual in my very being. Healing is rather the movement toward a fuller awareness, a fuller expression, and a fuller enjoyment of my wholeness and Spirituality. Understood in this way, healing is not just for obviously "sick" or "injured" people — rather, as the on-going process of Spiritual Self-realization, healing is for everyone. From this perspective, we are *always* in the process of healing, always under way toward a fuller expression of wholeness and Spirituality in our lives — overt sickness or disease is but one aspect or phase of this on-going healing process.

Removing the Blockages to Health

Obstacles to the full awareness and expression of wholeness and Spirituality in my life could include my Separative-Technological beliefs, my fears, and my tendency to think of language as an opaque description of the world. I can also be blinded by my attachment to my desires and aversions — the more I am completely preoccupied with chasing after and grabbing at some things and some experiences, and fleeing from and avoiding others, the less likely I am to fully appreciate the sacredness of *all* things. This is not a question of whether or not I have preferences (which may be simply one expression of my own uniqueness), but whether or not I am "lost" in my desires and aversions. For instance, when I try to see everything as a face of Spirit, it often seems to me that some faces are more translucent than others — that some things (or people or events) let their Spirituality shine through brightly, whereas others seem very "unspiritual." But whenever I look more deeply, I discover that the unspirituality of something is only a reflection of my own unspiritual way of looking at it — a way that has been filtered through my own presuppositions, fears, and desperate longings.

In the healing process, it is the self-revealing Spiritual wholeness itself that does the healing, as it comes to fuller awareness and expression. A medical doctor cannot force a broken bone to mend, nor can a psychiatrist force a broken psyche to heal — at best, they can try to create the conditions that allow the intrinsic health and wholeness of body and mind to fully express themselves. We can never force the process of healing — we cannot force Spirit to reveal itself. We can only create the conditions that allow the intrinsically self-revealing Spiritual wholeness to more fully express itself in our lives — the conditions that allow us to be open to its own self-revelation. Creating these conditions can include both removing the obstacles and presuppositions that block my awareness of Spirit, and actively cultivating my openness and receptivity to Spiritual awareness — actively creating a lighted clearing within which Spirit can reveal itself. One important part of creating such a lighted clearing for myself is my choice of ideas and beliefs — for instance, the light choices of "wholeness" and "Spirit" themselves. For example, in my own life, when I remember the phrase, "everything is a face of Spirit," my perception shifts and I become more open to experience the Spirituality-possibilities of each thing in my world. In addition to my conceptual light choices, I find that an attitude of reverence, trust, and unconditional love is also a necessary part of creating the clearing within which Spirit can reveal itself — opening my heart as well as my mind. Once I have created this clearing, Spirit (either

Spirit in general, or Spirit manifesting as a particular person or thing) can emerge and show itself in my experience.

As I become more attuned to the Spiritual wholeness of the world, I myself can add my own unique energy and creativity to its emergence. Ultimately, this is the essence of my "soul-gift," my unique contribution to the greater whole of which I am a part. It is a *soul*-gift rather than an ego-gift, since its source is explicitly and unhiddenly Spirit itself — the gift arises out of my interrelatedness to all things and is directed back toward serving the greater whole. My contribution to the healing process of myself and the world is to let the greater Spiritual wholeness express itself through me — and ultimately not just to let it, but to actively assist it. From the Spiritual perspective, what I creatively send forth from myself is also an expression of Spirit — the Spirit-as-me adding its own unique contribution to Spirit-in-general; the Spirit-as-me acting in concert with the Spirit-as-everything-else. But my soul-gift, like everything else in my life, exists only as possibility — a possibility that I can realize more or less fully, or perhaps not realize at all. Becoming aware of my own Spirituality — my own unique place and role in the greater scheme of things — may be a necessary first step toward discovering and expressing my soul-gift. But I also have to choose to actively *live* this awareness, in order to fully realize this deepest and most authentic possibility of my truth.

Opportunities to Heal Your Life

In my college days, I used to body surf off the coast of California. When I interpreted or read the ocean correctly and was at the right place at the right time, I had an exhilarating ride to shore. But if I was out of touch with the ocean's rhythms, I either missed the exciting ride, or else was actually ground into the sand as the wave crashed over me. It is important to recognize that the ocean did not intentionally hurt me in order to punish me or teach me a lesson. The ocean itself was offering a wonderful opportunity — any suffering I experienced was simply the natural consequence of my not being attuned to its nature and rhythms.

When the intrinsic thrust of wholeness toward self-awareness and self-expression is thwarted by my ignorance or fear, the wholeness awakens me to my resistance with a sense of dis-ease. But this is not a "punishment." From the perspective of the lighted clearing of healing, this lack of ease arises out of my denying or blocking my own wholeness. In this context, my dis-ease — which can take the form of physical disease, negative emotions, dysfunctional relationships, or a sense of alienation from Nature — can be understood as the birth pains of my emergent wholeness and

Spirituality, trying to somehow break through or overcome my barriers and my resistance.

Understood in this way, any form of dis-ease is ultimately an opportunity — an opportunity to stop thinking and doing those things that are somehow out of synch with my Spiritual truth (my truth as a be-ing of Spirit), and to begin thinking and doing those things that are in synch. A health "crisis" — whether a physical, mental, emotional, relationship, or financial crisis in our lives — forces us to reflect on, re-evaluate, and change our current routines and thought patterns. A health crisis often makes it impossible to hold on to our old routine — in order to experience peace and well-being, we have to make some kind of change. From the Spiritual-Holistic perspective, every health crisis is ultimately a gift and an opportunity — it is the self-revealing presence of your truth pushing through your unawareness and resistance, so that you can experience a deeper and fuller life, a life of more peace and love and joy.

From this perspective, sickness or dis-ease is not necessarily a "breakdown" or a step "backwards," nor is someone who is overtly sick somehow "worse off" or "less Spiritually evolved" than someone who seems completely well. A health crisis may signal that I have become healthy enough to "evolve" to a deeper level of healing and wholeness — to move "forward" in my journey toward Self-realization. "Getting sick" does not necessarily reflect that you have made some new mistake, nor does the persistence of symptoms reflect a "failure" on your part. Some people seem to have developed deep insight and Spiritual Self-realization, without resolving all of their symptoms — for instance, even though Ram Dass cannot physically do all of the things he could before his stroke, he has evidently healed his life at a very deep level (see his recent book, *Still Here*). Even death itself might be one step on an on-going healing journey, rather than the "end" of the journey — might be the emergence of the next level of wholeness and Spirituality, rather than a "failure" to heal. For the Spiritual-Holistic perspective, the criterion of healing is the quality of your life experience, your inner level of peace, well-being, love, and joy.

To say that an experience of dis-ease is ultimately a reflection of our Spiritual truth trying to emerge through our resistance into fuller expression must not be understood in the sense of blame — as if all of your diseases and crises were your "fault." For the Spiritual-Holistic perspective, to be "human" means to be in the process of awakening from an illusion of separateness (separate from Spirit, and from the world) to the truth of your Spiritual wholeness. This does not mean you are bad or wrong while you are still lost in illusion — as a human being, you are simply in the midst of the process of waking up to your truth. You are motivated to wake up only by discovering that you are asleep — you are motivated to remember your Self only because Truth Itself somehow reminds you that you are forgetting. From within the perspective of forgetting, the impulse to remember can seem foreign and unpleasant — one who is comfortably asleep often tends to resist and resent being shaken awake. For the Spiritual-Holistic view, this resistance and discomfort is ultimately only your own attempt to hold on to your illusions — to hold on to your sleeping dream, because you mistakenly believe that awakening is a threat to your identity and happiness.

From this perspective, your dis-ease is not an occasion for guilt or self-judgment, but an opportunity to more fully recognize and express your Spiritual wholeness. You simply are who you are here and now. You did not create yourself, nor did you create the ideas and beliefs of the Separative-Technological thought-system in which you find yourself. There is no blame involved here — it is simply the kind of existence and the state-of-mind you find yourself in here and now as this particular human being. But since your Spiritual truth is intrinsically self-revealing, you are never lost in your current level of Spiritual unawareness. Spirit will continue to expose the limitations of your understanding, the limitations of your ability to fully experience and express perfect peace, love, and joy. The exposure of these limitations is often manifested in your life as some form of dis-ease — otherwise, you would have no motivation to expand your awareness or wake up to your truth as a be-ing of Spirit. So it is never a matter of blame. It is always simply a matter of your responsibility — your ability to respond to the revelation of your current limits by opening your mind and heart to a deeper truth. For the Spiritual perspective, every health crisis — every experience of dis-ease in any area of your life — is an opportunity for you to reclaim your responsibility as a Spiritual being, to reclaim your ability to realize and send forth your truth as a be-ing of Spirit. From this perspective, blame is always an inappropriate response to illness or dis-ease. Blaming — whether blaming myself, or someone or something else for my dis-ease —misses the point. The point is *always* to wake up — *starting from here and now*, to let go of all blockages to Spiritual awareness, and actively turn your awareness back to your Spiritual truth. For the Spiritual-Holistic view, that is the message and the gift of dis-ease — or more generally, that is the message and the gift of *every* life experience. Blaming is merely a negative reaction (reflecting a pathology orientation) that serves no positive or constructive purpose — merely blaming someone or something for the darkness brings you no closer to seeing the light.

The more I am unaware of the wholeness and Spirituality of myself and my world, and the more I block their emergence, the more I will tend to experience suffering in my own life and the more I will tend to reinforce the ignorance and suffering of others. To whatever extent the lighted clearing of my life actively denies or precludes Spiritual joy and peace, I will tend to experience unhappiness and lack of peace, and I will also tend to influence others in such a way that they are blinded to the joy and peace of their truth — the light or lack of light in my own clearing contributes to the light or lack of light in the world. From the perspective of the lighted clearing of healing, my negative emotions are more than just the discomfort of a dissatisfied ego — they are my wake-up calls to once again re-member and re-claim the wholeness and Spirituality of myself and my world. Re-lighting a situation in order to feel more peace, love, and joy in my life is thus much more than just a technique to help myself feel a little better — from this perspective, it becomes a way to discover and more fully realize the truth of myself and my world, and to contribute to our healing.

I have defined healing as the movement toward a fuller expression of wholeness and Spirituality, toward greater health, toward more peace, love, and joy in my life. But this does not mean that the process of healing always feels pleasant and comfortable. The physical healing process can sometimes involve discomfort — for example, when the body generates a fever to help fight off an infection. This is a healthy response of a body seeking to take care of itself — and to merely repress this response with medication may actually interfere with the body's own healing process. In your mental and emotional healing, the journey toward wholeness often involves coming to recognize and reclaim parts of yourself that you have long since repressed or denied out of fear. The process of encountering those lost or disowned parts of yourself can be terrifying and painful.[18] It can sometimes be difficult to distinguish whether a given physical or emotional symptom signals a blockage that you need to attend to, or reflects a natural healing process that should best just run its course without interference. There is no simple formula to know the difference between these two alternatives in a given situation — the best you can do is to be deeply receptive to the Mystery of your own being for guidance. But note that in either case, the discomfort can be seen as the birth pain of the emergence of your Spiritual wholeness — and just as in the birth of a baby, it is important to know when to actively push to help the birth process, and when to just breathe, relax, and allow the womb's own natural contractions to bring forth new life.

❖ The Wholeness of the Body

From the Holistic perspective, each distinguishable whole is also an integral part or component of a still greater whole. Thus, we can speak of a hierarchy of levels of wholeness — for instance, the wholeness of my body, the wholeness of my Self (body, mind and emotions), the interpersonal wholeness of a group of people, and the wholeness of Nature itself. Just as every part of a holographic plate contains the information of the whole plate, so too does every level of wholeness reflect all of the other levels of wholeness — each microcosm expresses and reflects the greater encompassing macrocosm. What this means for our discussion is that the various levels of wholeness and healing should not be understood as a *linear* hierarchy — as if, for instance, I first had to heal (or facilitate the healing of) my body, and second had to heal my whole Self, and third had to heal my relationships with others, etc. In the Holistic model we are considering here, the health of each part both affects and reflects the health of the greater whole, just as the health of each cell in my body both affects and reflects the health of my whole body. So even though our discussion will proceed from one level to another, it is important to remember that the healing of all of these levels is occurring simultaneously, and that healing at any level affects all of the other levels as well — ultimately you are healing your whole life, and not separate "pieces" of your life.

In the field of health care, the Technological view tends to be reflected as a "mechanistic" approach to the body, whereas the Spiritual view takes a more "vitalistic" approach to health. The mechanistic approach views the body as merely a complex machine, which occasionally breaks down and must be "fixed" by a "health care mechanic," using the tools of modern technology. Fixing involves either adding something to the body (drugs), or taking something from the body (surgical removal of tissues and organs), and/or replacing body parts. Often "fixing" simply means getting rid of the symptoms — such as taking an aspirin to suppress a headache or to force a fever to come down. In health care, technological "power" means power "over" the body — the power to "make" the body function in a certain way, or the power to suppress unpleasant symptoms.

In the vitalistic approach, however, a living body is seen as more than just the atoms and molecules that make it up. There is also an intelligent life force, which monitors everything in the body and the environment, and coordinates and controls all of the life functions in the body — a life force that is inherently self-organizing, adaptive, self-healing, and self-regenerating. From the vitalistic perspective, health care is not a matter of controlling the body or "making" it do what we want, but rather of allowing and enabling the body to more fully express its own innate ability for healing and health. From this perspective, symptoms are understood as a way that the body tries to get our attention, to let us know that it is time to change something in our lives. As such, symptoms are not enemies to be conquered or eliminated, but rather friendly messengers to be heeded and understood — they are an expression of the body's intrinsic wellness trying to overcome some obstacle or resistance. To merely mask the symptoms with drugs or other palliative treatment, without discovering their underlying message, ultimately interferes with healing and the full expression of health — from a vitalistic perspective, for any treatment to be truly effective, its ultimate goal and intent must be to facilitate the body's own healing process. Moreover, from this point of view, health means much more than merely the absence of symptoms — health is positively defined as the full expression of life. Being healthy is much more than merely not feeling sick — it means living your full potential for energy, vitality, and joy.[19]

❖ The Wholeness of the Self

The next "level" of wholeness we will consider is the wholeness of my Self — the wholeness embracing my body, my mind, and my emotions. It is important to recognize here that "my Spirit" is not a fourth component of my Self on the same level as the other three. My Spirit is not a part, but rather a quality or dimension of every part — it is the dimension of interrelatedness, of sharing a common essence, of sacredness. In this sense my Spirit is not something separate from my body, mind, and emotions — my body, mind and emotions are manifestations of Spirit. The Spirituality of my body, mind, and emotions is their sacredness, their essential interrelatedness with all that is — in other words, my Self *intrinsically* includes a dimension of my relatedness to others.

The first step in reclaiming the wholeness of my Self is to recognize the interrelatedness of my body, mind, and emotions — to realize that the health of each component both reflects and affects the health of the others. I cannot, for instance, expect my body to be truly healthy if my emotions are unhealthy. (A good example of the opposite view here is a sign I once saw in a very mechanistically oriented doctor's office. It said, "Please don't talk to the doctor" — as if any expression of the patient's mental and emotional life would merely interfere with the purely physical process of fixing his body.)[20]

Reclaiming the wholeness of my Self also involves recognizing and reclaiming those parts of myself that have been disowned, repressed, or covered over. Since this repression is often at a deep subconscious level, I do not recognize these parts of myself as "me" at all. In contemporary psychological terms, reclaiming my wholeness involves "healing my wounds." For the Spiritual-Holistic view, there is not, and could not be, any real "damage" to my wholeness — my eternal Spiritual truth cannot be "scarred" by worldly events. Thus, in this context, a wound is a fear or a limiting belief that keeps me from realizing and expressing my wholeness. From this perspective, my active holding onto a belief that "I have been somehow damaged and am now un-whole" is what prevents me from fully experiencing the unchanging truth of my Spiritual wholeness now — the "wounds" and "scars" I feel reflect my lack of awareness of my wholeness, rather than any real lack of wholeness.

According to psychological theory, our early childhood experiences "teach" us that in order to feel accepted and safe, we must both disown or repress some parts of ourselves, and also develop certain inauthentic possibilities (pretenses) that seem to make us more "acceptable." As a very young child, whenever we felt threatened by harm or abandonment — whether the threat was real, or was merely imagined by our childish minds — we made decisions that we had to either do certain things and/or not do certain things, in order to survive at all. This decision was backed up by sheer terror — the terror of the threat of death. These decisions are buried in the pre-verbal history of our earliest years, and form the personae we live as adults — and for the most part, they remain unconscious, unless we make a deliberate effort to rediscover them.

From the perspective of the lighted clearing of healing, my wholeness intrinsically moves toward full expression. I will feel my resistance to the emergence of my wholeness as discomfort and lack of peace, and maybe even physical illness. But the intrinsic emergence of my wholeness will "push" me to uncover what I have covered over, and to reclaim what I have disowned. Often, this is a terrifying process — encountering my own deepest and most primordial terrors, which keep the lost and buried parts of myself unconscious. We see this general theme again and again in fairy tales: that I must encounter the fiercest dragon (the terror of my own wound), before I can gain the greatest treasure (my own wholeness, my own Self). In this process, I discover that, "my wound is the womb of my gift."[21] My wounds act as doorways to my wholeness — their fear and discomfort guide me to rediscover and reclaim those parts of myself that have been buried or repressed. Moreover, what I learn in healing my own woundedness gives me the insight, compassion, and empathy to help others facilitate their own process of healing.

As I reclaim my own wholeness and become more aware of my own lost and buried possibilities, I benefit in several ways. I no longer fight against myself, no longer sabotage myself with mere defensive reactions. To the extent that my wounds are unconscious, they are the source of my defensive reactions. Someone can "push my button" only if I have a button to be pushed — only if I have a subconscious wound that is sensitive and reactive.[22] Moreover, as I reclaim those lost possibilities, I am able to use them in a positive or constructive way to more fully enjoy my life, to fulfill my purpose and to contribute to others. Furthermore, as I recognize and reclaim the wholeness underlying my wounds, I am better able to recognize the underlying wholeness of others as well. I am less judgmental of their wounds and defenses. The more I acknowledge and affirm their own underlying wholeness, the more I become a positive influence in their lives, helping them to better recognize and realize their own truth.

Reclaiming my wholeness includes accepting those parts of myself that I don't like, that I condemn as somehow wrong or bad (whether I see them as "bad" qualities of myself, or unconsciously project them as the "bad" qualities I condemn in another). From the lighted clearing of healing, my dis-ease and dissatisfaction with these rejected parts of myself — my dislike or even hatred of them — can be seen as the birth pains of a healthier, more whole Self trying to emerge. To see something in myself that I don't like implies that there is something more to me than this "character defect" — a deeper me that can see that part as somehow deficient, somehow falling short of a deeper potential. If I didn't have this implicit deeper perspective, I simply would not care — for instance, I would not care if I were irritable with my children or defensive with my spouse. My very dissatisfaction is the expression of a self-revealing deeper potential for health. To merely reject what I don't like about myself can never help me to truly heal — I cannot reclaim my wholeness by trying to throw away parts of myself. Moreover, for the Spiritual view, the parts of myself that I don't like can be understood as distorted, fearful expressions of my deeper essence. From that perspective, not only would I not want to reject or ignore a part of myself I didn't like, but I would actually want to discover and reclaim its sacred essence. In terms of the Possibility Model, I would want to create a lighted clearing that could highlight the Spirituality-possibilities of the rejected part of myself, so that I could become aware of and realize its sacred potential in my life.

In *Emmanuel's Book*, Pat Rodegast and Emmanuel offer one very helpful way to create such a clearing for yourself. It involves asking yourself two questions: "What is the fear underlying this rejected part of myself?" and "What is the longing underlying that fear?" Recently, for instance, I was feeling very angry with my wife for something she had said to me, which I had interpreted as harsh and unkind. But when I looked at the situation from the lighted clearing of the underlying fear and the underlying longing, I discovered that beneath my anger was the fear that she didn't really love me, the fear that she would abandon me. Underlying this fear was the longing to love and to be loved by her. From this deeper perspective, I was able to see my own negative emotional reaction as an opportunity to become aware of and heal my underlying fear. Furthermore, as I became more aware of the longing underlying this fear, I discovered a new horizon of possible responses. My anger, after all, left me two choices: either to act it out by yelling and screaming, or to withdraw into a stony, "manly" silence — fight or flight. But neither of these reactions would actually help me to realize my deeper desire to love and to be loved. Discovering my underlying longing gave me an opportunity to respond in a way that truly served me. Instead of merely reacting in anger to what I didn't want, I could respond and proactively live toward what I truly desired.

If, however, I had simply rejected the angry, defensive part of myself, and tried to merely forget the whole thing, I would have deprived myself of valuable clues for reclaiming my wholeness. The fear underlying my anger — the fear of being abandoned — was probably an expression of a childhood wound. To merely ignore the wound meant that it would continue to fester in my subconscious and continue to sabotage all my relationships. Asking the question about the underlying fear allowed me to become aware of this wound and opened up the possibility of healing it. Also, insofar as I merely rejected my defensiveness and tried to forget the whole thing, I would, to some extent, throw out the longing that was its very essence, the longing to have a loving relationship with my wife — for it was this longing for love that was the true passion behind my anger. Asking the question of the underlying longing created a lighted clearing within which I could discover the deeper truth of my negative reaction. Insofar as I could identify this underlying longing, I could find more positive and constructive ways to express it. That longing was a very precious and important part of my truth — something that I didn't want to lose touch with or disown. Once I was more fully aware of this longing, I realized that aggression (whether active or passive) was not the best way to move toward its realization. This discovery came from going to the heart of what I didn't like about myself, rather than simply ignoring or rejecting it.

In addition to discovering new possibilities of responding, I also discovered new possibilities of experiencing the world. As I moved out of the lighted (or perhaps, darkened) clearing of my defensive anger, and into the lighted clearing of my underlying longing to love and to be loved, I became more aware of my wife's many expressions of love for me. Presumably these possibilities had been present and potentially experiencable prior to my shift of awareness, but my reactivity had blinded me to them. In the lighted clearing of unconditional love, however, not only was I more able to freely give love, but I was also more able to freely recognize and receive it.

This is the fundamental shift in perspective involved in the lighted clearing of healing: to see each symptom or dis-ease as the expression of an emerging greater wholeness. This is a shift of perspective from hating my mistakes and shortcomings, to loving my deeper emerging Self — to seeing each "imperfect" part of my life as my deeper perfection in its process of self-becoming. I cannot reclaim my wholeness by throwing away some of my parts — in merely rejecting them, I not only blind myself to my own wholeness, but I also hide from myself the very clues that could guide me to reclaim it.

❖ Interpersonal Wholeness

Our modern culture tends to be Separative and individualistic. Since our culture defines the individual person as the fundamental unit of reality, it can be relatively easy for us to think about such concepts as the "life force" or "innate intelligence" of an individual body, or even the "whole Self" of an individual person. But from the Separative view, a group of people is only a collection of separate individuals. Therefore, it may be relatively more difficult for us to think of the Self or soul of a group — a group soul that is somehow more than just a collection of all of the individual souls. This level of wholeness stretches and challenges the limits of our cultural Separative beliefs. In terms of our Possibility Model, the Separative view creates a lighted clearing that precludes any possible experience of levels of wholeness beyond the individual.

Several years ago, I did a vision quest program with the Animas Valley Institute out of Durango, Colorado. The traditional purpose of a vision quest is to discover your own unique soul-gift and how you can best "perform it for your people." Part of this program was done in a group setting, and part of it involved solitary time in the wilderness. Whenever our vision quest group gathered in a circle to share our experiences, we referred to our circle as a "Medicine Wheel." In this Native American phrase, "Medicine" does not refer to pills or drugs, but to healing in general, and "Wheel" indicates a circle, the symbol of wholeness. So the "Medicine Wheel" of our group was the healing wholeness of our group. In many Native American teachings, the Medicine Wheel is a general symbol for the healing wholeness of the whole universe. Every particular Medicine Wheel — for instance, the Medicine Wheel of our vision quest group — is a healing wholeness that mirrors the Great Medicine Wheel of Nature. As we sat around in our circle, we were all "spokes of the Medicine Wheel." For me, this phrase, "spokes of the Medicine Wheel" is a powerful metaphor that creates a lighted clearing within which I can perceive new possibilities of myself and others. It allows me to experience the group itself as a whole living being, as a greater manifestation of the human Spirit. Here, "human Spirit" refers to the Spirituality of humanity in general, the "soul of humankind" — the unique way in which human beings manifest and express Spirit. Every individual human is a particular "face" or manifestation of human Spirit, which in turn is a specific manifestation of Spirit in general. But in between the levels of individual Spirit and the human Spirit, it is possible to think of various groups as faces of Spirit as well — and each level has its own wholeness, its own soul.

As I sat in the Medicine Wheel of my group, I became aware of a deeper and fuller experience of Self. For me, it was as if the people in our Medicine Wheel represented different facets of a whole human Self — they reflected the various strengths and talents and weaknesses and fears of a human being (or of human be-ing in general). I learned a great deal about my own possibilities and wholeness simply by listening to others share their own truth — that sense of "Yes, that's true for me too! I never thought of it quite like that before." As I saw others living their own talents and gifts, I discovered previously unknown possibilities in myself — either because I had actively disowned those possibilities, or because I had simply failed to cultivate and realize them as my own. In a sense, our group expressed a more complete and healthier (more whole) human Self than any of us expressed individually. The group Self was thus a teacher and a healer for each of us in our individual journeys toward reclaiming wholeness.

Where this became especially powerful for me was with regard to those people in the group I felt most critical of. At one point in our group discussion, our guide had told me that I could find a clue to healing my own wounds by looking at my critical judgments of others. I was especially critical (at least in the seeming privacy of my own thoughts) of one woman in our group, who seemed to be "overly emotional" — and here, "especially critical" means that I myself had a strong emotional (but, of course, not an overly emotional) reaction to her. During part of my solo time in the wilderness, I explored my judgmental feelings toward that person — not so much as a reflection of her, but rather as a reflection of my own disowned emotionality. This exploration ended up being very difficult, painful, and terrifying, as I encountered one of my own childhood wounds — the fear that expressing my emotions, at least past a certain "safe" level, could lead to abandonment and even death. This, of course, sounds a bit histrionic in the cold light of rational adulthood — but these conclusions had been drawn by an infant, who was "frightened to death." Fully recognizing that part of myself and giving myself permission to embrace those authentic possibilities of myself *as my own* possibilities was one of the hardest and most frightening things I have ever done — there was a brief time out in the desert when I firmly believed that I was actually going to die from sheer terror. This was one of the fierce dragons I had to encounter, before I could gain the treasure — before I could reclaim my own wholeness. Given the terror that guarded this disowned part of myself, it is not surprising that I simply hadn't been aware of it as part of "me" at all. I could only see it in others — and since it was "bad" and "dangerous" to my infantile judgment, I tended to be very critical and judgmental when I saw others as being overly emotional. In psychological terms, I projected my disowned part onto others, and I rejected it in them just as I had rejected it in myself. The passion behind my critical judgment of that woman in our group was a distorted reflection of my own terror — the terror that kept my disowned possibility unconscious. This discussion is not to say that she either was or wasn't actually "overly emotional." There is obviously no objective way to establish a "correct" level of emotional expression for anyone. Her own healing journey would determine whether her level of emotional expression was authentic, or was partially due to the defenses and pretenses she had adopted as a child in order to cope with the perceived stresses and threats of her environment. My healing journey, however, was to discover why I felt compelled to be so vehemently judgmental of her personality.

To the extent that I projected this onto her in my critical judgment, I remained alienated from my own wholeness, and was blind to her own wholeness as well, since I saw her only as a mirror of my own fragmentedness. Moreover, I was blind to the wholeness of the two of us, the wholeness of our friendship. As I came to acknowledge and embrace that disowned part of myself, I became healthier and more whole, more able to more fully live the truth of my being, freer to express my emotions. Since my experience of her was now less distorted by my fearful projections, I was able to more fully see and accept her as a whole person — able to more fully receive her own unique soul-gift. This in turn allowed the two of us to develop a deeper, fuller friendship, which opened both of us to a deeper awareness of our truth.

Since we were all "spokes of the Medicine Wheel," the group also enabled each of us to discover and reclaim our part-ness, our participation in something larger than our individual Selves. As we participated in the group, it seemed to have a soul and life of its own. We were not merely the separate parts that added together to make up the whole — the whole itself seemed to add something to each of us as well. The group itself created a lighted clearing within which we could more fully discover our own truest possibilities and our own soul-gifts.

I am using my vision quest group as an example, because it was one of the deepest group experiences I have had. But I believe that such an experience is always possible within any relationship or group, if we can but create the lighted clearing that allows it to emerge.[23] It is important to remember in the present discussion that "group soul" is not to be understood as a label that refers to some soul-thing — not to be understood as an attempt to describe "how things really are." The idea of a group soul is rather one way of opening myself to a range of possible experiences — experiences which can teach me more about myself and my participation in the world; experiences which can heal my feeling of alienation from myself and from others.

The Lighted Clearing of Prayer

Earlier, we looked at the body, mind and emotions as interrelated aspects of an overall whole — i.e., the whole Self. Within the wholeness of the Self, the health of each of these interrelated aspects affected and reflected the health of the others — for instance, the health of my thoughts and emotions could affect the health of my body. An interesting implication of interpersonal wholeness — my wholeness with other people — is that my thoughts could affect not only the thoughts of others, but also their bodies. Larry Dossey's book, *Healing Words*, documents many scientific studies that validated the healing efficacy of prayer. These are controlled, double-blind scientific experiments — and, as often as not, were conducted by skeptical scientists who originally set out to debunk the myth of "the healing power of prayer." From the perspective of the lighted clearing of wholeness and healing, the effectiveness of prayer is not a matter of one separate individual mind sending a prayer "to" a separate God, who in turn sends healing "to" another separate individual's body.

Rather, it is seen as one aspect of a greater Spiritual whole affecting another aspect — seen in terms of the essential interconnectedness of the person who prays, the person who is prayed for, and the divine source of the healing. (Similarly, ESP would not be merely my separate mind somehow "sending" thoughts across space and time "to" your separate mind — from the perspective of wholeness, the communication would take place in the non-local sphere of our common essence.) Some proponents of creative visualization claim that merely visualizing and affirming the health of someone else can have a healing effect. What differentiates prayer from mere affirmation, and perhaps what makes prayer so effective, is that it includes, by definition, a focus on the Spiritual dimension of life — whether this Spiritual dimension is conceived as a general sacred living Presence of all things, or as a supreme being (God, Goddess, Allah, etc.) who is the creator, sustainer, and benefactor of all life. The intentional focus on the Spiritual dimension is the openness to what we share in common, whether we think of it in terms of a sacred common essence or in terms of a common divine source. In terms of our Possibility Model, this openness-to-Spirit creates the clearing that allows it to more fully express itself, and thus allows healing.

From a strictly mechanistic-Technological point of view, only the actual physical technique employed is important in the physical healing process — for instance, as long as your surgeon uses the proper surgical techniques, it makes no difference whether she loves you or hates you, no difference whether she is focused on your healing, or is thinking about her golf game or her recent fight with her husband. But from the larger perspective of interpersonal wholeness, the healer's thoughts and intentions can play a significant role in the healing process. In one lecture, Dr. Dossey said that once he had learned of the scientific evidence that validated the healing efficacy of prayer, he couldn't in good conscience not pray for each of his patients. In general, we could say that the healer's own health — her attunement to the wholeness and Spirituality of her own life — is an important factor in assisting another's healing, helping another to more fully realize the wholeness and Spirituality of his own life. Your own openness to Spirit helps co-create the openness for another, so that their own wholeness can more fully express itself. In this sense, taking care of your own individual physical, mental, and emotional health is an essential part of how you can serve others and contribute to their healing.

The process of helping others heal themselves also plays an important role in your own healing. To the extent that there is an interpersonal wholeness embracing you and the other person(s), then an essential component of your own identity is your relatedness to the other person(s)

— you are, in your very being, a part of a greater whole. An essential element of your individual health (including both the health of your body and the health of your whole Self) is the health of your relationship to others. Just as a cell cannot be fully healthy unless the whole body is healthy, so too "you" cannot be fully healthy unless "we" are fully healthy. This implies that helping others to remember and reclaim their own health is not altruistic self-sacrifice. Loving service is a way that you yourself become healthier — helping others to heal themselves is also a way that you help yourself to heal. Earlier I said that healing was not just for "sick" people — healing, defined as the on-going process of Self-becoming, is for everyone. Now we see that an essential part of Spiritual Self-becoming and Self-healing is being a healer (or a healing facilitator) for others. In that sense, everyone is a healer — not just doctors and other health care professionals, but everyone. In terms of our Possibility Model, we could say that everyone has healer-possibilities — and it is only in realizing your healer-possibilities that your own life becomes fully healed, that Spirit and wholeness can be fully expressed in every aspect and at every level of your life.

How does one concretely help to create a lighted clearing of healing for himself and others? As I have already indicated, my intention to heal and be healed can create an openness allowing the emergence of that level of wholeness and Spirituality that includes both me and the other person. The intention to enter a healing relationship with others — a relationship which can allow a common sacred wholeness to express itself through us — helps to transform our experience of a group of people from a mere collection of separate individuals to a Medicine Wheel, a whole which is greater than the sum of its parts. The intention itself helps to create the lighted clearing within which the Spirituality-possibilities of the world can emerge. This is one way to interpret the Biblical scripture, "For where two or three are gathered in my name, there am I in the midst of them" [Matthew, 18:20]. From the Spiritual perspective, every relationship or group is, in truth, a holy relationship, a Medicine Wheel. It is only my belief in separateness and valuelessness — only my active denial of and hiding of wholeness and Spirit — that prevents me from experiencing the sacred truth of each relationship and group. Moreover, my lighted clearing also influences others, either by reinforcing their fearful illusion of separateness, or by illuminating their truth of wholeness.

Another way to create a lighted clearing of healing is through the ideas and theories we use to light our path. For myself, for instance, phrases such as "we are all spokes of the Medicine Wheel" and "everything is a face of Spirit" open me to more fully experience our common essence.

This does not mean that I am blind to our differences. In fact, as we have seen in the examples above, our differences can be an important part of healing ourselves — both in helping me to discover parts of myself I was previously unaware of, and in helping me to realize and appreciate my own unique identity and soul-gift among the great diversity of unique identities and soul-gifts. But for the Spiritual view, the differences between us do not separate us from one another — rather, our differences reflect the diversity and richness of the sacred. Earlier I noted that although everyone is a face of Spirit, some disguises seem to be much better than others — and I have found that the opacity or translucence of a disguise depends on my own fears and desires and aversions rather than on "objective" factors. In my workshops, I sometimes use the following example to illustrate this point. Imagine you are a doctor and have just stepped into the treatment room to help your next patient. Which of the following "disguises" would make it difficult for you to remain focused on the Spirit-within? Ghandi, Mother Theresa, a powerful world leader (consider one whom you admire, and one whom you detest), a sexy movie star, an obese person, a thin person, an old person, a person of a different race and ethnic background from yourself, a gay or lesbian person, an extremely wealthy person, a homeless person, a person with AIDS, a person who is physically or mentally challenged in some way, a "mentally ill" person, etc. From the perspective of the lighted clearing of healing, observing your own reactions to the various people you see or think about in your life can give you valuable clues to your own blinders — to those prejudices and wounds and attachments that prevent your full awareness of the wholeness and Spirituality of others and of yourself.

Healing and Unconditional Love

When I discussed the Spiritual view earlier, I said that the corresponding ethics — the way of living that most unhiddenly expresses the Spirituality of all things — is unconditional love. In the context of our earlier discussion of responsibility, conditional love is always a reaction, rather than a response. If who someone is, or what they say or do, is acceptable to my desires and defenses and cultural prejudices, then I feel positive toward them — and when I feel very positive, I call it love. I love only those people that somehow make it through all of my personal and cultural filters that define "lovable." My "heart goes out to" only those people who are the "right kind" of people, who act the "right way," and who treat me "right." In a sense, conditional love can be seen as a form of hatred. Conditional love says, "I will love you only if you fulfill certain conditions (and otherwise I will not love you)" — not-loving is the baseline reality of any relationship, and it temporarily becomes loving only when, and as long as, you actively meet my special conditions. Many people also project this idea of conditional love onto God, believing that they have to be or act some special way before God will love them.

The word conditional means dependent on conditions. This always implies a dualistic framework — i.e., some conditions are "right," and others are "wrong." For the Spiritual view, any framework of thought that is dualistic and conditional — any framework of thought that believes that certain qualities and attributes and circumstances make someone or something good and lovable, and others make them bad and unlovable — is focused only on the differences between the various forms (appearances), and is blind to their common Spiritual truth or essence. From the lighted clearing of Spirit, conditional love simply makes no sense — it is just as if you were to decide to love or hate a person based on the color of his eyes or the size of her shoes. From the Spiritual perspective, conditional love is not truly a form of love at all. It is only the emotional reflection of your projection of your own dualistic ideas — a projection that blinds you to the truth of Spirit, both in yourself and in the world. Because it hides the wholeness and holiness of yourself and the world, conditional love can be seen as a kind of attack — ultimately an attack on yourself, which prevents you from experiencing perfect peace, love, and joy. This way of understanding "conditional love" can also be applied to peace, joy, and goodness — i.e., "conditional peace" (a temporary and arbitrary truce in the midst of the on-going reality of struggle and war), "conditional joy" (a temporary and artificial state of happiness when circumstances just happen to be "right"), and "conditional good" (when, by special effort, someone temporarily rises above his underlying truth of selfishness).

Unconditional love is proactive rather than reactive. In this sense, love is not merely how I "happen" to feel in reaction to certain circumstances or certain people — it is a way I can choose to send forth who I am in truth, regardless of the situation. It is not dependent on, or caused by, what happens to me — it arises in the gap between stimulus and response, as my creative expression of my truth as a be-ing of Spirit. Unconditional love is my affirmation that the underlying essence of each person and each thing in my life is Spirit — that each person and thing, seen in its full truth, has an essential dimension of sacredness. In the metaphor, "everyone is Christ in disguise," unconditional love would express my proactive commitment to remain focused on the Christ within, rather than to get derailed by the disguise. In terms of our Possibility Model, we could say that unconditional love creates a lighted clearing

210 — Lighted Clearings for the Soul

within which each person's Spirituality-possibilities can reveal themselves. In this sense, unconditional love functions as a means of my awakening to my Spiritual truth. Moreover, since Spirit can be characterized as the Being of love, unconditional love is also the expression of my awakening— the living expression of my own truth as a be-ing of love. (See the glossary for summaries of conditionality and dualism.)

Healing and Forgiveness

In the context of the lighted clearing of healing, forgiveness becomes one way of healing both myself and the other. In terms of our Possibility Model, we could say that my forgiveness of another person creates a lighted clearing that allows possibilities of healing to emerge — healing for me, for him, and for us. Conversely, holding a grievance or grudge against him creates a lighted clearing that tends to exclude those possibilities of healing (note that the phrase, "*holding* a grudge *against* someone," implies an active assault — from the Spiritual perspective, an assault on his truth). Earlier in my discussion of the Spiritual view, I said that forgiveness, in this sense, is not "letting someone off the hook" or "pardoning a sin" — for that way of defining forgiveness implicitly affirms the reality of the sin as something truly bad that needs to be pardoned. From the perspective of the Spiritual view, however, his "sin" was just a mistake, made out of ignorance and fear — for if he truly perceived the Spirituality of himself and the other person, he would not have tried to attack or harm or cheat that person in any way.

Likewise, my judgment of someone as a "bad" person, rather than simply as one who is mistaken, is also a mistake. (Many people claim they are judging only the act, and not the person. But any judgment of "sin" or "wrongdoing" implies a judgment about the intention of the person committing it — a judgment that that he acted deliberately for selfish motives, and/or that he knowingly chose to harm or cheat another in some way for his own advantage.) If I judge and condemn any person, including myself, for his mistakes, then I am basically identifying him with his misunderstanding. When I hold a grievance against someone, I am implicitly denying the truth of Spirit within him — I am saying that what is most real and what most deserves my focus and attention is the filter over his light, rather than the light itself.

Since my grievance against another blinds me to some aspect of his Spirituality, I cannot be fully open to Spirit in general — I cannot be fully open to either my own essence or to the essence of all things. I can be fully open to the Spirit within any particular thing or person only when I am fully open to the Spirit in *all* things — this would mean that I can truly appreciate and love the saint or the Messiah only to the extent that I can unconditionally forgive and love the worst "sinner."

To whatever extent I judge and condemn someone as sinful, I am blind to the Spirit we share in common. Thus, my blindness prevents the full expression of Spirituality and wholeness in my life and interferes with my own health and healing. My forgiveness of another can facilitate healing in two ways. First, since as my judgment of him as a sinful person was my mistake, my forgiveness heals my perception — allows me to see him and myself more truthfully. In that sense, my forgiveness of him is a gift to myself — a gift of truth and healing. My forgiveness of him is not a matter of letting go of his sinfulness, but rather letting go of my own misperception — my forgiveness of him is first and foremost my acknowledgment of my own mistake. Second, my condemnation of him could tend to make him even more fearful and defensive. It doesn't necessarily "cause" him to be fearful and defensive — he always has the ability to respond from his own truth, from that gap between stimulus and response. But my hostile judgment of him could tend to reinforce and validate for him whatever Separative and fearful ideas he already believes. Within the context of the lighted clearing of healing, I cannot be truly healthy unless he, too, is truly healthy. Therefore, anything I do to make him feel more fearful and separate will interfere with the full expression of his wholeness — and if he is not fully healthy, then *we* cannot be fully healthy either. Thus, my forgiveness of him is a gift to both of us — and I benefit not only from my gift to myself, but also from my gift to him. The fundamental motivation behind forgiveness is not some arbitrary moral imperative — as if I am supposed to forgive others because some spiritual authority said so. From the perspective of the Spiritual view, the lighted clearing of forgiveness allows me to experience myself and the other person more truthfully (unhiddenly) — and this truthful experience allows the healing of both of our lives.

Self-Forgiveness and Self-Love

It is very important to extend my unconditional forgiveness and unconditional love to myself as well. When I judge, condemn and reject myself, I hide my own Spirituality from myself. For the Separative person, self-condemnation or guilt seems to be a kind of insurance policy, which helps guarantee that the mistake will not be repeated — he believes that his selfish inner self is raging to burst out and is barely held in check only by the sheer force of his angry and determined self-condemnation. But for the

Spiritual person, guilt and self-condemnation obscure both the truth underlying the mistake, and the specific nature of its distortion (i.e., the specific way it could teach him to more fully express his wholeness and Spirituality). For the Spiritual view, my self-forgiveness is not a matter of "letting myself off the hook," but rather the choice to see myself as truthfully as possible. Whereas self-condemnation is an obsessive focus on my untruth and limitations, self-acceptance is the affirmation of, and openness to, my truth.

For the Spiritual perspective, my guilt blinds me to who I truly am, and in doing so it obstructs my healing, obstructs the full emergence of my wholeness and Spirituality. I can see this very clearly in my own life. Like most other people in our culture, I was raised to believe that a good person nurtured his guilt. On the one hand, this sense of guilt set me apart from the "bad" person, who didn't even care that he was bad. The "good" person was also sinful, but he somehow made up for it by feeling awful, by his self-condemnation and self-hatred. On the other hand, I believed that the more guilty I felt, the less likely I was to repeat my "sins." Ironically, I discovered that the more I focused on my "imperfections," the more I tended to repeat them — in general, we tend to experience more of whatever we focus our attention on. Thus, guilt, far from insuring me against making the same mistake again, actually appeared to make a repetition more likely.

Far from helping me to become more the person I wanted to be, I found that my feelings of guilt interfered with my own Spiritual growth, my relations with others, and my perception of the world. I noticed, for instance, that the more guilty I felt, the less I was able to receive love from others. Whenever someone said something kind or supportive to me, I felt that his opinion was simply based on an illusion — the illusion that I was worthy of love. I felt that if he really knew how imperfect I was, he could not possibly love me — his love for me was only a reflection of his ignorance, and had nothing to do with who I really was. Thus, the less I loved myself, the less I could accept love from others. I was also very sensitive to what I perceived as criticism from others, because deep inside I felt that I actually deserved their condemnation and attack — in a sense, my perception of another's attack on me was only a projected reflection of my prior attack on myself. This hypersensitivity caused me to be defensive, reactive, and paranoid. One of the primary ways I tended to defend myself was by attacking others — for I believed that they were just as guilty and sinful as myself. Therefore, I tended to be very critical and judgmental of others, at least in the seeming privacy of my own mind.

Often guilt and shame can be largely subconscious. You may believe at a conscious level that you do not carry any guilt or shame from your past, and yet have a subconscious sense of guilt and shame that undermines your ability to give and receive love. Once again, the key to recognizing such subconscious thoughts is the emotional tone of your life. Guilt and shame will always be emotionally reflected as negative feelings — including negative feelings about yourself (feeling unworthy, unconfident, vulnerable; or feelings of depression or self-pity), and negative feelings about others (anger, condemnation, fear, hatred). For the Spiritual-Holistic view, negative emotions are always a sign that you are unaware of your Spiritual truth, and are a reminder to shift your focus back to your deeper truth. Ultimately, the form of your illusion does not really matter — and for the Spiritual-Holistic view, guilt is merely one form of the illusion of your unwholeness and unholiness. Whatever the form of the illusion, the solution is always the same: return to awareness of your Spiritual truth.

For me, one of the clearest examples of how guilt can distort perceptions and obstruct Spiritual growth came to light in the way my own self-judgment affected my relationship with my first daughter. Like all parents, I've made mistakes in the course of raising my children, and it seems that I made the most mistakes with my first child. Although I was perhaps no better or worse than most other parents, I felt all of my "failures" acutely. As the years went by, I agonized under an ever-growing burden of accumulated guilt — but I believed that my self-condemnation would somehow guarantee that I wouldn't repeat my mistakes. I found, however, that the more I constantly affirmed for myself that I was a bad parent and the more I kept my guilty awareness focused on this image, the less I was able to positively direct my energy and attention toward becoming a better father. Furthermore, the more guilty I felt, the more I tended to see my daughter as "damaged goods" — emotionally damaged, perhaps irreparably, by my mistakes. To the extent that I related to her as somehow damaged and deficient, I not only supported whatever feelings of inadequacy and insecurity she had, but I may have missed precious opportunities to help her realize her own beauty and truth. Thus, my guilt, which I had voluntarily assumed for the purpose of making myself a better parent, actually acted as sand in the gears, as a constant impediment to realizing my highest potential as a loving father. As I came to better understand this whole dynamic, my initial reaction was to feel guilty over the fact that I had allowed my previous sense of guilt to "ruin" so much of my life. But I realized that the underlying truth of my feeling of guilt was my love for my daughter — and the ultimate purpose of recognizing my past mistakes was so that I could be a kinder and more loving parent *now*, and could cherish, nurture, and encourage the inner truth of myself and my daughter.

It is important to note here that "letting go of guilt" does not mean simply ignoring your conscience. From the Spiritual perspective, my conscience can be thought of as the quiet voice of Spirit, which gently reminds me that I have made (or am making or am about to make) a mistake — and here, mistake is defined as any way of thinking, speaking, or acting that hides my truth as a be-ing of Spirit. The purpose of this reminder of conscience is to allow me to heal the ignorance and fear and misperception that gave rise to the mistake. Guilt in the form of prolonged self-condemnation is an extra burden that our frightened egos have added to Spirit's gentle loving reminder. For the Spiritual view, it simply makes no sense to blame yourself for what you didn't see in the dark. Self-forgiveness is the decision to let go of your condemnation of your mistakes, so that you can begin to learn from your limitations in the wondrous process of outgrowing them.

Unconditional self-love is the affirmation of the truth of your Spirit — the truth of the perfect longing underlying your every mistake. Since the Separative view identifies the self as a separate ego, it interprets self-love as a form of egocentricity. For the Separative person, self-love means focusing my attention on a separate "special" me, which is exclusive of others — loving myself more than, or even instead of, everyone else. For the Spiritual view, however, self-love means to honor my deeper Spiritual nature, which is the truth of everything I do — honoring my capacity for unconditional love, my perfect longing for joy and peace. It is not glorifying myself in my separate specialness as if I am somehow better than others, but rather appreciating my uniqueness as one expression of the Spirit in all things. Thus, for the Spiritual view, loving my deepest and truest self is a way that I affirm and celebrate my connection with all things, my wholeness. Loving my deepest and truest self involves loving and accepting it in all of its phases of development, in all of its current "imperfect" modes of expression. By acknowledging and affirming the perfect truth of my imperfections, I encourage and nurture a more perfect expression of my Spirituality — this does not mean passivity in the face of my mistakes, but rather an on-going commitment to continually expand my capacity for unconditional love.

❖ The Wholeness of Nature

As we saw earlier, for the Technological view, everything non-human exists as mere "stuff" to be used by man. From this perspective, non-human Nature, in and of itself, has no intrinsic value. Humans, as the users and value givers, stand above or outside of the rest of Nature. For the Spiritual view, on the other hand, everything is a face of Spirit, an expression of the sacred living Presence of the world. "Everything" includes both human and non-human, both living (as defined by biology) and non-living. Each being and each thing is a unique face of Spirit, a unique voice of the sacred, through which the Mystery can offer wisdom and guidance. From this perspective, humankind is not above the rest of Nature — it is one strand in the great web of life, one spoke on the great Medicine Wheel of Nature.

When we say "everything is a face of Spirit," "everything" includes the inventions and products of science and technology, as well as the things and beings of Nature. Nevertheless, a Spiritual person may turn to the natural world as a relatively clearer and more translucent expression of the sacred living Presence of the world. Most of our man-made inventions have arisen out of the framework of Technology — as such, they tend to reflect a worldview of domination and control. Far from showing any reverence for the Spirituality of the natural world, many of the things of modern civilization are actually destructive to the natural world and the ecological balance. Such things are therefore symbolic of the implicit denial of the inherent value and holiness of all things. The natural world, on the other hand, is a relatively more unhidden expression of Spirit, and thus a Spiritual person will often turn to the things and creatures of Nature to discover and deepen his experience of his own Spiritual identity and truth. All of this is not meant to be misunderstood as a blanket rejection of modern inventions, nor an appeal to return to more "primitive" conditions. The real question is how we can use our technological inventions mindfully and carefully, and with reverence for the Spirituality of all things. For the Spiritual view, the problem is not so much in the inventions which have grown out of the attitude of Technology, as in the attitude itself — and the Spiritual antidote for this Technological attitude is to re-discover or remember the sacredness of all things.

From the Spiritual perspective, *everything* that exists is a face of Spirit, and thus has an intrinsic dimension of Mystery — in other words, everything offers us opportunities for Spiritual discovery. But we tend to be unaware of the dimension of Mystery in man-made things — we tend to believe that we fully understand our technological inventions and

216 — Lighted Clearings for the Soul

constructions, since we ourselves designed and built them. Since we do not pretend to ourselves to fully understand the natural world, however, Nature still holds a dimension of Mystery for us — and this openness to the unknown creates a lighted clearing that can allow us to experience possibilities outside the narrow horizon of our rational understanding and our past experiences. This element of Mystery is what is meant when we refer to the natural world as "the wild" or "the wilder-ness." When we encounter the natural world, we tend to have relatively fewer presuppositions filtering out the Spirituality-possibilities — the Spirituality-possibilities of both the world "out there" and ourselves "in here." The wilderness outside of me reflects and calls forth the wilderness within me — it helps me to discover and appreciate both the limits of my understanding, and the sacred Mystery that lies beyond.

For many indigenous peoples, Nature is the clearest and deepest expression of Spirit, and is the primary source of the Spiritual archetypes of their religions. The things of Nature are often spoken of as "people" — thus, in addition to the human people (the two-legged people), there are, for instance, the four-legged people, the winged people, the finned people, the creepy-crawler people (snakes, bugs, etc.), the plant people, the stone people, and so forth. The word "people" indicates the presence of living Spirit, and thus points to a deep kinship between humans and other beings. This idea of kinship is further emphasized by using family metaphors — Mother Earth, Father Sky, Grandfather Sun and Grandmother Moon, Grandfather Fire, Brother Tree, and Sister Eagle. Speaking of Nature in terms of our family invites us to approach all creatures with reverence, respect, and love. For the Spiritual perspective, such an attitude of reverence not only opens us up to a truer and deeper experience of the world, but also allows us to tap into wondrous sources of non-human power, guidance and wisdom. But to speak of these ideas as "metaphors" does not mean that they are merely clever and colorful literary devices that fall short of direct description. In the context of the Possibility Model, we cannot accurately describe "how things really are." At best, we can use words to create a lighted clearing of experiential discovery. From this perspective, an explicit metaphor can be more truthful than an idea which claims to describe reality — precisely because the metaphor does not pretend to be a substitute for direct experience, it implicitly turns us back into our own openness and invites us to explore new dimensions of our experience. In our example, the underlying intent of the family metaphors in talking about Nature is to open us to a deeper truth, a deeper unhiddenness within which we can discover and experience our Spiritual kinship with all things. (I do want to emphasize here that the Spiritual view, as I am defining it, does not imply some particular form of Nature worship, nor is it a Nature religion. It simply regards the natural world as one especially clear expression of Spirit, which can provide an important way to remember our deeper truth.)

The Technological person will tend to think of this whole approach to Nature as romantic nonsense, as a pleasant imaginative fiction. He considers animals to be merely complicated machines, and he explains their actions in terms of the basic biological drives of hunger, thirst, sex, etc. Those actions that he cannot understand or explain are labeled as "instinct" — a word which means that some obscure mechanical principle is driving the dumb animal to do certain things, and man doesn't yet have a rational explanation for how it works. Plants are merely complicated photosynthesis machines. Things like rocks are even further down the scale — mere collections of dead, mindless atoms, bound together by electromagnetic forces. The Earth itself is just a dead ball of dirt and water hurtling through space, and the sun is just a nuclear fusion machine in which lifeless atoms go through meaningless chemical reactions to create heat and light. For the Technological view, the idea that humans could communicate at all with these things of Nature, let alone actually learn from them, is simply uneducated foolishness — whether that of primitive man or of a modern New Age idealist. Man may enjoy these things for his own purposes, and may even choose to call them "beautiful" — but in and of itself, the natural universe has no intrinsic value or meaning. For the Technological view, the physical universe, with all of its beauty and marvelous mathematical complexity, can be a very bleak and lonely place to live.

For the Spiritual view, this blanket denial of the Presence and sacredness of the non-human world is itself superstition and pretense. Even though both views might be considered "equally valid" according to the criteria of objective experience and logical proof, there is a radical difference between them in terms of the quality of life they each engender. The lighted clearing of healing raises important questions and issues for our modern Technological culture. What if there is more to Nature than mindless atoms and soul-less machines? What do we lose by actively denying and screening out other possibilities of experience? Might we be depriving ourselves of invaluable learning and healing possibilities of companionship, guidance, and love?

For the Holistic view, one's individual health is interdependent with the health of the greater whole of which he is a part. In the present context, this would mean that caring for the ecological balance of Nature was an intrinsic part of one's personal health care. From this perspective, my active participation in the greater whole of Nature is not a noble act of self-sacrifice, but an intrinsic part of my own Self-realization and Self-healing — I truly become myself only in realizing the truth of my participation in a greater whole. The greater truth of Nature *is* my greater truth. In terms of our model of healing, the lighted clearing formed by the unity of the human and the non-human provides an even greater opening for the self-revelation of the wholeness and Spirituality of the world.

Since the Technological person sees the things of the natural world only as objects to be used, he tends to feel alienated or cut off from Nature — a recurrent theme in our modern culture is how we can "reconnect" or "bridge the gap" between ourselves and Nature. But for the Spiritual view, there is no *real* gap or separation to overcome. To reconnect with Nature means simply to *remember* and realize the connectedness and Spiritual identity that *already* exist. Dis-covering or un-covering the connectedness that *already* exists is fundamentally a matter of letting go of the *illusory* belief in separateness and alienation that is hiding the truth of wholeness from our awareness. The indigenous way of relating to Nature as our Spiritual family is one possible way to let go of that illusion of separation and alienation.

In modern times, we hear a great deal said about dysfunctional families. For the indigenous view of Nature, however, everyone has a very real and very functional Spiritual family, regardless of (their interpreted memories of) their personal biological family. From this perspective, one primary way to heal the pain of one's personal family history is to become reacquainted with the loving extended family of Nature — Mother Earth, Father Sky, and all of our various brothers and sisters of the natural world. Like a plant, if we lose our connection to Earth and Sky, we cannot bloom — we cannot realize and celebrate our full potential. In truth, of course, we can never really lose our connection to Earth and Sky — we simply lose sight of it temporarily, blinded by our beliefs in our superiority, in our separateness and alienation. Meanwhile, the greater Spiritual family of Nature patiently waits to welcome us back, like its returning (or awakening) prodigal sons and daughters.

CHAPTER 14

CHOOSING TO TRUST

❖ Trust

In the last two chapters, we have explored two kinds of re-lighting approaches. The first approach was to shift my attention to the positive elements that are already present in my life, but which I have been ignoring because of my preoccupation with the negative elements. This enabled me to have a truer or more unhidden experience of my whole situation. Sometimes this more complete view is enough to change the emotional tone of my life and to allow me to more fully live my purpose and realize my truth. In other situations, this truer experience of my life can serve as the starting point and foundation for further re-lighting. In the last chapter, we explored the lighted clearing of healing. Within this clearing, my negative emotions were understood as signaling the emergence of a greater truth — the birth pains of a greater wholeness and Spirituality in my life. From the Spiritual perspective, the "pain" of this birth is not an intrinsic quality of wholeness and Spirituality, but is merely a reflection of my own frightened resistance to awakening. Thinking of my experiences of struggle and suffering in this way highlights intrinsic positive possibilities of my seemingly negative situation. It also enables me to see my negative emotions as clues and stepping-stones to a deeper and more fulfilling experience.

This whole process of re-lighting is founded on trust — the trust that every situation contains positive and life-enhancing possibilities. Moreover, from the Spiritual-Holistic perspective, only these positive possibilities are truly valid. The seemingly negative possibilities you experience are ultimately only the reflection (or projection) of your denial of the truth of wholeness and Spirituality. But when you are in the midst of experiencing those negative possibilities as the whole truth, the belief or trust that there are "equally valid" positive possibilities of experience can be a necessary first step in opening yourself to deeper Spiritual awareness.

One way to discover the positive possibilities of any situation is "the lighted clearing of trust." It is created by your choice to believe that the universe is basically purposeful and benevolent. In this context, Spirit is not just a passive ethereal substance but is rather an active, living Presence — it is intelligent and intentional, and acts through the world for the benefit of all things. And as I have defined it, "Spirit" is not a separate supernatural being that stands apart from everything else and somehow controls and directs it for everyone's benefit — rather it is a dimension of purposefulness and benevolence *intrinsic* to reality itself.

The analogy of dreaming is one good way to begin to understand the lighted clearing of trust. I believe that many of our nightly dreams are somehow created and orchestrated by a deeper part of ourselves, in order to symbolically communicate to us what we need for our growth and healing — I choose to believe this theory (theoros) because it creates a lighted clearing that allows me to discover meaningful healing possibilities in my dreams. Every dream event and every dream character are created to somehow teach me, or to bring me a message from my deeper Self. The response of my dreamed-self (the "me" that is in the dream) to the dreamed world can play a co-creative role in the unfolding and the meaning of the dream. For instance, sometimes in the midst of a dream I become aware that I am dreaming — i.e., my dream shifts from a non-lucid (un-self-aware) to a lucid (self-aware) dream. When I am having a non-lucid dream, I tend to get caught up in all of the ups and downs of my dreamed character — some events seem good and make me happy, while others seem bad or tragic and make me unhappy; I conditionally love those people who cooperate with my agenda, and I hold grudges against those who do not. But when I become aware that I am dreaming, my whole perspective changes. In a lucid dream, I interpret all of the events in the dream as being created and orchestrated by my deeper Self, in order to guide me in my soul's growth. From this perspective, I am no longer lost in the emotional roller coaster of my dreamed ego, desperately chasing after some things, and desperately running away from and trying to avoid others. What might have previously seemed bad to my dreamed ego is now seen as a lesson or a message, an opportunity to find deeper resources in myself for courage or love. Because of my shift of awareness, I am able to more fully receive the gifts offered by my dream.

In this analogy, the dreaming consciousness would be analogous to Spirit in the waking world — the wise and benevolent Presence that creates, sustains, animates, and guides all that is. The dreamed self would correspond to the ego — when I am unaware of my truth as a be-ing of Spirit, I believe that I am a separate, independent ego in the midst of other independent egos, all competing and battling for our "share of the pie." This sleepwalking lostness in my ego-identity would be analogous to having a non-lucid dream. Being aware of the truth of all things as be-ings of Spirit — being Spiritually awakened — would correspond to having a lucid dream. The lighted clearing of trust we are exploring here — choosing to see all of the people and things and events of my life as ultimately purposeful and benevolent — involves a shift of perspective from the forms and appearances of my experience to their underlying Spiritual source and essence.

"Mere Coincidences"

Those who are skeptical about the idea of "the purposefulness and benevolence of Spirit," may contend that everything that happens is merely random — just one random event causing another in a meaningless linear sequence. From that perspective, any seemingly significant connections are dismissed as mere coincidences. But it is important for us to note here that terms like "random" and "mere coincidence" are intrinsically deceptive. They seem to be definite descriptive terms: to call something a "random" event or a "mere coincidence" implies that we know that it has no underlying purpose and no meaningful connection to other events. But that is not the sort of thing that we could actually know — at best, we could know that we don't yet know of any purpose or connection. Thus, terms like "random" and "mere coincidence" hide our not knowing under the pretense of knowing. I am reminded here of a joke I heard about a group of atheists who wanted to produce a TV Christmas special entitled "Coincidence on 34th Street." Like "coincidence," the idea of "miracle" also points toward the limits of human knowledge. But "miracle" connotes that there is something beyond what we understand, and implicitly acknowledges those limits. "Coincidence," however, implies that we completely understand the situation.

The belief that "everything is random" is just as much of a leap of faith as a belief in underlying purpose. A random approach to the world will tend to regard any belief in the purposefulness of the world as a "mere superstition." But like mere coincidence, mere superstition also pretends to know something that cannot be known. To call something a "mere superstition" implies that we know there is no validity to it — that, for instance, the so-called "omen" was not really an omen at all, but merely a random unrelated event that happened by mere coincidence. But since there is no way to perceive or prove the absence of significance, to call something random or mere coincidence is just as superstitious as to call it an omen or a sign. As I mentioned earlier, many indigenous peoples have claimed that our "civilized" view of the world as random and meaningless is merely our modern superstition — and one that blinds us to the deeper wholeness and sacredness of the world around us. We want to be especially careful of ideas like mere coincidence and mere superstition, which pretend to know. In hiding our ignorance, such ideas conceal the belief choices we are already making, and prevent us from realizing that we have any choice at all. Critics of the Spiritual view might claim that a faith in the essential goodness of the universe blinds us to the "real" meaninglessness of life. But it could be equally argued that a belief in the meaninglessness of life can blind us to any possible experience of its intrinsic significance and benevolence. Every view has its price tag. Again, the real question here is, what view truly serves *you*?

Evaluating "Good" and "Bad"

A story from the Chinese Taoist tradition illustrates the faith involved in any evaluation of our life events as either good or bad. There was a farmer whose prize stallion jumped the fence one night and ran away into the hills. The farmer's friends came to him the next day and said, "We're so sorry for you. That had to be the unluckiest night of your life when your horse ran away." The farmer simply replied, "We'll see." A couple of weeks later, the stallion returned from the hills, bringing with him an entire herd of wild mares. The farmer now had more horses than he had ever dreamed he would. His friends came to him and said, "We're so happy for you. That had to be the luckiest night of your life when your horse ran away." Again the farmer replied, "We'll see." In the next several weeks, the farmer's son was very busy, training all of the new horses. But one especially feisty mare threw him to the ground, breaking his leg. The farmer's friends came around again and said, "We're so sorry for you. That had to be one of the unluckiest nights of your life, when your horse ran away." The farmer replied, "We'll see." A week later, the emperor's soldiers came to the farm. They were conscripting every young man in the province for a war against a neighboring state. The farmer's son could not go because of his broken leg. It turned out to be a brutal and devastating war, and nearly all of the emperor's soldiers were killed. Again the farmer's friends came around, saying "We're so happy for you. That had to be one of the luckiest nights of your life when your horse ran away." And again the farmer replied, "We'll see."

What this story illustrates is that whether something is good or bad is not immediately apparent. To fully evaluate any event, we would need to see all of its consequences, to see how it fits into the whole of our lives. We might also want to know how it affects the lives of our families and friends. Ultimately, we would even want to know how it affects our community, our nation, and our world. But we can't know all of these global and future consequences with any certainty. We don't even know what will happen in the next few minutes of our own lives, let alone the more distant future of ourselves and others. Thus, it would seem that the only way we could possibly evaluate something as good or bad is to *presume* that we know its short-term and long-term effects — in other words, any such evaluation involves an element of belief and faith. In the context of re-lighting, this is an important reminder that our initial evaluation of something as "bad" is ultimately just as much of a leap of faith as our attempt to see it in a more positive light.

The lighted clearing of trust involves more than just the belief that there is some underlying purpose or meaning to the events in my life. It explicitly specifies that this underlying purpose is *good* — that the events of my life happen in the best interests of me and everyone else. From this perspective I would approach each event with the question, "How can this contribute to my growth, my awakening, my healing?" The very asking of such a question creates a lighted clearing within which I can discover possible answers. A belief in randomness, on the other hand, presupposes from the outset that there is no overall purpose to the events in my life. It is not, as it often pretends, a merely neutral position — it actively *denies* that there is any greater purposefulness to events. Thus it tends to preclude any possible discovery of a deeper purpose or good — both because I am not looking for any deeper purpose, and because I will discount any possible indication of such a purpose as "mere coincidence." The difference between the benevolent and the random views is especially important when seemingly adverse events happen in our lives. A random approach will tend to take the event at face value — and in labeling the event as "bad" or "tragic," it locks us into a passive, victim mentality. The best we can do is to cope with the frequent garbage and suffering that randomly come our way. From the lighted clearing of trust, however, we would ask such questions as, "How can this seemingly awful event be seen as a lesson in disguise? What is or could be its underlying meaning or purpose? How can it contribute to my growth? How can I see it as a gift and an opportunity?" Asking these questions opens up the horizon of possible discovery.

❖ Opportunities for Healing

Several years ago, I attended a powerful and transformative workshop offered by the Option Institute, founded by Barry Neil Kaufman. We learned how our belief choices and interpretations determine our feelings — in particular, determine our happiness or unhappiness.[24] In one exercise, each participant sat down with a partner and told her about something that he had done in the recent past that he felt badly about. I recounted a painful incident that had happened with my daughter about a week before. I had been feeling generally stressed and irritable for quite a few days, and that particular day had been especially difficult for me. With all of the stress I was experiencing in my life, I ended up getting very upset over some trivial thing my daughter did, and began to yell at her about it. Right away I knew in my heart that I wasn't really acting the way I wanted to; I wasn't really living my truth. But instead of stopping, I escalated. I went to great lengths telling her why she was wrong, getting louder and more assertive. It was almost as if my inner sense that I was acting inauthentically made me fight more desperately to vindicate myself and to prove that I was right. Soon afterwards I apologized to my daughter, but days later I still carried some painful guilt inside. As I told this story to my partner, I felt ashamed, embarrassed, and very petty. I cried for my daughter's pain and for my own failing as a parent. I love my children so very much, and yet I felt this was just one more example of how my own limitations and mistakes were inflicting emotional scars that I feared might permanently cripple my children. As I explored and felt the pain of this one past event, I also felt the weight and pain of all of my other past mistakes as a parent. When I finished my story, my present felt dark and heavy, and my future and my daughter's future seemed very bleak.

Then the workshop leader had us all change partners. With our new partner, we were to relate the same incident, but with a different perspective. We were to tell our new partner about the "wonderful opportunity" that had happened to us — an event which may have seemed very challenging at the time, but which was really an exciting opportunity, filled with the bright promise of self-discovery, growth, and joy. We were to retell the story with as much enthusiasm and happiness as possible, the story of this wondrous blessing and gift in our lives. This was a difficult transition for me — to wipe away my tears, and somehow present this dark moment of shame as a blessing and an opportunity. The difficulty, of course, stemmed from my conviction that my previous version of this story had been the whole truth — a completely accurate description of what had "really" happened, of "what the photo really looked like." But in the spirit of the workshop, I threw myself into this exercise with all of the enthusiasm of an actor giving an Oscar-winning performance (although what started off as mere pretending ultimately created an openness that allowed me to actually experience a new level of truth).

I told my partner of this challenging but wonderful event that had happened in my life. I told him of how I had only been dimly aware of how much stress and tension were building up beneath the surface, until I finally exploded. The outburst had given me the opportunity to discover the tension and unhappiness, and to make some important changes. It had also helped me to rediscover how much I really loved my daughter and how very unimportant were those occasional teenage mistakes she made (or at least what I interpreted as mistakes). That event also gave me an opportunity to talk with her about her own reactions to my outburst — how she tended to feel frightened and constrained by someone else's display of anger. I could point out to her that my outburst had little or nothing to do with her — that it was simply me dealing with my internal stress (and not dealing with it very well at that). It did not reflect on her worth, nor was it a true reflection of how I felt about her. We could also talk about some of the beliefs that underlie anger — and this could be important for both of us, since we both had a tendency to get angry when things didn't go our way. And we could reaffirm the deeper truth of our love for each other. The event was an opportunity to heal my own life, and to learn and grow together with my daughter.

This is not to say that the angry outburst itself was wonderful. But once it had *already* happened, I had a choice of seeing it merely as a failure and a wrong on my part, or as an opportunity to respond with forgiveness and love. The "opportunity" involved is always an *opportunity to respond.* In his book, *Still Here*, Ram Dass says (p. 5), "Healing is not the same as curing, after all; healing does not mean going back to the way things were before, but rather allowing *what is now* to move us closer to God."

By the time I am aware of a situation, it is *already* happening or has *already* happened. My choice at that point is how I will respond to it — how I will choose to see it (what light I will send forth from myself) and what I will choose to do about it. Basically, I have two choices here. I can choose to see the situation as "bad," and can use this judgment as a reason to attack — either attack myself in the form of shame and guilt, and/or attack another in the form of condemnation, anger, or violence. Or I can choose to let go of my self-righteous judgment of the badness or wrongness of the situation, and ask how I can respond in a way that is healing to myself and everyone involved. For the Spiritual perspective, opportunity means the *opportunity to heal* — the opportunity to respond in a way that allows the underlying truth of Spiritual wholeness to come to light. "Wonderful," in this context, refers to the healing, and not to the situation that elicits my response. The very fact that there is a need to respond in a healing way implies that I initially perceived the situation as un-wonderful and un-Spiritual.

It might seem that seeing my angry outburst at my daughter as a wonderful opportunity could be misused as an excuse to heedlessly repeat the same mistake over and over, thus giving myself more and more wonderful opportunities. But in fact, as long as I simply carried the event inside myself as a painful source of guilt, I was much more likely to make the same mistake again — to the extent that I focused on myself as a bad parent, and on my daughter as a "damaged" child, I tended to overlook our deeper Spiritual truth and wholeness. By choosing to see my mistake as an opportunity to heal, however, I opened myself to a different way of experiencing myself and my daughter — a new lighted clearing of experience, within which those kinds of mistakes simply did not exist. I might still occasionally lapse back into the lighted clearing of defensive anger — but since I had actually *experienced* an alternative that was more true to my own heart, I was less likely to simply get lost in my reactivity.

From the perspective of the lighted clearing of trust, everything that happens in our lives is a purposeful and benevolent expression of Spirit. Seeing every event or situation as an opportunity for healing is one way we can open ourselves to discover and experience this Spiritual character of reality. As I said earlier, given our limited knowledge and our limited perspective, it is equally a leap of faith to judge a situation as either a blessing or a curse, as either wonderful or tragic, as either good luck or bad luck. There is no way we can prove whether reinterpreting a situation as a wonderful opportunity for healing is more correct than seeing it as tragic and bad. But asking, "What is the healing opportunity in this situation?" can open me to a horizon of possible experience I might otherwise be unaware of.

"Past," "Present," and "Future" Healing Opportunities

This healing-opportunity approach can be used to re-light the events of the past. From the lighted clearing of trust, you can choose to look at your whole collection of memories at any given time — including both your personal memories and our collectively shared historical memories — as a kind of treasure chest which has been given to you in the present to help you discover your own truth, your own deepest capacity for love and joy. You can choose to believe that Spirit, in its wisdom and goodness, has provided you at every moment with the perfect past for your present awakening. For instance, instead of seeing your present in light of the apparently limiting events of your past — "I am who I am now.... *because* I had a 'dysfunctional' family, or *because* I was an alcoholic, or *because* I made 'wrong' choices as a youth" — you could choose to see your past in the perspective of your present process of Self-realization; choose to see the events of your past as opportunities to broaden and deepen your present horizon of possibility and vision. From the perspective of the lighted clearing of trust, each event contains potential seeds of healing and self-awareness that can not only make your own life richer, deeper, and more joyful, but can also help you to contribute to the healing of others. The joyful potential may seem more difficult to discern in some events than in others — especially when it is wrapped in layers of pain. Yet to choose to believe that the seeds of healing and growth exist in *every* event can open us up to deeper possibilities of our past. You can access these possibilities by entering into the lighted clearing created by asking yourself such questions as, "What is or could be Spirit's (or my deeper Self's) purpose for choosing this particular past and these particular memories? How can these past events enrich my life now and enable me to contribute to others?" Earlier we said that "your wound is the womb of your gift" — what transforms the wound into a womb is the choice to see it as an opportunity for growth, healing, and service.

Seeing every situation as an opportunity can also be applied to the present. This can include all of those seemingly negative situations in our lives, such as an unexpected flat tire, a financial crisis, a traffic jam, a sickness, a divorce, a job loss, or the death of a loved one. Seeing a situation as an opportunity for healing opens me up to possibilities of positive response. So long as I see a situation simply as a stroke of bad luck, I am basically limited to variations of anger or self-pity — the lighted clearing of victimhood limits my possibilities to fight or flight. But when I choose to affirm a situation as an opportunity, I am open to experience those possibilities that could help me to learn and grow, to fulfill my purpose and realize my truth.

Within the lighted clearing of trust, every person, thing, event and situation in our lives is a potential opportunity to experience the blessings of Spirit. From this perspective, our belief in, and openness to, grace (the freely given benevolence of Spirit) is what allows it to shine through every minute of our lives, whereas our doubt and distrust tend to block our awareness of its holy light. Actually *living* the Spiritual view is the only way to discover its possible truthfulness for ourselves. The lighted clearing of trust is more than merely a faith that I will "sometime in the future" see the purpose and goal of what is happening now — from the Spiritual perspective, it is a shift of perception that can allow me to see the grace that is *already* present in every detail of my life *now*.

This technique of reinterpretation can also be applied to the future — that is, to the future as it exists for me now. I once saw a bumper sticker that said, "Worry is a form of atheism." The various negative feelings we have about the future, such as worry, anxiety, and dread, are all forms of distrust. They are based on the belief that the world is random or even hostile, and that we can realistically expect bad things to happen to us. The Spiritual view, however, asserts that everything that happens is informed and guided by the wise and benevolent power that lives in and through all things. As we have seen, it is equally a leap of faith to anticipate the future as either a blessing or a threat. Affirming that my future is a potential opportunity does not mean passive acceptance of whatever may happen. To the contrary, it orients me to actively look for every possibility of growth and healing for myself and others. The prospect of a job loss next year, for instance, could be seen as an opportunity to explore new possibilities of livelihood and Selfhood. The prospect of the destruction of the ozone layer could be seen as an opportunity to learn our role in a true ecology, and actively work together toward healing our planet.

"Mistakes" and "Imperfections" as Opportunities

Earlier, we explored how looking for the underlying fear and the underlying longing of a seeming "imperfection" in myself could help me discover its deeper Spiritual potential — its underlying opportunity for growth and healing. This same approach can also help me to discover the hidden Spiritual possibilities of seemingly "unspiritual" persons or events in my life. In my earlier example, I said that underlying my defensive angry reaction to my wife's seemingly harsh words was my own insecurity and fear of abandonment. And underlying this fear was my true longing to live a loving relationship with my wife. Discovering the fear and longing underlying my anger opened me to possibilities of healing my reactivity, so that I could more fully live and express my deeper truth. Furthermore, in that situation I also chose to see my wife's angry outburst (or what I interpreted as her angry outburst) from the lighted clearing of its underlying fear and its underlying longing. Insofar as I discovered her own underlying fear and underlying longing, I was better able to help her heal her own wounds and more fully express her own truth. In other words, choosing to see the whole event as an opportunity rather than simply as a lousy thing that happened "to" me, enabled me to discover and realize deeper possibilities for healing my life, her life, and our life together.

From the lighted clearing of trust, I can look at my own and others' "mistakes" and "imperfections" as opportunities — opportunities to learn, to grow, to love, to serve, to heal. With respect to my own mistakes, the very fact that I recognize my mistake as a "mistake" implies that I have somehow already grown beyond it — that I now have a deeper or broader perspective that enables me to see that what I had previously done or said does not truly serve my best interests. My ability to recognize my mistakes is the foundation of my ability to grow beyond them. Thus, whenever I recognize that I've made a mistake, I have a choice — I can choose either to focus on guilt and self-condemnation, or to see the mistake as an opportunity to more fully realize my implicit deeper understanding. I can also choose to respond to (what I perceive as) the mistakes of others from the lighted clearing of trust — I can choose to see their mistakes as opportunities for me to extend unconditional forgiveness and unconditional love. As I respond to another from the lighted clearing of trust and unconditional love, it can enable him to be less judgmental and more accepting of himself — my trust of the other can help him to trust himself.

According to the Spiritual view, everything that happens in my life becomes sanctified when I choose to see it as a gift and a lesson of Spirit — "sanctified" not because it itself changes, but rather because I become more aware of its Spiritual truth. "Everything" includes all of the things and people and events in the "outer" world, as well as everything I think and feel "inside" myself. Each moment I am able to choose what these things *mean* to me and what role they play in my life. The lighted clearing I create with my focus and my beliefs enables me to see each thing (person, event, situation, feeling, etc.) as either an opportunity or an enemy, as either a stepping stone or a stumbling block to my peace of mind — I can choose to see each one in the light of Spirit or in the shadow of fear. The true value of the Spiritual view is that it constantly reminds me that, regardless of what I or others have done or said or thought or felt, and regardless of what has happened or is happening, I can *always* re-choose forgiveness, love, trust, peace, and joy. For the Spiritual view, all of reality, in its deepest truth, is Spirit's gift of love freely offered to us in each moment in the most perfect form — and my choices determine how much of this on-going blessing I allow myself to experience.

❖ Guidance and Synchronicity

An intrinsic part of the lighted clearing of trust is the belief that guidance is always available — the belief that everything that happens is purposeful and meaningful, and that Spirit always provides us with clues and directions to help us find our way. From this perspective, there is a principle operating in the world that is at least as important as the principle of causality — what Carl Jung called the principle of "synchronicity." His theory of synchronicity maintains that all of the elements of any given situation are meaningfully connected. Thus, two events in a given situation, which may not have any causal connection with one another, can still be related or connected, insofar as they both will reflect the meaning of the situation. It is as if the meaning or the final purpose of a situation acts as an invisible force, orchestrating and organizing everything that happens, so that all of the events move toward the same end. Synchronicity can be understood as *meaningful coincidence*, as opposed to "mere or meaningless coincidence," which implies that there is no relation between the two events.

Many rituals of asking for guidance or seeking deeper insight are grounded in a belief in synchronicity. For instance, a person who asks God a question and then opens the Bible at random for his answer, assumes that the passage he finds will be related to the question he asked — in this case, God is assumed to be the invisible agent coordinating all of the events toward a meaningful end. One ancient Chinese ritual for consulting the *I Ching* involves tossing three coins a total of six times — and then the various combinations of heads and tails in each toss direct the questioner to a certain passage in the book. According to the principle of synchronicity, the results of these seemingly random coin tosses will reflect the intention of the question, and will lead one to just the answer he needs. From a strictly causal perspective, this would all be sheer nonsense, since there is no demonstrable causal connection between the question and the results of the coin tosses — and thus the answer you would arrive at through this ritual would be completely random, and any relevance to the question you asked would be "mere coincidence."

One explanation for this seeming guidance is that the focus of my own question serves as an interpretive filter, so that I am more aware of any possible connections. Someone who is skeptical about the *I Ching* ritual, for instance, might say that all of the readings in the book are very general and vague, and serve as a kind of poetic Rorschach ink blot that we can interpret any way we choose. This position is another variation of the random view, for it still maintains that the events leading to a certain passage are essentially random, even though we may be able to interpret the answer in a way that is helpful to us. For the lighted clearing of trust, however, the universe itself is purposeful and benevolent, and lovingly offers guidance and support, although it is up to us to receive and understand this help. The central issue here is whether I choose to believe that my ego is essentially on its own in a random universe, or that there is some source of available wisdom, guidance, and support that is beyond my rational calculation.

The random view will argue that there is no way to perceive through the five senses or to logically prove the principle of synchronicity — there is no way to perceive or prove that an overall meaning or an intrinsic purposefulness is orchestrating and guiding the seemingly disconnected events of a situation. But we could equally argue that there is also no way to perceive or prove the absence of any underlying significance or purpose, and thus no way to disprove the principle of synchronicity. Calling something a "mere coincidence" is just as much of a leap of faith as calling it a "meaningful coincidence." For that matter, there is no way to perceive or prove the principle of causality either. Philosophers from Berkeley and Hume through Kant pointed out that we cannot perceive a causal connection between events — we may perceive a consistent linear sequence of events, but we cannot perceive or prove they are *necessarily* connected.

There are many possible variations of the lighted clearing of trust, depending on how we define the ultimate source of the goodness and purposefulness of the events of our lives. One version claims that my deeper Self or higher Self benevolently orchestrates my life down to the finest details. Another version claims that there is a higher being outside of myself — for instance, God, Allah, Jehovah, etc. — who directs all the events in my life for the highest good of everyone involved. Still another version defines this outside source in terms of various beings or forces, such as angels, devas, or power animals — which are often thought of as intermediaries or agents of a higher spiritual power. In terms of Spirit as I have defined it, the purposefulness and benevolence is an *intrinsic* dimension of the nature of reality itself — reality itself, as an expression of Spirit, inherently unfolds toward the benefit of all things. But regardless of how we might define this source, the common theme in these variations is that there is some guiding force "behind" or "above" or acting "through" all things — a force which is wise and good, and which transcends the limited perspective of our conscious rational egos. Moreover, this wise and benevolent source is always offering guidance and direction and insight. This is the promise of virtually every religious tradition — seek and ye shall find, knock and the door will be opened. There are many ways to seek such guidance, from the sacred simplicity of prayer, to listening to my intuition, to observation of the omens and signs of the natural world, to shamanic journeys into other dimensions of reality, to more elaborate rituals such as the *I Ching* or the Tarot or the Sacred Path Cards. Each approach has its own language, its own ritual, its own form of receptivity, and its own way to interpret the answers. But regardless of the particular rituals and interpretations, these various approaches share the common vision that there is something beyond all of my "figuring out" — something that can and does offer me guidance, insight, and support. From the perspective of the lighted clearing of trust, possibilities of support, guidance, and love are being offered in every moment of our lives, whether we happen to be consciously asking a specific question or not — they are available if we can but receive and understand them.

Ultimately, you must discover your own unique ways of asking for, receiving, and interpreting the guidance of the sacred Mystery — your own rituals that allow you to be open to Spirit's grace-ful promptings. There is no right or wrong way to do this — you have to follow the guidance of your own heart, and the sincerity of your intent may well be more important than the specifics of your ritual. The process of asking a question of Spirit is always a dynamic balance of concentration and openness. On the one hand, you want to formulate your question or request for guidance as specifically as possible. The very process of making your question as specific as possible helps you to focus clearly on what you truly desire, and thus better defines the lighted clearing of possible answers you can discover. Also, the more specific your question is, the more specifically you can interpret the answer you receive. On the other hand, however, once you have formulated your request, you want to remain as open as possible to receiving your answer in whatever form it may arrive. Sometimes, the answer may come in an unexpected way — something you "happen to" observe in the natural world, something you "accidentally" overhear in the seemingly casual comments of a stranger, or a passage you read in a book opened "at random."

From the Spiritual perspective, our questions and our requests for guidance are *always* answered *because* Spirit is benevolent and responsive, although the answer may sometimes be at odds with our egos' hopes and desires. It is up to us to create and discover our own ways of receiving and interpreting this guidance. In so-called "primitive" cultures, this often involves a complex system of beliefs about omens and portents and signs — for instance, a crow might be a reminder to remain open to the Mystery; a deer might signal a message of love; and the unexpected appearance of an owl might be a portent of death. From the perspective of these indigenous traditions, the beliefs about what various things and events mean are not just arbitrarily made up — they grow out of a deep communication with the beings and forces of Nature. The meaning of each thing is not invented, but discovered. Our modern culture tends to dismiss these kinds of beliefs as mere superstitions, since they cannot be "objectively" proved — they cannot be proved outside of the context of belief in which they occur. For the Spiritual view, however, such beliefs function as personal and collective agreements with Spirit that certain beings and events have a certain meaning — a personal and collective symbolic language that the living Presence of the world can use to communicate its guidance to us. If I believe, for instance, that a hawk "means" or conveys a message of vision and wisdom — again, not as something I arbitrarily invent, but rather as a meaning I discover in a reverent communication with Nature — then the higher source of all guidance will make sure that this creature crosses my path when I need to be reminded of its particular lesson. For the random view, it would merely be a dumb creature driven by instinct or need. The Spiritual view does not claim that this animal necessarily makes a conscious decision to meet me at a certain time, or to do just the right thing to give me the message I need to receive — it is rather that Spirit or the Oneness itself is friendly and benevolent, and the various natural creatures are simply the vehicles and forms of its expression. Which view is superstitious? Is it really safer or better to deny all deeper meaning to life's events, simply to avoid occasionally misinterpreting some of them? Or is the belief that there is no meaning perhaps the biggest misinterpretation of all? Again, each person must choose according to what she feels truly serves her and her world. The lighted clearing of trust can provide us with a foundation for re-establishing communication with the world — for discovering the possibility of being on friendly speaking terms with the universe.

CHAPTER 15

THE TRUTH OF YOUR OWN
EXPERIENCE

The idea of the lighted clearing itself creates a lighted clearing within which I can discover and realize the very openness of my own being — to experience my very possibility of experiencing at all. As I become more aware of the truth or unhiddenness that enables me to experience myself and my world, I can discover a greater range of possibilities. I am no longer simply locked into the narrow circle of the experiences of my past, or into the prejudices of my culture — I can begin to better appreciate the "possibility nature" of my experience. Within any particular clearing, there is a tendency to think that I am experiencing all that there is to experience in that situation, simply because I am experiencing all that there is to experience within that clearing. The idea of the lighted clearing, however, shifts my focus from what I am experiencing in my clearing, to the possibility boundaries of the clearing itself — shifts my focus to the unhiddenness or clearing-ness of my own being, which makes experience possible at all.

I have emphasized throughout that my ideas and theories are not intended to "tell" you your truth — to tell you what you will experience in the unhiddenness of your own being. I don't pretend to know "how things really are," or "what's true for everyone," or "what's true for you." Moreover, I don't believe that the richness and depth of experience can be fully captured and described in words, or that there is any one right way to "speak the truth." As I said earlier, my ideas and theories are meant to help you create your own lighted clearing for yourself, within which you can discover and explore possibilities of yourself and your world. These ideas are in no way a substitute for the actual experience — they represent merely one possible map that you may find helpful in your on-going process of discovering which possibilities of experience best serve you and your purpose. Any theory about Spirit, no matter how comprehensive and inspiring it may be, is still only a finger pointing at the moon — its true value is only the extent to which it facilitates your own direct experience of the Spiritual dimension of your life.

The main ideas I have discussed in this book — ideas such as possibility, unhiddenness, lighted clearing, responsibility, wholeness, Spirit, healing, gratitude, opportunity, and trust — are the trailmarkers I personally use to re-create a specific lighted clearing for myself. This clearing enables me to be more open to a certain range and kind of possible experience — a particular horizon of possible experience that not only brings more peace, love, and joy into my life, but which feels deeply and profoundly true. When I am truly *living* from this clearing (as opposed to merely thinking about it), it feels as if I am seeing through to the very heart and soul of myself and the world. For some unknown reason, however, I do not seem to remain in this lighted clearing of authenticity. I seem to cycle in and out of forgetting who I truly am, and then re-remembering — and for me the ideas in this book are an important part of my active role in this re-remembering process. I do find that as the years go by, I tend to catch myself faster when I am falling into forgetfulness, and I can more quickly re-create the lighted clearing of remembering. This is presumably the value and wisdom of experience — although this experience seems to be not so much a matter of one's age, as rather the fruit of an on-going commitment to waking up. I am alerted to my own need to re-remember by feelings of uneasiness and lack of peace — these emotions signal me that I am no longer remembering my truth. I do not know why I again and again forget. Perhaps one's deepest truth is ever-evolving, so that one level of remembering becomes a kind of forgetting relative to the next deeper remembering — and perhaps this is an on-going creative process that has no final end point; the infinite, eternal expansion of Spirit. I heard a beautiful metaphor during a weekend workshop with Pat Rodegast and Emmanuel. Emmanuel said, "We come to Earth to walk in dappled light." By this, I believe he meant that the purpose of human life was to move in and out of remembering, in order to both repeatedly re-experience the joy of remembering our truth, and to become better at being able to remember. Experiencing this cycle also gives us greater compassion for the forgetting and the mistakes of others — and as I learn and re-learn how to remember myself, I am better able to help others in their remembering. Often the very act of helping another to remember his or her own truth is what enables me to remember my own more deeply. Perhaps this oscillation of light and dark is somehow the perfect be-ing or becoming of an ever-deepening remembering, which is a reflection of the perfect be-ing or becoming of the ever-expanding Self-revelation of Spirit.

From this perspective, it may be more appropriate to speak of the journey *toward* remembering my truth, for it is unclear whether there is a final fixed destination. My choice to believe the Spiritual view, for instance, is an on-going choice to love and trust unconditionally — a choice that is not simply made once and for all, but must be chosen anew moment by moment. From the Spiritual perspective, it is time to renew my choice for Spirit whenever I begin to feel a lack of peace in my life — whenever I am feeling anything but unconditional love for myself and others, and anything but unconditional trust in the wisdom and benevolence of Spirit. These feelings are not an occasion for discouragement or guilt, nor do they reflect a "failure" on my part. For me, these feelings are the way Spirit gets my attention and wakes me up to the fact that my life is temporarily inauthentic. My negative feelings signal to me that I am still alive, that I am still growing — tell me that there is still more joy and peace possible for me than I can yet imagine. For the Spiritual view, the essence or truth of everything in this whole process *is* Spirit, including the "we" who are provided with the opportunities, the opportunities themselves, and the Mystery that provides them — Spirit is the sleepwalker, the wake-up call, and the wise and benevolent source of the awakening. We can use only myth and metaphor when speaking of that which is beyond the limits of language and understanding — and the inevitable inexactitude of our concepts will be indirectly expressed as paradox.

But these are just the ideas and theories that work for me now. "Work" is a most appropriate term here, since the value of these ideas lies only in their ability to create a lighted clearing within which I can remember my truth. It is also important to say that they work for me "now," since the ideas and theories that facilitate my remembering seem to evolve and change with time. This may be because ideas sometimes tend to become stale and dogmatic over time — they somehow become important in and of themselves, and no longer serve as a dynamic living opening to the truth of experience. Or, it may be that as I grow and change, I need different ideas and theories to help me remember each deeper dimension of my truth. But the on-going focus is the *experience* itself. The ideas simply serve as vehicles that allow me to discover and make sense of possible realms of life experience.

These are my stories, my theories, my tools, and my explanations — "mine" not in the sense that I made them up all by myself, or that I own them, but mine insofar as they work for me. *Your* question, however, is what works best for you? Which ideas and theories and beliefs best enable you to experience the deepest and richest possibilities of yourself and the world? Which ones best enable you to fulfill your own unique life purpose? Which ones best enable you to perform your own unique soul-gift and to serve others in your own unique way? Which ones best enable you to realize your own authentic visions and dreams? Before you can begin to answer these kinds of questions, you have to provisionally clarify your own purpose and dreams for yourself. Then you have to experiment and explore. Use whatever ideas from this book seem promising, in whatever combinations work best for you. But remember throughout that your ultimate criterion is the *depth and richness of your own experience*, and not the political or metaphysical correctness of your theories. From the basis of your experience itself, you will create your own ideas and beliefs — your own trailmarkers that help you find your way back to that clearing of experience. For some, the trail is marked with the concepts of formal metaphysics — ideas like the Void, Non-Duality, Emptiness, and Being. For others, the more elaborate images of religion can form the polestar that guides them back home. Of course, it isn't always necessary to use words at all — some may rediscover their truth through playing music, or walking in the woods, or working in the garden.

Mystery

Just as your dogmatic ideas can become a prison limiting your possible experience, so too can your familiar experiences become a barrier to exploring new ideas and theories. You cannot critique the possible validity of someone else's experiences for yourself, unless you actually live within the lighted clearing of those experiences. From outside of that clearing, it is merely someone else's story about someone else's life. The point here, of course, is not that we should simply throw out all of our critical discernment and naively believe whatever anyone says, but that truly exploring an alternative belief or worldview is always an act of courage and faith. From within your familiar clearing of experience, you seem to yourself to be experiencing all that can possibly be experienced, because that clearing defines the very limits of your possibility. Nothing in that clearing will justify venturing forth into a new clearing — the experiences that could justify and validate the new clearing, if they exist at all, are accessible only from within that new clearing. Sometimes this process can feel very threatening. An intrinsic part of the seeming security of the familiar realm of experience is the belief that the familiar is all that there is — the belief that the familiar represents the total range of possible experience. Even if you are not completely happy with your familiar realm of experience, there is a comfort in its familiarity — at least you know "what's what." Beyond the familiar lies the strange, the unknown. To discover a fundamentally new possibility of experience doesn't merely add one more experience to your inventory. The familiar itself is transformed. It is no longer the whole of how things are — it is now relegated to one possible experience of how things are. In this transformation, the familiar loses its sense of security. It is as if the Mystery that once seemed to lie beyond the boundary of the familiar has now "infected" the familiar itself. In terms of my earlier reference to talking with trees, if I actually communicate with a tree, it can never again be just a piece of wood for me. Since it has now become for me an expression of the living Presence of the world, it can no longer be dismissed as "just a tree" — for there is now a dimension of Mystery at its very core.

Moreover, the Mystery is not merely in the world "out there" — it is also a part of your very being as well. One of my own experiences during my vision quest dramatically brought this home for me. Our guide had told our group that traditionally a village would choose some person or persons to go out beyond the boundaries of the familiar — to go out into the wilderness, in order to bring back a little bit of chaos, a little bit of the sacred Mystery. This little bit of the beyond introduced an element of the strange and unknown, the divinely creative element that kept the village from becoming stagnant. When I left for my own solo time in the wilderness, I had this romantic fantasy of returning to my village as a triumphant warrior, carrying a glowing piece of the divine Mystery in my cupped hands to offer to my people. During my time in the wilderness, I looked deeply into myself. At one point, when it seemed I had gone to the very limits of my soul, I discovered (and *experienced*) that it did not have any definite boundary. It was bottomless — in its depths it opened into, and was continuous with, the Mystery that lives through all things. When I later returned to my village, I did not bring back the unknown in my cupped hands as some kind of offering or object I could pick up and put down as I pleased. In the open-endedness of my soul, I discovered that the Mystery was living in the depths of my own heart. I didn't carry back a bit of the Mystery to transform my village — I myself was transformed. It wasn't that I was a different person or a different somebody — I could no longer think of myself as a completely definite somebody at all. I hadn't totally lost the boundaries of my ego and myself — I could still function in the world. But my boundaries had become porous and permeable. Whatever transformation might happen in my village as a result of my quest will not come from something I carried back with me, but from my very being itself.

In exploring the unknown, you always run the risk of losing the seeming stability, security, and knownness of the familiar. I say "seeming," because my experience was not so much that I had lost something real, but rather that I discovered that I and my world were not as definite and solid as I had previously imagined. In the everyday familiarity of things, it seems as if each thing in my lighted clearing merely reflects back the light of my understanding — it exists only as those possibilities that my worldview allows to emerge into actualization. But as I become aware of a deeper Mystery interpenetrating all things, it is as if each thing in my lighted clearing is shining with an inner light of its own — I and the world become more luminous. In addition to the known possibilities that filter through my beliefs, there is a dimension of Mystery — a "something more," which calls forth from me a reverent receptivity.

According to the Spiritual view, everything that happens in our lives is purposefully designed and exquisitely timed to guide us toward discovering and remembering our truth. Each detail in our lives is a clue and an opportunity to deepen our capacity for unconditional love, for peace and joy. As the word opportunity suggests, we are never forced to discover our truth — rather, we are provided with moment-to-moment possibilities for awakening, possibilities which we can choose to realize or not. Every thing, every event, and every feeling is an opportunity for awakening, including, especially, those things that seem most negative to us. For the Spiritual view, my negative judgments and feelings indicate the limits of my current capacity for unconditional love and forgiveness, and thus provide clues for further growth.

"Sacred" and "Ordinary" Reality

We often tend to separate our lives into two categories of reality. On the one hand, there is a special kind of reality, which we consider to be sacred and Spiritual. This is the kind of reality we may experience in certain dreams, on a vision quest, during a shamanic journey, in a sweat lodge ceremony, in a prayer or meditation retreat, or on a holy walkabout in the outback of the sacred Mystery. In this "sacred" reality, every detail is seen as meaningful — each event, each feeling, each word is inspired and informed by Spirit to awaken us to truth and to guide us home. There are no mere coincidences, nothing is taken for granted, and nothing is insignificant — there is an implicit message of love and truth in every minute detail. On the other hand, there is what we call our "ordinary" or "everyday" reality. What distinguishes ordinary reality from sacred reality is not so much its content, but rather its significance for us. Ordinary reality is "merely" the familiar reality we encounter every day. There is nothing very special about it — it simply happens according to familiar patterns, with no particular significance or meaning for our lives. There is nothing operating behind the scenes, no guiding force, no overall wisdom or purpose. In ordinary reality, a bird flying across my path is not seen as a meaningful omen or a message of Spirit, but merely as an insignificant mindless creature driven by instinct to seek food or shelter. A rude clerk at the grocery store is not a purposeful opportunity given to me to expand my capacity for unconditional love, but merely another harried, inconsiderate person with his own egocentric agenda. Many people find it very difficult to return to ordinary reality after an inspiring seminar or workshop — to return from a wondrous environment of loving community and Spiritual illumination to the meaningless and mind-numbing grind of everyday reality.

According to the Spiritual view, however, *all* reality is an expression of Spirit. Sacred reality is not a special reality that is separate from profane reality — for the Spiritual view, *all* reality is sacred. What happens in our so-called everyday reality is just as much a manifestation of Spirit as is anything else — every event is a potential blessing, a lesson, a message, an opportunity; and every detail is ultimately a loving expression of the sacred Mystery. Ordinary and sacred are simply two possible ways of *experiencing* life, depending on the lighted clearing we create — depending on whether our focus and our beliefs are hiding or revealing Spiritual truth. For the Spiritual perspective, our Spiritual "journey" is not really a movement from some here to some other there — for instance, from my ordinary, mundane reality to some separate and extraordinary sacred reality. The Spiritual journey is simply a process of awakening to the truth of what is *already* here — it is not a journey away from ordinary reality, but rather deeper into its truth. Moreover, this journey toward discovering my truth is not some special endeavor I pursue in addition to the other activities of my everyday life — it is how I live my life toward Spirit in *everything* I think and say and do.

There will be many situations in the unique unfolding of your life that are not specifically addressed in this or any other book. But from the perspective of the lighted clearing of trust, guidance is always available for the asking. As human beings who are under way toward creating and discovering our truth, we are always in the midst of a leap of faith, choosing either love or fear, either forgiveness or grievance, either trust or doubt, either the Mystery of Spirit or the seeming knowledge and security of some familiar worldview. We are choosing to see each situation either as a blessing and an opportunity, or as a random, meaningless event that threatens and victimizes our happiness. We are choosing either to be open to some deeper guidance, or to simply be driven by the fears of our egos.

The Separative-Technological view promises us safety at the expense of keeping our fears — the Spiritual-Holistic view promises peace and joy at the expense of surrendering to trust and love. No one can prove to us which view is better or which choices we "should" make. For those who choose the Separative-Technological view, the way is clear and well-traveled — it is the view that almost everyone takes for granted in our culture, and you have only to read the daily newspaper or watch television for directions down this frightened path. If you choose an alternative such as the Spiritual view, however, you have to discover and create your own unique path of awakening. Any book or theory or philosophy is but a map that can lead you to the next threshold of your on-going journey of coming home to your own truth. The ending of any teaching is the beginning of your next step into the unknown of the Sacred Mystery. Remember, though, that you are never alone on this journey — Spirit's loving voice is guiding you every moment in the gentle promptings of your heart and in every sacred whisper on the wind.

EPILOGUE

During my vision quest, I had an experience that helped me define for myself the purpose and soul of this book. I was in the beautiful red-rock canyonlands of southern Utah. In the middle of the night I suddenly awoke, feeling that I was somehow being called forth into the wilderness. I left my warm sleeping bag and ventured into the darkness, following my heart's guidance. When I was far from camp, I lay down on my back and looked up at the wondrous profusion of stars. As I lay there, the stars spoke to me:

"We create patterns of light against the Mystery of the black sky, to help travelers who are lost in the darkness find their way home. We do not tell them where their homes are, or how to get there. We only provide the light patterns, so that those travelers in the night can remember where they are and where they are going.

"Likewise, your purpose is not to tell others who they are, for that you cannot know. You will craft starwords to create patterns of light against the Mystery of existence, which can be used by those who are lost in the darkness of forgetting to remember their truth."

I lay there on the ground for a long time, crying with joy for the grace and generosity of the Star People. I thanked them for their teaching, and I asked if there was anything I could do for them to express my deep gratitude.

They replied, "Tell our story."

FOOTNOTES

[1] This philosophical view of Being is consistent with the discoveries of modern science. Physics, for instance, no longer considers an electron to exist as a particular actual particle (or wave) in a particular place, but understands it more like a "smear of possibilities." An electron is experienced as a particular actuality in a particular location only when it is actually observed under particular conditions. Under one set of experimental conditions, an electron will be experienced as a particle; under another, it will be experienced as a wave. But it doesn't incrementally change from a particle to a wave between the experiments, nor can we ever catch it in the middle — rather at one time we actualize its particle possibility, and at another time its wave possibility. Likewise, in one observation, we may find the electron in one location relative to an atomic nucleus, and in a later observation find it in another location. But according to physicists, the electron doesn't "move" from one place to the other — it simply actualizes another spatial possibility within its horizon of probability. As the conditions of observation change, so does the experienced form and location of the observed electron. For a discussion of modern physics, see *The Tao of Physics* by Fritjof Capra, and *The Dancing Wu Li Masters* by Gary Zukov.

[2] In Western philosophy, we find this emphasis on experience in the tradition of phenomenology, from Hegel down through Husserl and Heidegger.

[3] In its own defense, the thought-creates-reality model might argue that the Possibility Model also makes an unverifiable claim about the metaphysical nature of reality — namely, that reality, in and of itself, consists of a "field of possibilities." Moreover, it might further argue that, in order to verify the Possibility Model for myself, I would have to somehow step outside of my experience in order to witness the process of a possible experience becoming an actual experience. But the difference here is that the Possibility Model does not claim to be an accurate description of how things really are. In its own terms, it is just one possible *way of thinking about our experience of the world* — a way whose value is determined by the kind and range of experiences it allows or enables us to have. In the thought-creates-reality model, however, it is presumed that thought-creates-reality describes what's *really* going on. (That the thought-creates-reality model intends to be a description of how things really are can be illustrated in the following example. Suppose I happened to think that reality really consists of merely given material objects existing outside of myself, which are totally unaffected by my thoughts. Would my thinking such a thought make it so? "No," the thought-creates-reality model would answer, "because what's really going on is that your thoughts create reality, whether you happen to be aware of the fact or not." This suggests, paradoxically, that there is some non-thought-created frame of reference, that somehow defines and limits the creative power of

our thoughts — we cannot, for instance, create a reality in which thoughts are powerless.) There are versions of the thought-creates-reality model that claim that there are other minds in addition to mine, and/or that there are other levels of mind in addition to that of the conscious ego (for instance, my subconscious mind, the mind of my deeper Self, various group minds, and even a universal mind). All of those other minds and other levels of mind are busily thinking their own thoughts, which help to define the reality I experience. Such a position seems to be able to maintain the basic claim of thoughts create reality, without falling into individual subjectivism or egocentricity. But this apparent solution generates some difficult questions of its own: Do the thoughts from these other minds and levels sometimes supersede or override my own thoughts in the creation of the universe? What active or creative role do I actually play in this creation? If I simply have to accommodate or adapt to the reality created by others, how is this different from merely accommodating to some supposedly external material reality? If I am merely given some already pre-created reality that I have to somehow deal with, doesn't the whole notion of "my thoughts create reality" lose much of its power and meaning?

[4] The concept of truth as unhiddenness is mentioned by Plato. It is also discussed extensively by Heidegger in *Being and Time*.

[5] The idea that human be-ing exists as possibility is a central theme in Heidegger 's *Being and Time*.

[6] Compare also, the related German words *denken* ("to think" — which originally meant "to illuminate something so as to make it clear and evident"), and *danken* ("to thank").

[7] In the history of Western philosophy, Thomas Hobbes' analysis of social relations is a good example of the Separative view.

[8] In modern philosophy, Nietzsche discusses this theme in detail.

[9] On the topics of unconditional love and forgiveness, see the Selected Reading List: *A Course In Miracles*, and books by Gerald Jampolsky, Gail Straub, Kenneth Wapnick, and Marianne Williamson.

[10] "Spiritual-Holistic" and "Separative-Technological" are not strictly parallel constructions (for them to be strictly parallel, I would have to use either "Holistic-Spiritual" or "Technological-Separative"). But I have chosen to name these two views, the "Spiritual-Holistic" and the Separative-Technological," because in each case the primary term comes first. The essence of the Spiritual-Holistic view is the Spiritual nature of Being. The essence of the Separative-Technological view is separateness — because only insofar as I am separate from the other things of the world, can I treat them as mere objects and assign meaning and value to them.

[11] For more on the topics of mindfulness and meditation, see the Selected Reading List for books by Thich Nhat Hanh, and Shunryu Suzuki.

[12] This phrase was coined by Jerry and Esther Hicks, in their book, *A New Beginning II*.

[13] The phrase, "a path with heart," comes from the writings of Carlos Castaneda.

[14] Heidegger discusses the topic of experiential time in *Being and Time*.

[15] See *Spiritual Economics* by Eric Butterworth for a discussion of affirmations as a way of aligning oneself with Spiritual truth.

[16] For an excellent discussion of affirmations, limiting beliefs, and turnaround beliefs, see *Empowerment* by David Gershon and Gail Straub.

[17] In the history of Western philosophy, this philosophical position of naïve realism is exemplified by John Locke.

[18] For more on the topic of healing, see *The 12 Stages of Healing*, and *Healing Myths Healing Magic*, by Donald Epstein.

[19] Chiropractic, at least in its original definition and intent, is a good example of a holistic and vitalistic approach to health care. This is especially evident in the form of chiropractic called Network Spinal Analysis (often referred to simply as Network Chiropractic), developed by Dr. Donald Epstein.

[20] On the topic of mind-body health, see the Selected Reading List: books by Joan Borysenko, Deepak Chopra, Donald Epstein, Louise Hay, and Bernie Siegel.

[21] I am indebted to Nick Gordon for this phrase and this insight.

[22] See *The Mastery of Love* by Don Miguel Ruiz for an excellent discussion of healing emotional wounds.

[23] For discussion of interpersonal healing within a couple relationship, see *Getting The Love You Want*, Harville Hendrix.

[24] On the topic of how our happiness is affected by our beliefs, see the books by Barry Neil Kaufman and Andrew Matthews in the Selected Reading List. Also the seminars and workshops offered by the Option Institute (Barry Neil Kaufman) are excellent and life-transforming.

SELECTED READING LIST

Anthony, Carol K. *The Philosophy of the* I Ching. Anthony Publishing Company, 1981

Black Elk, Wallace. *Black Elk: The Sacred Ways of a Lakota.* Harper, 1991.

Blakney, Raymond (translator). *Meister Eckhart.* Harper Torchbooks, 1941.

Blofeld, John. *The Zen Teaching of Huang Po: On The Transmission of Mind.* Grove Press, 1958.

Borysenko, Joan. *Minding The Body, Mending The Mind.* Bantam, 1987.

Boyd, Doug. *Rolling Thunder.* Dell Publishing, 1974

Butterworth, Eric. *Spiritual Economics.* Unity School of Christianity, 1983.

Byrom, Thomas (translator). *The Dhammapada: The Sayings of the Buddha.* Alfred A. Knopf, 1976.

Cameron, Julia. *The Artist's Way.* Penguin Putnam, 1992

Capra, Fritjof. *The Tao of Physics: An Exploration of the Parallels Between Modern physics and Eastern Mysticism.* Shambhala Publications, Inc., (Fourth Ed.) 2000.

Castaneda, Carlos. *Journey To Ixtlan.* Washington Square Press, 1972.

———. *Tales of Power.* Pocket Books, 1974.

Chung-yuan, Chang (translator and commentator). *Tao: A New Way Of Thinking.* Harper and Row, 1975.

Chopra, Deepak. *Ageless Body, Timeless Mind.* Harmony Books, 1993.

———. *The Seven Spiritual Laws of Success.* Amber-Allen Publishing, 1993.

Covey, Stephen R. *The 7 Habits of Highly Effective People.* Fireside, 1989.

Dass, Ram. *Be Here Now.* Newspaper Printing Corporation, 1971.

———. *Grist For The Mill.* Unity Press, 1977.

———. *Still Here.* Riverhead Books, 2000.

Dass, Ram and Gorman, Paul. *How Can I Help?* Alfred A. Knopf, 1985.

DeMello, Anthony. *Wellsprings.* Doubleday, 1984.

Dossey, Larry, M.D. *Healing Words.* HarperSanFrancisco, 1993.

Epstein, Donald M. *The 12 Stages Of Healing.* Amber-Allen Publishing, 1994.

———. *Healing Myths, Healing Magic.* Amber-Allen Publishing, 2000.

Feng, Gia-Fu and English, Jane (translators). *Tao Te Ching.* Vintage Books, 1972.

Fields, Rick, et. al. *Chop Wood Carry Water.* Jeremy P. Tarcher, Inc., 1984.

Foundation For Inner Peace. *A Course In Miracles.* Foundation For Inner Peace, 1975.

Gawain, Shakti. *Creative Visualization.* Bantam, 1979.

Gershon, David and Straub, Gail. *Empowerment.* High Point Press, 1989.

Goldsmith, Joel S. *The Art of Meditation.* (Copyright 1956) HarperSanFrancisco, 1990.

———. *The Art of Spiritual Healing.* (Copyright 1959) HarperSanFrancisco, 1992.

———. *Practicing The Presence.* (Copyright 1958) HarperSanFrancisco, 1991.

———. *The Thunder of Silence.* (Copyright 1961) HarperSanFrancisco, 1993.

Hanh, Thich Nhat. *Peace Is Every Step.* Bantam, 1991.

———. *The Miracle of Mindfulness.* Beacon, 1975.

Harner, Michael. *The Way Of The Shaman.* HarperSanFrancisco, 1980.

Hay, Louise. *You Can Heal Your Life.* Hay House, 1984.

Heidegger, Martin. (Translated by Macquarrie, John and Robinson, Edward) *Being and Time.* Harper and Row, 1962

———. (Translated by Lovitt, William) *The Question Concerning Technology.* Harper Colophon Books, 1977.

Hendrix, Harville. *Getting The Love You Want.* HarperPerennial, 1988.

Hicks, Jerry and Hicks Esther. *A New Beginning I.* Crown Internationale, 1994.

———. *A New Beginning II.* Crown Internationale, 1994.

Ingerman, Sandra. *Soul Retrieval.* HarperSanFrancisco, 1991.

———. *Welcome Home.* HarperSanFrancisco, 1994.

———. *Medicine for the Earth.* Three Rivers Press, 2001.

Kabat-Zinn, Jon. *Wherever You Go There You Are.* Hyperion, 1994.

Kaufman, Barry Neil. *Happiness Is A Choice.* Fawcett Columbine, 1991.

———. *PowerDialogues*(SM), Epic Century Publishers, 1991.

———. *Son-Rise: The Miracle Continues,* H J Kramer Inc., 1994.

———. *To Love Is To Be Happy With.* Fawcett Crest, 1977.

Kapleau, Philip (compiler and editor). *The Three Pillars Of Zen.* Beacon Press, 1965.

Kurtz, Ernest, and Ketchum, Katherine. *The Spirituality Of Imperfection.* Bantam, 1992.

Jampolsky, Gerald G., and Prather, Hugh. *Love Is Letting Go Of Fear.* Celestial Arts, 1988.

Levine, Stephen. *A Year To Live.* Bell Tower, 1997.

Matthews, Andrew. *Being Happy.* Stern Sloan Publishing, 1990.

Millman, Dan. *No Ordinary Moments.* H. J. Kramer, 1992.

———. *Sacred Journey of the Peaceful Warrior.* H. J. Kramer, 1991.

———. *Way of the Peaceful Warrior.* H. J. Kramer, 1985 .

Myss, Caroline. *Anatomy Of The Spirit.* Random House, 1997.

Patanjali (translated by Swami Prabhavananda). *How To Know God* Mentor, 1953.

Patent, Arnold. *You Can Have It All.* Celebration Publishing, 1987.

Prather, Hugh. *The Quiet Answer.* Dolphin, 1982.

———. *Spiritual Notes To Myself.* Conari Press, 1998.

Ponder, Catherine. *Dynamic Laws of Prosperity.* DeVorss & Co., 1988.

Reps, Paul (compiler). *Zen Flesh, Zen Bones.* Doubleday Anchor, 1961.

Rodegast, Pat. *Emmanuel's Book.* Bantam, 1985.

———. *Emmanuel's Book II.* Bantam, 1989.

———. *Emmanuel's Book III.* Bantam, 1994.

Ruiz, Don Miguel. *The Four Agreements.* Amber-Allen Publishing, 1997.

———. *The Mastery of Love.* Amber-Allen Publishing, 1999.

Rumi (translated by Barks, Coleman and John Moyne). *The Essential Rumi.* HarperSanFranscisco, 1995.

Sams, Jamie. *Sacred Path Cards.* HarperSanFranscisco, 1990.

Shri Purohit Swami (translator), *The Bhagavad Gita.* Vintage Books, 1977.

Suzuki, D. T. *Manual Of Zen Buddhism.* Grove Press, 1960.

———. *Outlines Of Mahayana Buddhism.* Schocken Books, 1963.

Suzuki, Shunryu. *Zen Mind, Beginner's Mind.* Weatherhill, 1970.

Siegel, Bernie, M.D. *Peace, Love & Healing.* Harper and Row, 1989.

Spangler, David. *Everyday Miracles.* Bantam, 1996.

———. *Blessing: The Art and the Practice.* Riverhead Books, 2002.

Straub, Gail. *The Rhythm of Compassion: Caring for Self, Connecting With Society.* Charles E. Tuttle Co., 2001.

Trungpa, Chögyam, *Cutting Through Spiritual Materialism.* Shambhala Publications, Inc., 1973.

Walsch, Neale Donald. *Conversations With God* Putnam, 1996.

Wapnick, Kenneth. *Forgiveness and Jesus.* Foundation For A Course In Miracles, 1998.

Wilhem, Richard (translator and commentator). *The I Ching.* Princeton University Press, 1950.

Williamson, Marianne. *A Return To Love.* HarperCollins, 1996.

Yoder, William. "Toward An Ontology And Epistemology Of Mysticism." Ph.D. dissertation, SUNY Buffalo, 1978.

Zukav, Gary and Finkelstein, David. *The Dancing Wu Li Masters: An Overview Of The New Physics.* Bantam, 1994.

GLOSSARY

The glossary summarizes the meaning of key terms as they are used in *Lighted Clearings for the Soul.* Table 1 at the end of the glossary summarizes some of the main differences between the Separative-Technological view and the Spiritual-Holistic view. Boldface items within a definition have their own glossary entries.

Actuality Model: The Actuality Model is the **theory** that Being consists of a fixed, actual, material reality, which exists external to us and independent of our experience of it. Our goal is to perceive and describe it as accurately as possible — and this is called, being "realistic."

Affirmation: To af-firm means to make firm. Typically, the practice of "doing affirmations" involves writing or saying a statement repeatedly, in order to make it firm in your subconsciousness and/or consciousness.

For the **thought-creates-reality model**, you use affirmations to control your thoughts, so that these affirmed thoughts will create the reality (the things and circumstances and relationships) that you desire.

For the **Possibility Model**, doing affirmations is a way to consciously choose, create, and reinforce a specific **lighted clearing**, a specific horizon of receptivity.

For the **Spiritual view**, doing affirmations is a way to create a lighted clearing of Spiritual Self-discovery. From this perspective, the key to true happiness is not manipulating reality to "get stuff," but becoming fully aware of your own truth as a be-ing of Spirit.

Aletheia: Aletheia is the ancient Greek word for **truth**, which literally means, "unhiddenness." The "truth" of anything (for instance, of any idea or **theory**) for you is the specific openness it creates in your life.

Alienation: Alienation refers to the belief that you are somehow separate (alienated) from other people, from Nature, and from God, and usually with the connotation that this separateness causes you some degree of discomfort — you feel "alienated," or a "sense of alienation".

For the **Separative-Technological view**, separateness is merely a fact of reality. Feeling alienated is the emotional reflection of being realistic. You can form temporary and tentative alliances with others, but the fundamental fact of your separateness and your essential aloneness remains unchanged.

For the **Spiritual-Holistic view**, separateness is merely a way of *thinking about* reality — a way of thinking that is based on a denial of the Spiritual wholeness of Being. From this perspective, alienation is simply the **illusion** of the absence of Spiritual wholeness. There is no need to solve the problem of alienation (to somehow **"bridge the gap"**) — you only have to recognize that alienation is not, and could never be, true at all.

Bad (as the opposite of "good"): See "Good and evil."

Best Day exercise: The Best Day exercise is a way to "exercise" your **responsibility** — exercise your ability to consciously and deliberately send forth your truth from yourself back to the world. In every situation throughout the day, you ask yourself, "How would I respond to this on my Best Day? How can I best send forth my truth in this situation?" This includes your response to the external events and circumstances that happen "outside" you, as well as to the thoughts or **feelings** that happen "inside" you. The Best Day exercise is a practice of deliberately and self-consciously choosing and living your **truth** throughout every moment of the day.

Blame: To blame someone is to accuse or condemn him for being at fault. Typically blame is used in one of two ways:

(1) To blame someone or something for causing you to feel unhappy ("She *made* me mad"): For the **Possibility Model**, however, your **feelings** are the emotional reflection of the **lighted clearing** you have created. You and only you can determine how you interpret things, what they mean to you, and how you feel about them. From this perspective, blame reflects your lack of self-awareness.

(2) To blame someone for doing something "wrong": For the **Spiritual view**, to condemn another as wrong (**bad, un-Spiritual**) reflects your own misperception, your own blindness to her essential Spirituality. When you find yourself blaming or condemning another, the only true **response**, the only way to send forth your truth, is to release any mistaken **judgments** of the other's (or of your own) un-Spirituality — to **forgive**. (See also "Grievance, grudge.")

Bridge the gap: A pervasive theme in psychology, philosophy, and literature is how we can "bridge the gap" of separation and **alienation**.

For the **Separative view**, you are separate from others, from Nature, and from **God**. This can lead to a feeling of discomfort and a sense of alienation. Thus, you try to somehow "bridge the gap" that seems to separate you from them — you try to find a way to think about and act toward them that creates a feeling of relatedness (non-isolation, non-loneliness) and comfort, even though the underlying reality of separateness and aloneness remains unchanged.

For the **Spiritual-Holistic view**, alienation is simply the **illusion** of the absence of **wholeness** — there is, in **truth**, no gap to be bridged. Trying to "bridge the gap" only makes this thought-created gap seem more real, as something that must somehow be bridged.

Christ-in-disguise: For the **Spiritual view**, this is a metaphor for seeing everything as a form or expression of **Spirit**, rather than as a separate thing-in-itself. It is a way to focus on the underlying shared **truth** of another, rather than only on the qualities of his form that seem to make him different from you. To whatever extent you see another as **un-Spiritual**, the other is "in disguise" for you. But ultimately the disguise is only your own misperception of his **truth**.

Co-create: In the **Possibility Model**, you co-create your *experience* of reality. Your beliefs and your focus of attention contribute the specific **lighted clearing** of discovery, and the **Mystery** contributes the possible experiences that can emerge-into-awareness within that clearing.

The Possibility Model is in contrast to the **thought-creates-reality model**, which claims that your thoughts unilaterally create reality itself.

Coincidence: For a **mechanistic** worldview, the fact that two events happen to occur together in time and space is considered mere random chance or coincidence, if there is no direct causal connection between them. The word, "coincidence," implies that you actually know that the events have no meaningful connection with one another; you know that it was mere random chance that they happened together. But you cannot positively perceive or know the absence of connection — at best, you can know that you are unaware of any connection. So words like "random" and "coincidence" hide your not-knowing under a pretense of knowing. (Compare this to "miracle," which connotes that there is something beyond what we understand. "Miracle" implicitly acknowledges the limits of our knowledge, whereas "coincidence" implies that we completely understand the situation.)

Conditional/unconditional: Conditional means dependent on conditions, and always implies a **dualistic** framework. For instance, to say someone or something is conditionally **good** implies that certain conditions are being met; but in the absence of meeting these conditions, he would be not-good (bad, **evil**). Conversely, dualism always implies conditionality — if you define good only relative to evil or bad, you are implicitly claiming that there are certain conditions and qualities which *really* differentiate one from another ("really" differentiate implies that the differences are of essence and content, rather than mere differences of form or appearance).

Unconditional means independent of all conditions and circumstances, and implies a non-dualistic framework. For the **Spiritual-Holistic view, Spirit** is the ultimate non-dualistic and unconditional idea — there simply is no such thing as not-Spirit, and nothing in its **truth** is un-Spiritual or un-sacred. Another way to say this is that for the Spiritual view, all differences — all possible conditions — are only differences of form and appearance, not differences of content, essence, or truth. The opposite of the non-dualistic **truth of Spirit** is the dualistic belief in the reality of *both* Spirit *and* not-Spirit (or, the belief in the reality of *both* good *and* evil). This dualistic belief system will be emotionally reflected as dualistic pairs of feelings: conditional **peace** *and* lack of peace (conflict), conditional love *and* lack of **love** (hatred, fear, anger), and conditional **joy** *and* lack of joy (unhappiness, depression). For the Spiritual-Holistic view, the **negative feelings** in each of these pairs are merely the emotional reflection of the **illusory** experience of the lack of Spirit. But even the positive half of each pair (conditional peace, conditional love, conditional joy) is only a limited and conditional feeling — for instance, you feel conditional love only insofar as, and as long as, you judge another person to be exhibiting those particular qualities or behaviors that make him worthy or deserving of love according to your definition. Unconditional love, on the other hand, is not dependent on any conditions or particular qualities or behaviors — and it has no opposite whatsoever. Unconditional love is the unconditional and universal extension of goodwill, blessing, and kindness to all. Ultimately, it is the truth of your being (Spirit-as-you) extending unconditional love to the truth of another being (Spirit-as-another). (See "Peace," "Love," "Joy," and "Good and evil" for examples of conditional and unconditional qualities.)

Constructive: To see something as constructive or in a constructive light means to see it in a way that truly serves you — that helps you fulfill your **purpose** and realize your true desires. For the **Spiritual view**, this means to see something in a way that helps you to realize and express your **Spiritual truth**. Since Spirit is **self-revealing**, the only way that Spirit could be unrealized or unexpressed is if you were somehow actively hiding it from yourself. For the Spiritual view, every situation has constructive-possibilities waiting to be realized — this is the Spiritual truth of the situation waiting on your openness so that it can emerge into your awareness. (See also "Grow" and "Opportunity.")

Cynicism: In the context of this book, cynicism refers to the blanket denial of wholeness and **Spirituality**. It bases its denial on the fact that wholeness and Spirituality cannot be perceived with the body's senses, nor can they be logically proved. But as the **Spiritual view** points out, the absence of Spirituality and wholeness cannot be perceived or logically proved either.

Dogmatic/experiential: There are two possible ways that you can understand a **theory** or belief system — either as an arbitrary metaphysical description without an experiential foundation (i.e., dogmatic), or as a lighted clearing for direct experience. Whether a theory is dogmatic or experiential for you depends not so much on the theory itself, as rather on how you think about it and understand it. The **Possibility Model** and the idea of **truth** as **unhiddenness** provide a way to understand any idea or theory experientially. (See also "Fingers pointing at the moon," and "Theory/theoros.")

Dualism/non-dualism: A dualistic concept is one that is defined only relative to its opposite. For instance, dualistic **good** is defined only relative to dualistic **bad**. Dualism always implies conditionality — if you define good only relative to evil or bad, you are implicitly claiming that there are certain conditions and qualities which distinguish one from another. For the **Spiritual view**, *the* fundamental non-dualistic idea is "Spirit" itself. **Spirit** is the essence and **truth** of everything — there simply is no such reality as not-Spirit. From this perspective, the foundation of any dualistic thought system is the distinction between Spirit and not-Spirit (or between the Spiritual and the non-Spiritual), and the belief that both halves of this distinction are equally real. For the Spiritual view, however, this dualistic distinction involves two mistakes. First, it mistakenly asserts that the non-Spiritual is real in itself, and actually exists in some way. From the Spiritual perspective, the non-Spiritual is merely an **illusory** idea, in that it points toward nothing real at all — it represents only the hiddenness of (i.e., your unawareness of) the truth of Spirit. Second, the dualistic idea of Spirit (Spirit as merely one half of the Spirit/non-Spirit pair of concepts) defines Spirit only in dualistic and **conditional** terms, and thus hides the non-dualistic, unconditional **truth of Spirit**. (A similar line of reasoning can be applied to the conditional and unconditional concepts of **good, peace, love,** and **joy**).

For the Spiritual-Holistic view, all misjudgment and misperception ultimately arise out of the mistaken belief in **dualism** — the mistaken belief that there is some reality or causal power besides Spirit; that both Spirit and non-Spirit, both good and evil, truly exist. Your **negative emotions** are your **feedback system**, which reminds you that you have lapsed back into dualistic thinking and experiencing. (See also "Conditional/unconditional," "Forgiveness/unforgiveness," "Joy," "Love," and "Peace.")

Ego/egocentric: Ego refers to your identity as a separate, independent being, with its own will and its own agenda. Egocentric refers to a way of life whose primary focus and reference point is one's own ego.

For the **Separative view**, the ego (your separate, independent identity) is simply a given reality. Thus, the corresponding **ethics** (the way of life that would most truly express that view) would be essentially egocentric. For many Separative-Technological persons, this egocentric way of life is tempered with a morality of cooperation and altruism, and they are sincerely and genuinely kind and loving people. But since this view believes that separateness is the fundamental reality, selfless service always means some form of self-sacrifice (although you might believe that what you will gain from your sacrifice will be worth more than what you gave up).

For the **Spiritual-Holistic view**, the experience of separateness is only the **illusory** experience of the absence of wholeness. In terms of the Possibility Model, the mistaken idea of separateness creates a lighted clearing that actively excludes the experience of wholeness. Thus for the Spiritual-Holistic view, the ego is merely a mental fiction — how you mistakenly conceive your identity within the illusory context of separateness. An egocentric life, far from truly serving you, would actually block Spiritual awareness, and prevent you from experiencing perfect **peace, love,** and **joy**. For the Spiritual-Holistic view, an ethics of unconditional love is authentic self-expression — and far from being a form of self-sacrifice, it is the source of all true happiness.

Emotions/feelings: Emotions are your feedback system that lets you know how you are doing — the feedback system that reflects the quality of your life. (See also "Positive emotions" and "Negative emotions.")

From the perspective of the **Actuality Model**, your feelings let you know how the world is treating you, and what is happening to you. Positive feelings indicate that what is happening is in your own best interests; negative emotions indicate that what is happening is not in your own best interests.

For the **Possibility Model**, your feelings reflect the quality of your life experience within the **lighted clearing** you are creating with your beliefs and focus of attention. By changing your lighted clearing — by re-choosing your beliefs and focus — you can change the feelings you are experiencing.

Eternal/eternal truth: The eternal is not to be confused with the non-temporal of the dualistic **temporal/non-temporal** pair of concepts. The eternal is a non-dualistic idea referring to the **truth** or essence of now-ness itself — the "always, already now," which transcends all distinctions of past, present and future. For the **Spiritual view**, eternal truth is the **truth of Spirit**. Awareness of eternal truth is emotionally reflected as perfect **(unconditional, non-dualistic) peace, love, and joy**. Eternal truth, by definition, is always already now, and is thus available for you to experience in any moment you are open to it. Nothing external or circumstantial can prevent you from experiencing perfect peace, love, and joy in any moment — nothing except your own closed-off-ness to the awareness of your truth. (See "Grace and Karma" and "Temporal/ non-temporal.")

Ethics: One of the meanings of the ancient Greek word, "ethos," is "**true (unhidden)** character." Thus, to speak or act ethically means to speak or act truthfully — i.e., in a way that expresses and reflects the truth of your being. Ethics is to be distinguished from mere morality (from the Latin, "mores," meaning convention or custom), which is a set of rules for "right living" that is imposed on you from without (by social custom, by God, etc.). For instance, "to love your neighbor as yourself" would be a moral rule for the **Separative-Technological** view, but an ethical principle of authentic Self-expression for the **Spiritual-Holistic** view.

Evidence: We typically look to our experiences as "evidence" to support and validate our beliefs — for instance, you might believe that you are justified in thinking that people are basically selfish, because you see so many selfish, greedy, **egocentric** people. But according to the **Possibility Model**, your beliefs create the **lighted clearing** which allows and enables you to have specific meaningful experiences at all. From the perspective of that model, your experiences are not evidence of the correctness of your beliefs, but are simply an experiential reflection of those beliefs.

Evil: See "Good and evil."

Experiential: See "Dogmatic/experiential."

Family of Nature: This is a **metaphor** for a way of thinking about all of the beings of Nature as family members —seeing not only humans as your brothers and sisters, but also seeing the non-human beings of Nature as family (Mother Earth, Brother tree, Sister eagle, etc.). For the **Spiritual view**, the **truth** and value of this metaphor is that it can create a **lighted clearing** that allows and enables you to experience the common Spiritual truth or kinship of all beings.

Fear: Fear is the basis of all **negative emotions.**
For the **Separative-Technological view**, fear is simply the emotional reflection of being realistic. Since the world really is separate, hostile, and threatening, it would be dangerous and foolish to be unafraid.

For the **Spiritual-Holistic view**, fear is the emotional reflection of the **illusion** of the absence of **love**. Since everything is an expression of Spirit, there is, in truth, no real absence of love. But you can believe that there is an absence of love — you can choose to believe that reality is made up of independent, valueless beings (you can choose to believe that wholeness and Spirituality do not exist). This belief will be reflected in a life experience of separateness, threat and fear. Since the basis of every negative emotion is fear, and fear arises only out of your unawareness of your truth, the way to heal any negative emotion is to return to the awareness of your truth.

Fear-based and love-based approaches to life: A "fear-based approach to life" is based on the belief that you are somehow missing or lacking what you need to experience **peace, love,** and **joy** now. You, in and of yourself, are not enough, and you can experience happiness only by achieving and maintaining certain circumstances and conditions. If you do not do this, your life will continue to be deficient and lacking. From this perspective, your goals and dreams are essentially fearful and desperate, since you believe that you "have to" succeed in order to be enough, and in order to experience peace, love, and joy. And even when you do succeed, you have to continually maintain and defend your success, because you believe that it is these conditions and circumstances that establish your worth and are the cause of your happiness.

A "love-based approach to life" starts from the belief and the awareness that you are, in your deepest **truth**, already enough, and that nothing needs to change for you to experience perfect peace, love, and joy now. Thus, everything you do in your life becomes an expression of your truth as a be-ing of peace, love, and joy, rather than a desperate, fearful attempt to somehow create or achieve or earn these feelings. (See "Fear" and "Pathology orientation/Vision orientation.")

Feedback (guidance) system: See "Emotions/feelings."

Feelings: See "Emotions/feelings."

Fingers pointing at the moon: This is a **metaphor** from the literature of Zen Buddhism — a metaphor which indicates that our concepts and **theories** can never accurately describe reality. At best, our ideas can evoke, or point our attention toward, the direct experience of reality. The intent of this metaphor is similar to that of the **lighted clearing**: to remind us to be receptive to the **truth** of experience itself, rather than to get lost in our concepts. It is important to note that these metaphors are not meant to be anti-conceptual or anti-thinking — they simply remind us to use our concepts as pointers and windows and clearings, rather than to mistake them as substitutes for direct experience itself.

Forgiveness/Unforgiveness:

For the **Separative-Technological view**, forgiveness means pardoning a sin of yourself or another, and "letting them off the hook." For this view, since the wrongdoing was real in the first place, forgiveness is actually a form of dishonesty — pretending that the wrongdoing and wrongdoer are not bad, when they really are.

For the **Spiritual-Holistic view**, the truth of all Being is Spirit. Thus, your **judgment** of another as bad or sinful (and unworthy of your **unconditional love**) can only be your own misperception of his **truth**. Your experience of his badness is merely the **illusory** experience of the absence of his Spirituality — it reflects only your self-created blindness to his **Spiritual truth**. You are unaware of it only because you are actively hiding it from yourself. This active hiding of his Spiritual truth from yourself takes the form of actively misjudging and misperceiving him as somehow un-Spiritual or **bad**. This kind of misjudging and misperceiving is what I call "doing unforgiveness," or actively being unforgiving. The resolution to this situation of condemnation and self-created blindness is to release your judgments — to **forgive**. Seen in this light, it is not so much a matter of "doing forgiveness," as rather "ceasing to do unforgiveness."

Your condemnation of the other also reflects your misperception of yourself — for you see yourself as a judge who is separate and different from the person he judges. You are blind to the common Spiritual truth you both share. Thus, forgiveness is simply releasing your misperception and misjudgment, so that you can be aware of the Spiritual truth of both yourself and the other. And ultimately, it is this awareness that is the source of any experience of perfect **peace**, **love**, and **joy**.

For the Spiritual-Holistic view, all misjudgment and misperception ultimately arise out of the belief in **dualism** — the belief that there is some reality or causal power besides Spirit; that there is *both* Spirit *and* non-Spirit, *both* good *and* evil. When you are in a dualistic framework, the idea of (dualistic, **conditional**) "**good**" is *relatively* more similar to the non-dualistic idea of Spirit (relatively more effective for evoking the experience of Spiritual truth) than is the idea of (dualistic, conditional) "bad." That means that your negative judgments of people hide their Spirituality from you relatively more than do your positive judgments. Thus, in the earlier stages of one's journey of Spiritual awakening, forgiveness is typically understood to mean releasing one's negative judgments. But ultimately, from the Spiritual perspective, the idea of dualistic, conditional good can also serve to block your full awareness of non-dualistic, unconditional good (can block your full awareness of Spiritual truth). Judgments of *both* conditional good *and* conditional bad implicitly define the truth of someone only in terms of certain attributes and qualities of his form or appearance, and thus overlook his **non-dualistic** and **unconditional** truth as a be-ing of Spirit. For the Spiritual-Holistic view, any belief that one being is truly and essentially different from another is a mistake. Thus, forgiveness, in its deepest sense, means releasing *all* conditional or dualistic judgments that are based on the belief in real difference — this includes the dualistic positive judgments as well as the dualistic negative judgments. In other words, forgiveness means releasing *all* judgments that interfere with your ability to extend *unconditional* love (which would include all judgments that in any way limit your full awareness of the common Spiritual truth of yourself and the other.)

Good and evil: From a **dualistic** perspective, good and evil are two separate realities or causal powers that co-define each other. For the **Spiritual view**, however, Spirit is the only reality and causal power. The goodness and **love** of Spirit have no real opposites — evil represents only the **illusory** belief that there is another reality and causal power in addition to (and opposing) Spirit. In terms of the familiar religious metaphor that every person is your brother or sister (i.e., shares a common Spiritual kinship with you), we could say that evil is always some form of the misunderstanding and misperception that someone is not your brother or sister — and thus you believe that you are justified in judging them or even harming them in some way. For the Spiritual perspective, the opposite of the truth of (**non-dualistic, unconditional, perfect**) Spiritual good is not evil (for there is nothing that is not-Spirit), but is rather the belief in the reality and separateness of *both* good *and* evil. (One interpretation of the Garden of Eden story is that humans lost their awareness of non-dualistic truth when they began to believe in the dualistic and conditional concepts of both good and evil.)

Grace and Karma: Karma (or the law of karma) refers to the law of cause and effect — the law that every action or event has, or causes, a corresponding consequence. In its broadest sense, karma includes both moral causality ("what goes around, comes around," "you reap what you sow") and physical causality. For the **Separative-Technological view**, karma represents the lawfulness, order, and coherence of reality itself — and it is what prevents reality from being utter chaos. For the **Spiritual-Holistic view**, however, Spirit itself is the only causal power. In truth, one separate thing (or action or event) does not cause another — everything that is and everything that happens is in truth an expression of, and is caused by, Spirit. (But this does not mean that everything that you experience is caused by Spirit. For instance, a mistaken belief that there is something apart from Spirit — a belief that not-Spirit is real in some way — will be reflected as illusory non-Spiritual experiences, for instance, experiences of separateness, conflict, meaninglessness, and evil. The seemingly non-Spiritual part or aspect of such experiences is not caused by Spirit, but is only an illusory projection of your own ignorance and unawareness.) Thus, for the Spiritual-Holistic view, what is called karmic law is not an "external" law (external either in the sense of a law built into external reality, or in the sense of a law imposed on us by an external creator-being). For the Spiritual-Holistic view, karma is a reflection of the internal orderliness and coherency of your thinking and experiencing — because you simply could not be aware of utter chaos at all. And from a Holistic perspective, this internal orderliness and coherency of worldly experience could be seen, in turn, as a reflection of the wholeness and unity of Being. But when you are unaware of Spirit, you will experience the manifestations and expressions of Spirit as separate, independent beings, each with its own separate causal power — and you will interpret the things and events in your experience as causing one another. Every time you blame another person or an external circumstance for your unhappiness (or even credit them for your happiness), you commit yourself to the belief in, and the experience of, karmic law — in effect, you make your life experience karmic. The key to becoming free of the law of karma is not by paying off all your "karmic debts," but rather by releasing *all* dualistic judgments that things are good or bad in themselves; releasing every judgment that anyone or anything outside of you can make you happy or unhappy — the key is **forgiveness**.

Grace: The Separative-Technological view tends to think of grace as a special gift that a separate creator-being can arbitrarily give you or not — and you may have to first pay some karmic debt, and/or subscribe to some particular religious belief, in order to qualify for the possibility of receiving this gift. For the Spiritual-Holistic view, however, grace refers to the eternally given gift of Spirit's love and benevolence — because Spirit *is* the eternal extension of unconditional love. In this sense, you are always in a state of grace, since Spirit's on-going extension of love is the very **truth** and essence of its Being.

The phrase, "state of grace" is also used to refer to a particular state of consciousness, in which you are fully aware of the eternal love and benevolence of Spirit (fully aware of Spirit's grace) as the very truth of your being. For the Spiritual-Holistic view, grace is eternally offered and available, *because* Spirit is the Being of unconditional love — and thus, the grace of perfect **peace, love,** and **joy** is available in every moment, *because* it is the very truth of your being. Your experience of Spirit's grace — your experience of perfect peace, love, and joy — awaits only your receptivity to it, your receptivity to the **Spiritual truth** of your being. You can't force this awareness to happen; you can only choose to be receptive to it. Since it is Spirit's own nature to emerge into full expression and awareness, only your resistance (in the form of your dualistic judgments, your beliefs in separateness and valuelessness, etc.) can block it from your own experience.

From the Spiritual-Holistic perspective, karma and grace are not two separate realms of reality, but simply two ways we can experience life — either hiddenly or unhiddenly. From the Spiritual-Holistic perspective, there is no karmic debt which must be satisfied before you can experience perfect peace, love, and joy — you need only shift your awareness from effects to cause, from forms to source, from the many separate appearances in the world to the one truth of Spirit. The past has taken nothing from you, nor will the future add anything to you — your truth and essence eternally *is* Spirit. (Also see "Ordinary reality and Sacred reality.")

Gratitude: Gratitude is the natural and spontaneous expression of your awareness of your **Spiritual truth**. For the **Spiritual view**, the **lighted clearing** of gratitude is also one of the most powerful tools you have for Spiritual awakening — one of the most effective means for remembering your Spiritual truth.

Grievance/grudge: To hold a grievance against someone means to judge him as **bad** (that is, undeserving of your unconditional love) for something he has done, and to continue to actively maintain this **judgment**. (Some people claim that they are only judging the act, and not the person. But to judge an act as a sin or wrongdoing rather than a mere mistake is to implicitly judge that the person who did it was acting from selfish motives and/or intentionally trying to harm or cheat another.) For the **Spiritual view**, however, the essence or truth of all beings is Spirit. The judgment that someone is bad or **evil** reflects only your misperception of his truth. Thus, when you notice that you are holding a grudge or grievance against someone — when you discover that you are feeling anger, hatred or **blame** toward him — it is an **emotional** reminder to you to release your mistaken judgment (i.e., to **forgive**), and to return to the awareness of the **Spiritual truth** of yourself and the other.

Grow: For the **Spiritual view**, personal growth means awakening to your **Spiritual truth**. To see anything, or anyone, or any situation from the **lighted clearing** of Spirit illuminates its intrinsic growth-possibilities (**opportunity**-possibilities, **healing**-possibilities) for you — allows you to see it in a light that enables you to move toward greater awareness and expression of your Spiritual truth, and thus toward the experience of perfect **peace**, **love**, and **joy**.

Grudge: See "Grievance."

Guidance system: See "Emotions/feelings."

Guilt: Guilt is the **emotion**al reflection of the belief and **judgment** that you have done something wrong, and are thus a bad (sinful) person — a person unworthy of **unconditional love**. For the **Spiritual view**, however, you are a be-ing of Spirit. You may misperceive this **truth**, and thus make mistakes based on your misperceptions. But this does not mean you are bad or **evil** — simply that you are speaking and acting out of **ignorance** and **fear**. Thus, for the Spiritual view, the feeling of guilt can be seen as an emotional reminder that you are not living in awareness of your truth, and you therefore need to return to this awareness. From within the awareness of your truth, any necessary corrections of speaking and acting will naturally occur. Likewise, when you notice that you are judging another to be guilty (when you are holding a **grievance** against him), the appropriate response is to **forgive** (release your misperception of him) so that you can become aware of his **Spiritual truth**.

Happy/unhappy: See "Joy."

Health/healing: Health is the full awareness and expression of wholeness and Spirituality. Healing is the process of wholeness and Spirituality emerging into full awareness and expression. For the **Spiritual view**, any perceived lack of wholeness and Spirituality you may experience is merely a misperception on your part, merely the **illusion** of an absence. Thus, healing ultimately means the healing of misperception, the dispelling or dissolution of an illusion.

Holistic view: The Holistic view is a way of thinking about and experiencing reality in terms of wholeness; a way of understanding all of the seemingly separate and independent beings as interconnected parts or aspects or manifestations of a greater whole. Even though the various parts of the whole may be distinguishable from one another, and may even have some relative degree of independence, they exist as *essentially* interconnected parts of a greater totality. "*Essentially* interconnected" means that the inner essence or **truth** of your being (your being in its deepest unhiddenness) *is* that it is a part of a greater whole. Your relationship to any other part of the whole is not somehow "outside" you, or "between" you and some separate other — being-related is an *intrinsic* dimension of your own being. For the Holistic perspective, to say that you are "part" of a greater whole does not mean that you are like one separate, interlocking piece in a huge puzzle of many separate interlocking pieces. Here, "part" means that you *are*, in your own being, one unique and distinct expression or manifestation of the greater whole. (Often the analogy of a hologram is used to illustrate this kind of part/whole relationship, since every "part" of a holographic plate contains the information of the whole holographic image.) (See also "Spiritual-Holistic view.")

Ignorance: For the **Spiritual view**, ignorance does not mean a lack of specific information, but rather a lack of awareness of your truth of Spiritual wholeness. This lack of awareness is usually disguised as the **illusory** experience of your separateness and valuelessness. Since Spiritual **wholeness** is intrinsically **self-revealing**, the only way you could be unaware of your truth would be if you were implicitly denying it and hiding it from yourself, (for instance, by creating a **lighted clearing** that prevents it from emerging into your awareness).

Illusion: An illusion involves confusing the true and the not-true (the merely seeming) — mistaking the not-true as the true, and/or the true as the not-true. What you judge to be illusory is defined only relative to what you judge to be true.

Joy: Joy is used in two very different senses: conditional and unconditional. These are not simply "smaller" and "bigger" versions of the same thing, but represent fundamentally different worldviews and life experiences. (See "Positive emotions" for a general introduction to ideas of peace, love, and joy)

Conditional joy (or conditional happiness) is based on a belief in lack or scarcity — the belief that your own nature is somehow lacking what it needs in order to be happy, and that certain conditions (certain external circumstances, and/or other people treating you in a certain way) have to be met in order for you to be able to feel joy or happiness. If these conditions are not met, you are unhappy. Thus, the belief in conditional joy leads to a **fear-based approach to life**, since the baseline nature of reality (when special conditions are not being met) is one of lack and unhappiness. Everything you do to try to achieve or create the conditions for your happiness is driven by the constant threat and **fear** of unhappiness. Even if you temporarily succeed at achieving these conditions, you will constantly live with the implicit threat and fear that things might change at any moment. Conditional joy is always based on a temporary and tentative set of circumstances, and is defined on all sides by the threat of change, loss, and death.

Unconditional joy: (Also called perfect or **non-dualistic** joy or happiness) For the **Spiritual-Holistic view**, joy is simply the emotional reflection of your awareness of your **truth**, and has nothing to do with particular circumstances and conditions. You are, in your **Spiritual truth**, a be-ing of joy. Since there is, in truth, no such thing as **not-Spirit**, any feeling of unhappiness or un-joyfulness can only be the emotional reflection of an **illusory** belief in (and fabricated experience of) "not-Spirit." The real and only cause of feeling unhappiness, then, is the belief that happiness is dependent on particular conditions. If you believe this, you will in effect make yourself feel unhappy whenever you believe that these necessary conditions are not being met.

(Note that for the Spiritual-Holistic view, peace, love, and joy are not separate emotions, but are interrelated aspects of Spiritual awareness. See also "Conditional/unconditional," "Dualistic/non-dualistic," and "Positive emotions.")

Judge/judgment/judgmental: In general, "to judge" someone or something means to categorize them within a **dualistic** framework — to judge someone as **good** or bad, in the dualistic sense of these terms. The phrase, "being judgmental," has the connotation that you are judging something as bad.

The **Separative-Technological view** tends to categorize everything in the world in a relativistic, comparative hierarchy of better and worse. It is important to know who is good and who is bad, who is friendly to your agenda and who is not. "Critical judgment" is a necessary part of your self-defense and self-protection in a potentially hostile world, as well as being the key to achievement and success.

For the **Spiritual-Holistic view**, if you see things only in terms of (in light of) your own dualistic judgments, you will be blind to their non-dualistic **Spiritual truth**.

Karma: See "Grace and Karma" and "Ordinary and sacred reality."

Leap of Faith: A leap of faith is a **metaphor** for any belief choice that cannot be justified or validated by sensory perception or logical proof.

Life purpose: See "Purpose."

Light Choice: In the metaphor of the **lighted clearing**, a light choice is a choice of belief and/or a choice of focus, which creates a specific lighted clearing of discovery.

Light spectrum: A light spectrum is a metaphor for a range of **light choices**, defined by two opposing beliefs: for instance, the spectrum of choices defined by the **Separative view** at one end, and the **Holistic view** at the other; or the spectrum of choices defined by the **Technological view** at one end, and the **Spiritual view** at the other; or the combined spectrum defined by the **Separative-Technological view** at one end, and the **Spiritual-Holistic view** at the other.

Lighted clearing: "Lighted clearing" is a **metaphor** for a specific horizon of receptivity and discovery. In the **Possibility Model**, your **light choices** (choices of belief and focus) create a lighted clearing that allows and enables you to experience some **possibilities** and not others.

Limiting belief: A limiting belief is any belief that creates a **lighted clearing** that artificially limits your experience.

For a **Separative** and materialistic point of view, limiting beliefs are those which limit your ability to create or receive fame, wealth, power, etc.

For the **Spiritual view**, a limiting belief is any belief that creates a lighted clearing that limits your awareness of your **Spiritual truth**.

264

Living Presence of the world: See "Presence."

Love: Love is used in two very different senses: conditional and unconditional. These are not simply smaller and bigger versions of the same thing, but represent fundamentally different worldviews and life experiences. (See "Positive emotions" for a general introduction to ideas of peace, love, and joy.)

Conditional love: Conditional love is a sense of affection that you extend to those who meet your standards and conditions of lovability. You love someone (i.e., you judge her to be worthy and deserving of your love) only if, and as long as, she meets certain conditions. Otherwise, you do not love her (and perhaps even hate her). Typically you extend this conditional love to someone because she has done something for you (i.e., as a reward to her), or because you believe that it is to your advantage to do so (i.e., as a kind of barter). In this sense, conditional love is basically reactive, and is dependent on either circumstances or on your ever-changing desires. Conditional love is really a form of "not-love" (or even a form of hatred), because it takes special circumstances and special effort for people to "qualify" for your love — their baseline reality, apart from any special circumstances or effort (who they are in and of themselves, apart from meeting your needs and conditions), is unlovable.

Unconditional love (also called perfect or **non-dualistic** love) is the universal and unconditional extension of goodwill, kindness, and blessing that you offer to all. No one has to earn your love, nor are you bartering in order to get something in return for it. For the **Spiritual view**, you *are*, in your truth, a be-ing of Spirit — a be-ing of unconditional love itself. Moreover, insofar as you see the Spiritual truth of others, you can do nothing but extend unconditional love to them. Unconditional love *is* the natural expression of your awareness of your Spiritual truth, as well as the natural expression of your awareness of the Spiritual truth of others. Whereas conditional love is a circumstance-dependent **reaction**, unconditional love is a true **response** (a sending forth from yourself), which is independent of any particular internal or external conditions.

(Note that for the Spiritual-Holistic view, peace, love, and joy are not separate emotions, but are interrelated aspects of Spiritual awareness. See also "Conditional/ unconditional," "Dualistic/non-dualistic," and "Positive emotions.")

Love-based approach to life: See "Fear-based and love-based approaches to life."

Mechanistic view: The mechanistic view is a way of thinking about the living body as merely a complicated machine, made up of physical parts (atoms and molecules), and physical, chemical, and electro-magnetic forces. On a larger scale, a mechanistic view of the universe sees it, too, simply as a huge collection of physical parts, and physical, chemical, and electro-magnetic forces — i.e., a giant mechanism or machine. A mechanistic view is the opposite of a vitalistic view (see "Vitalism").

Metaphor/poetic: For the **Spiritual view**, "Spirit" cannot be conceptually described.   Conceptual   description   necessarily   involves   distinction   and differentiation.   Spirit, however, is essentially **non-dualistic**.   At best, we can use language poetically or metaphorically to point toward the direct experience of our **Spiritual truth** — i.e., to create a **lighted clearing**, which allows us to discover and experience the **Spiritual dimension** of our lives.   (See also "Fingers pointing at the moon.")

Model: A model is a way of thinking about something.

The **Actuality Model** and the **thought-creates-reality** model are two opposing ways of thinking about "reality."   The Actuality model claims that reality is given and fixed, and that you have to somehow accommodate to the external facts of the world.   The thought-creates-reality model, however, claims that your own thoughts create reality — and that if you don't like reality, you can change it merely by changing your thoughts.

The **Possibility model** is a way of thinking about your *experience* of reality. It claims that your thoughts and your focus of attention create a **lighted clearing** of discovery, a specific horizon of receptivity that allows you to experience some **possibilities** and not others.

Mystery: "The Mystery" is an idea that points toward the ultimate source of all **possibilities**.   The Mystery can be "experienced" only as "that which is beyond all possible experience," and can be "understood" only as "that which is beyond all possible understanding."   For the **Spiritual view**, the Mystery is often referred to as the sacred Mystery, to indicate the essentially Spiritual nature of all Being.

Negative emotions/feelings: Negative emotions are those emotions that are forms or variations of the lack of **peace** (feelings of fear or conflict), the lack of **love** (feelings of hatred or anger), and the lack of **joy** (feelings of unhappiness or depression).   "Negative" does not imply that these emotions are bad or wrong.

For the **Separative-Technological view**, the **truth** of reality is separateness and valuelessness.   Therefore, at one level, negative emotions merely reflect your awareness of this reality; they are part of the necessary cost of being "realistic," of being intellectually honest.   At another level, negative emotions can act as a valuable **feedback system** which alerts you to potential threats; which reminds you to keep up your guard; and which indicates when it is time to change yourself or the world for the "better" (even if this "better" will be a temporary and tentative condition at best).

For the **Spiritual-Holistic view**, the truth of all reality is its Spiritual **wholeness**.   Awareness of this truth is emotionally reflected by the positive feelings of perfect peace, love, and joy.   Unawareness of this truth (i.e., the **illusory** experience of the absence of wholeness and Spirituality, which takes the form of the illusory experience of the presence of separateness and valuelessness) is emotionally reflected by negative feelings.   Ultimately, all negative feelings are based in **fear** — whenever you are unaware of the wholeness and Spirituality of Being, you will feel separate and threatened in a hostile universe.   You may experience this fear either as a form of fight (anger, hatred, aggression), or as a form of flight (self-pity, depression, withdrawal). For the Spiritual-Holistic view, negative emotions are your feedback system, which reminds you that you are unaware of your **Spiritual truth**. Since Spiritual wholeness is **self-revealing**, the only way you could be unaware of your truth would be if you were implicitly denying it and hiding it from yourself (for instance, by creating a lighted clearing that prevents it from emerging into your awareness). For the Spiritual-Holistic view, the appropriate **response** to any negative emotion is to let go of the **limiting beliefs** and **judgments** that are excluding the awareness of your truth (i.e., to **forgive**), and/or to proactively **affirm** for yourself those beliefs that will create a **lighted clearing** of receptivity to your Spiritual truth.

Non-dualistic: See "Dualism/non-dualism."

Non-temporal: See "Temporal/non-temporal."

Not-Spirit: See "Dualism/non-dualism" and "Spiritual view."

Opportunity: For the **Spiritual view**, opportunity means the opportunity to **respond** in a way that is **healing** for yourself and the world; in a way that allows Spiritual wholeness to more fully emerge into awareness, and to more fully and **unhiddenly** express itself. For the Spiritual perspective, every being and every situation has opportunity-**possibilities** (healing-possibilities), if you are only open and receptive enough to perceive them.

   Ordinary reality and sacred reality: **Dualistic** thinking distinguishes between two separate realms of reality: "ordinary reality" (in which there is no spiritual significance or deeper meaning to beings and events), and "sacred reality" (in which every being and every event has some deeper spiritual significance).

   For the **Spiritual view**, however, ordinary reality is not a separate realm of reality, but only a specific way of thinking about and experiencing your life — a way that implicitly denies and hides the universal **truth of Spirit**. Sacred reality, on the other hand, is how you experience your life when you are not hiding Spiritual truth (for instance, when you are living in the **lighted clearing** of the Spiritual view) — "sacred reality" is simply the unhidden or undisguised experience of the **eternal** (non-dualistic) truth of Spirit.

   From a Spiritual perspective, there is never a need to sanctify anything, for nothing in its truth is or could be **un-sacred**. Since Spirit is the source and essence of possibility itself, the un-sacred is impossible. From this perspective, the purpose and value of any religious or spiritual ritual of sanctification is to help ourselves remember and recognize the sacredness that is already eternally present as the very truth and essence of Being itself. (See also "Conditional/ unconditional," "Dualism/non-dualism" and "Grace and karma.")

   Original thought: Original thoughts are thoughts that you have discovered for yourself in the **truth** (**unhiddenness**) of your own direct experience. It is irrelevant whether they happen to be the same as, or different from, someone else's thoughts.

Pathology orientation/Vision orientation:
A **pathology orientation** is a way of thinking about and experiencing the world, that focuses on what is wrong; what needs to be fixed or overcome or destroyed; what you are moving away from. A pathology orientation is necessarily a **fear-based approach to life.**

A **vision orientation** focuses on what you desire to move toward. A vision orientation can be either a fear-based or **loved-based approach to life.** If you believe that you need to accomplish a goal or realize a dream in order for you to experience **peace, love,** and **joy,** your pursuit of your goal will be fear-based. (In a sense, what appears to be a vision orientation of moving towards your goal is actually motivated by a fearful moving-away-from what you believe to be your current lack.) But when you know that your very **truth** is the be-ing of perfect peace, love, and joy, and you pursue your goals out of the sheer joy of living your true desires, then you are living a love-based approach to life.

Peace: Peace is used in two very different senses: conditional and unconditional. These are not simply smaller and bigger versions of the same thing, but represent fundamentally different worldviews and life experiences.   (See "Positive emotions" for a general introduction to ideas of peace, love, and joy.)

Conditional peace: For the **Separative-Technological view,** reality is composed of separate, independent beings, each with his own will and his own individual agenda and goals. Therefore, conflict is inevitable. For this view, conflict is not merely one particular state of affairs, but is the on-going reality of separate beings, each competing and negotiating for his own good. "Peace" in this context always means conditional peace: a temporary and tentative truce, in the midst of the ongoing reality of conflict; a particular set of circumstances and conditions, within which you feel temporarily unthreatened. From this perspective, the idea of unconditional peace is a dangerous delusion that can lull you into dropping your guard against your ever-threatening and ever-attacking neighbors.   Realistically, the best you can hope for is an occasional conditional peace that can give you a brief respite.

Unconditional peace: (Also called perfect or **non-dualistic** peace) For the **Spiritual-Holistic view,** all beings are part of a greater whole and share the common **truth** or essence of Spirit. From this perspective, "conflict" is always an **illusion,** in which you fail to see the truth of **wholeness** and Spirituality.   In this illusion, you mistakenly believe and perceive that you and your neighbor are separate, independent beings, somehow competing with each other — and therefore you believe that conflict is not only possible but inevitable. But for the Spiritual-Holistic view, only the Spiritual wholeness of Being is true, and that means that conflict is impossible (even though you may project or fabricate the experience of it for yourself). The feeling of unconditional peace is simply the **emotional** reflection of your awareness of your Spiritual-Holistic truth.

For the Spiritual-Holistic view, conditional peace is an illusion, based on a belief in the possibility and reality of conflict. And since conditional peace is founded in a belief in the reality of conflict, it negates the very possibility of unconditional peace. The opposite of the non-dualistic (unconditional, perfect) peace of Spirit is not conflict. The opposite of non-dualistic peace is, rather, the illusory dualistic belief in the opposition and reality of *both* (conditional) peace *and* conflict.

(Note that for the Spiritual-Holistic view, peace, love, and joy are not separate emotions, but are interrelated aspects of Spiritual awareness. See also "Conditional/ unconditional," "Dualistic/non-dualistic," and "Positive emotions.")

Perfect peace, love, joy: Unconditional **peace**, **love**, and **joy**. (See "Conditional/unconditional.")

Poetic: See "Metaphor/poetic."

Positive emotions/feelings: Positive emotions are all of those emotions that are forms or variations of **peace**, **love**, and **joy**.

For the **Separative-Technological view**, reality is made up of separate, independent beings in conflict or competition with one another. Positive emotions reflect at best a temporary and tentative configuration of circumstances that is non-threatening — in this sense, all positive emotions are merely **conditional**. Positive emotions reflect at worst a person's unawareness of the potentially threatening nature of reality — e.g., "living in a fool's paradise" — and can cause one to become complacent and drop his guard.

For the **Spiritual-Holistic view**, positive emotions are simply the body-mind **feedback** that lets you know that you are living in awareness of your Spiritual truth. Although we tend to talk about them as three separate emotions (peace, love, and joy), they are interrelated aspects of the emotional expression of Spiritual awareness. Peace is the calmness or lack of **fear** that reflects awareness of the wholeness of Being — from within this context of experience, there is no separateness, no enemy, and conflict is impossible. But the calmness or lack of fear that characterizes Spiritual awareness is not merely an emptiness or lack. It is experienced as a positive fullness, as a sense of well-being and harmony — i.e., as joy. From the Spiritual perspective, when you are aware of yourself as a manifestation or out-picturing of Spirit, you experience yourself as full to overflowing, and can express this overflowing fullness only as the extension of good will and blessing to everyone you meet. In gratitude, you discover yourself so completely filled with Spirit's gift of unconditional love, that you can only let unconditional love flow through you and from you. The sense of receiving unconditional love from your source, and being so overfilled that you can only send it forth from yourself to the world, is the Spiritual meaning of **responsibility** — to send forth your truth back to the world *is* to be a channel of Spirit's unconditional love.

Possibility: In the **Possibility Model**, "possibility" means possible experience.

Possibility Model: The Possibility Model is a way of thinking about the *experience* of reality. For the Possibility Model, Being consists of a vast range of **possibilities** (possible experiences). You create the specific horizon of receptivity (**lighted clearing**) that allows some of these possibilities to become your actual experiences of the world, and excludes others.

Presence: Presence implies some level of self-awareness. One presence can encounter another, each with some level of self-awareness and awareness of the other — and thus with possibilities of sharing, comfort, and guidance. For the **Spiritual view**, **Spirit** has a quality of presence, or presenc-ing. But Spirit is not merely one presence (or one present being) among many. Spirit is the very Being of Presenc-ing itself that is expressed or manifested *as* the presence of every presence; the very "I-am-ness" of every "I am." In this sense, we can speak of Spirit as "the sacred living Presence of the world."

Purpose: This idea is used in two senses: "life purpose," and "the purposefulness of the world."

Your life purpose is your choice of who you are and how you can contribute or serve. Your life purpose is what you bring to every situation; what you send forth from yourself. Your life purpose is your primary reference point for all of your other choices and decisions. For the **Spiritual-Holistic view**, you are a unique be-ing of **Spirit**, and your life purpose is to realize and express your **Spiritual truth** in your own unique way.

Implicit in the **Spiritual-Holistic view** is a belief in "the purposefulness" of the world. Since **Spirit** is the only **truth** and the only cause, everything that happens, when seen in its deepest truth, can serve the purpose of **healing**. (To say that Spirit is the only true cause, however, does not mean that everything you experience is necessarily caused by Spirit, since your own mistaken ideas and misperceptions may lead you to have **illusory** "**un-Spiritual**" experiences.) The belief in the purposefulness of the world is a belief that it is always possible to discover healing-possibilities, no matter how un-Spiritual (e.g., bad, negative, tragic) the situation may seem — it is *always* possible to **respond** in a way that is healing for yourself and the world. In terms of the **Possibility Model**, we could say that the idea of "the purposefulness of the world" creates a **lighted clearing** that allows you to discover the intrinsic healing-possibilities of every situation. For the Spiritual-Holistic view, healing always means healing a misperception that there is some lack of **goodness, peace, love,** or **joy** — i.e., a misperception that there is, or could be, a lack of Spirit. (See "Opportunity.")

Question: A question is a way of focusing your awareness, which creates a specific **lighted clearing** of discovery. The "truth of a question" for you is the specific **unhiddenness** or opening of discovery it creates for you. Since the mind tends to either discover or make up answers for whatever question you ask, you want to make sure that the form and content of your question are creating the lighted clearing you truly desire — one that will allow you to discover the kinds of answers you truly desire to find.

Random: See "Coincidence."

Reaction: To "respond" means to send forth something from yourself back to the world. If you consciously and deliberately choose what you will send forth, it is a true **response**. If, however, what you send forth is merely dictated by your past conditioning rather than arising out of your present deliberate choice, it is a mere "reaction." (See "Response/ Responsibility.")

Reality, ordinary: See "Ordinary reality and sacred reality."

Reality, sacred: See "Ordinary reality and sacred reality."

Re-light: To re-light a situation or to re-light your life means to change your beliefs or focus of attention, so that you create a different **lighted clearing** of discovery, which allows you to see everything "in a new light" — to see it in a way that brings new **possibilities** to light. For the **Spiritual-Holistic view**, the purpose of all re-lighting is to become more fully aware of the **Spiritual truth** of yourself and your situation.

Response/Responsibility: To "re-spond" means "to send forth from yourself back to the world." "Respons-ibility" means "your ability to consciously and deliberately send forth your **truth** from yourself back to the world." Since a true response (as opposed to a mere **reaction**) is a conscious and deliberate sending-forth of your truth, it is not dependent on or limited by or defined by external circumstances.

Sacred Living Presence: See "Presence."

Sacred Mystery: See "Mystery."

Sacred reality: See "Ordinary reality and sacred reality."

Self-revealing: For the **Spiritual-Holistic view**, the Spiritual **wholeness** of Being inherently moves toward coming to light — moves toward more complete expression and awareness. You don't have to "make" it come to light — once you stop actively denying it and hiding it from yourself, it comes to light on its own.

Separative view: The Separative view is a way of thinking about and experiencing reality as a collection of fundamentally separate and independent beings, each with their own private agenda. The Separative view is typically not so much a conscious and deliberate choice, but rather an unconscious assimilation of one's predominant cultural worldview.

Separative-Technological view: The Separative-Technological view is a way of thinking about and experiencing reality that combines the **Separative** and the **Technological** views. It sees reality as a collection of fundamentally separate and independent beings, which have no intrinsic value in and of themselves, apart from that which is given to them by humans. The Separative-Technological view is typically not so much a conscious and deliberate choice, but rather an unconscious assimilation of one's predominant cultural worldview.

Spirit: See "Spiritual view."

Spiritual dimension: The "Spiritual dimension" of your being is that dimension of experience in which you experience the **Spiritual truth** of yourself. (See "Truth: Truth of Spirit.")

Spiritual truth: See "Truth: Truth of Spirit."

Spiritual view: The Spiritual view is a way of thinking about and experiencing reality from the **lighted clearing** of **Spirit**. Although Spirit transcends any conceptual distinction or precise definition, it can be characterized or pointed to with ideas such as "the common sacred essence of all things," "the sacred living **Presence** of the world," "the Being of unconditional **love**," and "the source, essence and **truth** of all beings" (see "Fingers pointing at the moon"). Spirit, in this sense, is not a being, but is rather the Being of all beings, the common (shared) essence that is expressed or manifested *as* individual beings. Therefore, Spirit, as used here, is not synonymous with "**God**" in the sense of "a separate creator-being" — Spirit is the common essence or **truth** of all beings and all distinctions, and thus Spirit includes "Spirit *as* creator" and "Spirit *as* the process of creating" and "Spirit *as* the created being." (It should also be noted here that some people use the term "God" not in the sense of a separate creator-being, but rather in the same sense that I use Spirit in this book.)

Since Spirit is the essence and truth of *everything*, it is non-dualistic. There simply is no such reality as **not-Spirit** (the **un-Spiritual** or non-Spiritual) — such terms merely refer to the hiddenness of the Spiritual.

Spiritual wholeness: See "Spiritual-Holistic view."

Spiritual-Holistic view: The Spiritual-Holistic view is a way of thinking about and experiencing reality that combines the **Spiritual** and the **Holistic** views. It sees the wholeness of the Holistic view as an essentially Spiritual wholeness. That means that the wholeness or relatedness of all beings *is* their common Spiritual source, essence, and **truth** — the connectedness of all beings *is* that they are all expressions or manifestations of *one* Spiritual source.

Synchronicity: The **theory** of synchronicity, developed by Carl Jung, is sometimes referred to as the theory of *meaningful* **coincidence**. It claims that there is another principle operating in reality (or at least in our experience of reality) in addition to the law of cause and effect. According to this principle, all the events and elements of any situation are somehow meaningfully connected. (For the **Spiritual view, Spirit** is the only causal power, and the "connectedness" of all of the elements of a situation is but a reflection of the "oneness" of Spirit.) From the perspective of synchronicity, to say that an event happened by "random chance" (i.e., that there is no meaningful connection) merely reflects our blindness to its deeper meaning and significance within the whole situation. (See also "Coincidence" and "Ordinary and sacred reality.")

Technological view: The Technological view is a way of thinking about and experiencing reality, which believes that the value of non-human things is simply human fabrication and projection. Non-human things have no value in themselves, apart from their usefulness to humans. For one variation of the Technological view, even some humans are considered merely things to be used, because of their religion, ethnic background, skin color, economic status, etc. The Technological view is typically not so much a conscious and deliberate choice, but rather an unconscious assimilation of one's predominant cultural worldview.

Temporal/non-temporal: "Temporal" and "non-temporal" are two ways you can think about and experience your life — two possible lighted clearings of experience. The temporal is the experiential realm of change, in which every experienced "now" or "present" is defined relative to "what has gone before" or "where you are coming from" (i.e., the "past"), and "what is still to come" or "where you are headed toward" (i.e., the "future"). In this experiential realm of temporality, the past and the future are not separate from the present, but are rather *intrinsic dimensions of the experienced now* (see Chapter 10 of the text for a more detailed explanation of this idea). The "non-temporal," on the other hand, focuses on the pure awareness that is the unchanging background, which allows you to experience change as "change." The dualistic ideas of temporal and non-temporal are to be distinguished from the **non-dualistic** idea of "the **eternal**."

Theory/Theoros: The ancient Greek word, "theoros," means "a view of the divine." A theory was not considered to be an accurate description (since the non-dualistic divine could not be accurately described with dualistic concepts), but rather a way to create an opening (or **lighted clearing**) that could allow you to "view" or directly experience the sacred.

Thought-creates-reality model: The thought-creates-reality **model** is a way of thinking about the nature of reality, which claims that your thoughts actually create reality.

Trust: For the **Spiritual view**, the **lighted clearing** created by your choice to trust the benevolence of **Spirit** allows you to discover the **purposefulness** of everything in your life — allows you to discover the **opportunity-possibilities** (**healing-possibilities**) of everything in your life.

Truth:
    For the **Actuality Model**, truth means accuracy — an idea is "true," if it accurately re-presents reality.
    For the **Possibility model**, truth means **unhiddenness**. (See "**Aletheia**"). The "truth of a theory or idea" for you is the unhiddenness it creates in your life. The "truth of yourself" is you experienced in your deepest unhiddenness. For the Spiritual-Holistic view, what you are in your deepest unhiddenness is a be-ing of Spirit — i.e., the "truth of yourself" is "your **Spiritual truth**."

Truth, eternal: See "Eternal."

Truth of meditation: The "truth of meditation" can be thought of as the **unhiddenness** of unhiddenness itself. For the Spiritual view, the "unhiddenness itself" is not a mere emptiness, but is the fullness of Spirit.

Truth of a question: See "Question."

Truth of Spirit: "The truth of Spirit" (or "Spiritual truth") is Spirit experienced in its deepest unhiddenness.

Similarly, "your Spiritual truth" is you experienced in your deepest **unhiddenness** as a be-ing of **Spirit**. Since the Spiritual truth or essence of your being is the same Spiritual truth shared by all, "your Spiritual truth" *is* (one unique expression or manifestation of) "the" Spiritual truth common to all. Your Spiritual truth is not something you have to learn or attain or earn, but something you simply awaken to, or remember.

Unconditional: See "Conditional/unconditional."

Unforgiveness: See "Forgiveness/Unforgiveness."

Unhappy: See "Joy."

Unhiddenness: See "Aletheia."

Un-Spiritual (un-sacred): See "Dualism/non-dualism" and "Ordinary reality and sacred reality."

Vision orientation: See "Pathology orientation/Vision orientation."

Vitalism: Vitalism is the view that a living body is more than merely the atoms and molecules, and the physical, chemical and electro-magnetic forces that make it up. There is also an intelligent life force that creates, sustains, and animates all the physical parts and activities of a living body. On a larger scale, a vitalistic view of the universe would see the entire physical universe as a living whole. It would see the universe as the unified physical manifestation of an intelligent life force, and would see every activity and event as being created, sustained, and animated by that intelligent life force. A vitalistic view is the opposite of a **mechanistic** view.

What truly serves you: "What truly serves you" is what helps you to fulfill your authentic **purpose** and realize your true desires. For the **Spiritual view**, "what truly serves you" is what helps you to fully realize and express your **truth** as a be-ing of **Spirit**.

Wholeness: See "Holistic view" and "Spiritual-Holistic view."

Wound: For the **Spiritual-Holistic view**, a wound is a **fear** or **limiting belief**, which creates a **lighted clearing** that limits your awareness of your **Spiritual truth**. Your wound can be seen as "the womb of your gift." In this context, "your gift" is your unique expression of the truth of Spirit — your unique way of being an expression of Spirit's **unconditional love**. Thus, your gift to the world is the unique way Spirit's **grace** expresses itself as, and through, your being for the benefit of all. All that prevents you from truly (unhiddenly) living and giving your gift are the fears and limiting beliefs (i.e. your wounds) that block your awareness of your Spiritual truth. Discovering and releasing those fears and limiting beliefs enables you to become aware of your truth, and thus to give your gift. Also, the process of recognizing and letting go of your wounds gives you a greater sense of understanding and compassion for the wounds of others — and thus enables you to better serve the **healing** of others (i.e., to better give your gift). Thus, your wound is "the womb of your gift."

TABLE 1: A comparison of how the two views understand the world

	Separative-Technological	Spiritual-Holistic
Alienation	Separateness and aloneness are simply a given fact of reality. Feeling alienated is the emotional reflection of your awareness of this fact.	Alienation is simply the illusion of the absence of Spiritual wholeness. Feeling alienated is the emotional reflection of your unawareness of the truth of Spiritual wholeness.
Emotions — positive (peace, love, joy)	At best, positive emotions reflect a temporary and tentative set of conditions that is non-threatening. At worst, they reflect the naïve and dangerous illusion of the absence of threat.	Positive emotions are the emotional reflection of your awareness of your Spiritual truth. Since Spirit is non-dualistic, positive emotions are unconditional (i.e., perfect peace, love, and joy)
Emotions — negative (lack of peace, lack of joy, lack of love)	Negative emotions in general are the emotional reflection of seeing "how things really are," of being "realistic." In some situations, they can also indicate that it is time for you to somehow change yourself or the world — to somehow "make" things "better."	Negative emotions remind you that you are temporarily unaware of your Spiritual truth. Negative emotions are the emotional reflection of living in illusion. They do not indicate that you need to change yourself or the world, but rather that you need to become aware of the truth of Spirit that is already and always present.
Ethics	Egocentric self-interest (although this may be tempered with a morality of altruism and cooperation).	Unconditional love.

	Separative-Technological	Spiritual-Holistic
Fear	Fear is the emotional reflection of being realistic. Since the world really is separative, hostile and threatening, to not feel afraid is foolish and dangerous.	Fear is the emotional reflection of experiencing the *illusion* of the absence of wholeness and Spirituality, the illusion of the absence of love. As such, fear (and all the negative emotions that arise out of fear) is a reminder to return to awareness of your truth.
Forgiveness	Pardoning a "sin" of yourself or another; letting them off the hook. But since the wrongdoing was real, forgiveness is actually a form of dishonesty — pretending that the wrongdoer is not bad, when he really is.	"Forgiveness" is merely the letting go of the illusion of sin — letting go of your own misjudgment and misperception, so that you can be aware of the Spiritual truth of yourself and the other.
Illusion	Experiencing what is not truly present (e.g., wholeness and Spirituality), and not experiencing what is truly present (e.g., separateness and valuelessness).	Experiencing what is not truly present (e.g., separateness and valuelessness), and not experiencing what is truly present (e.g., wholeness and Spirituality).
Joy (happiness, the good life)	Conditional joy: you have to achieve or earn your happiness by creating the proper conditions. But ultimately, conditional joy is only a temporary and tentative feeling, since the reality of separateness and threat are ever-present.	Unconditional joy. An emotional reflection of your awareness of your Spiritual truth.

	Separative-Technological	Spiritual-Holistic
Judgment	To judge means to categorize all the separate beings in the world in a relative, comparative hierarchy of "better" and "worse," depending on whether they are friendly to your current life agenda or not.	To judge means to see things only in terms of (in light of) your own dualistic concepts. Judgment blinds you to the Spiritual truth of yourself and the world.
Love	Conditional love: feeling and showing affection for another because you believe it is somehow to your advantage, or because you have judged them to be worthy of love (e.g., they are behaving in certain approved ways, and are exhibiting certain "good" qualities).	Unconditional love: extending good will, kindness, and blessing to all. Unconditional love is the emotional reflection of your awareness of your Spiritual truth (i.e., your truth as a be-ing of unconditional love).
Peace	Conditional peace: a temporary and tentative absence of conflict. Since reality, by definition, is separateness and conflict, every temporary truce is threatened on all sides by potential attack.	Unconditional peace. The emotional reflection of your awareness of the Spiritual truth of wholeness and unconditional love.
Purpose of life	Typically defined in terms of achieving, accomplishing, "getting" (e.g., fame, power, pleasure, acquisitions, wealth) for you and yours. In a separative, competitive world, your gain often means another's loss.	Radiating forth, (extending, sharing, giving) unconditional love. Living, expressing and manifesting your deepest truth as a be-ing of Spirit, a be-ing of unconditional love.

	Separative-Technological	Spiritual-Holistic
Relationship	An arrangement between two or more separate individuals, which usually involves some degree of self-sacrifice and compromise, so that each individual can get what they desire from the relationship.	Every relationship is an expression of the truth of wholeness and shared Spirituality. A relationship can create a "larger" lighted clearing, that can allow everyone involved to become more aware of their shared Spiritual truth.
Separative-Technological view	Being realistic; seeing reality as it is.	A view that is based on the denial of wholeness and Spirituality. Since it is unaware of this denial, it experiences the illusion of the absence of wholeness and Spirituality as the illusory presence of separateness and valuelessness.
Spiritual-Holistic view	An unrealistic fantasy with no basis in logic or sensory experience.	A lighted clearing that can allow you to experience Being in its truth (in its deepest unhiddenness).
Value	For the Technological view, the value of non-human things is simply human fabrication and projection. Non-human things have no value in themselves, apart from their usefulness to humans.	Since every being is a be-ing of Spirit, every being has an intrinsic absolute value, which you can experience only when you have let go of the relative, dualistic values you are making and projecting onto the world — i.e., when you forgive.

INDEX

Items in boldface are defined in the glossary.

ABOUT THE AUTHOR

William Yoder has doctorates in both philosophy and chiropractic. His doctoral dissertation on comparative mysticism was hailed by Dr. Huston Smith as "thoroughly rewarding, interesting, instructive, and original. It advances the philosophical treatment of mysticism."

He has taught Eastern and Western philosophy and religion at major universities, including Vassar College and Furman University. He and his wife currently practice Network Chiropractic at their clinic in upstate New York.

Dr. Yoder has explored and lived a spiritual path for over 35 years. His studies include both formal university training, and personal study with the Option Institute, and with such teachers as Ram Dass, Michael Harner, Gail Straub and David Gershon, Wallace Black Elk, David Spangler, Brant Secunda, and Thich Nhat Hanh.

For the last 15 years, he and his wife have developed a reputation as inspiring public speakers. They also teach highly acclaimed workshops in both the private and the corporate sectors on the topics of health and healing, human potential, self-actualization, and spirituality.

To book a speaking engagement or a workshop, or to receive information about already scheduled events, call 1-800-871-8802, or visit their website at lightedclearings.com.

 *QUICK* ORDER FORM

Fax orders: (315) 737-9009

Telephone orders: Call 1-800-871-8802 toll free. Have credit card ready.

e-mail orders: Visit our website at alightpublications.com for ordering information

Postal orders: Alight Publications, PO Box 524, Dept. A, Sauquoit, NY 13456. (Tel. 1-315-736-7990)

Please send the following books, disks, audio tapes, or reports:

_____

_____

Please send me more FREE information on:

☐ Other books   ☐ Speaking/workshops   ☐ Newsletter   ☐Other

Name: _____

Address: _____

City: _____ State/Province: _____ Zip: _____

Telephone: _____

e-mail address: _____

Special offer for first printing: Order *Lighted Clearings for the Soul* **directly from publisher, and receive autographed copy plus free shipping in U.S.** (Please request this special offer when you order.)

Sales tax: Please add 8.25% for items shipped to New York State.

Payment: ☐Cheque ☐Credit card:
   ☐ Visa ☐ Master Card ☐ Discover
Card number: _____

Name on card: _____ Exp. Date: _____

Visit our website at alightpublications.com to see our other titles, to get information on Dr. Yoder's upcoming lectures and workshops, and to sign up for his free newsletter.